CHRISTIANITY IN AFRICA

STUDIES IN WORLD CHRISTIANITY
The Edinburgh Review of Theology and Religion

This journal is designed to meet the new challenges to Western dominated Christian theology and religious studies, challenges which now come from: re-emergent religious cultures of the Non-Western world; the more intense encounters of religions that now occur in so many cultures, requiring each and all to go beyond the assessment of other religions simply as 'God's way of preparing others for my religion'; those social sciences and ideologies of the West which are themselves re-thinking the kind of ethos and view of reality too often imposed under their influence, sometimes to the detriment of essentially religious dimensions of cultures.

The journal aims to provide a truly international forum for a dialogue of equals, so that, by a common hearing of the voices of those who respond most positively to these challenges, each from his or her own place, the related disciplines of Christian theology and religious studies may advance.

OCCASIONAL ACCOMPANYING BOOKS

Studies in World Christianity will be accompanied by occasional books on theology and religion with the same focus and kind of contents as the review. The first of these is Kwame Bediako's *Christianity in Africa*. Please address enquiries to Edinburgh University Press; manuscripts should addressed to the editor of *Studies in World Christianity*, Professor James P. Mackey, New College, Mound Place, Edinburgh EH1 2LX

Christianity in Africa
The Renewal of a
Non-Western Religion

KWAME BEDIAKO

EDINBURGH UNIVERSITY PRESS
ORBIS BOOKS

To
Andrew F. Walls,
teacher, encourager, friend,
in gratitude

© Kwame Bediako, 1995
Edinburgh University Press Ltd
22 George Square
Edinburgh

Published in the United States of America by Orbis Books,
Maryknoll, New York 10545-0308

Typeset in Linotron Garamond
by Koinonia, Bury, and
printed and bound in Great Britain

Reprinted 1997

A CIP record for this book is available from the British Library
Library of Congress CIP Data is available
ISBN 0 7486 0625 4
ORBIS/ISBN 1-57075-048-3

The Catholic Foreign Mission Society of America (Maryknoll) recruits and trains
people for overseas missionary service. Through Orbis Books, Maryknoll aims to
foster the international dialogue that is essential to mission. The books published,
however, reflect the opinions of their authors and are not meant to represent the
official position of the society.

Regnum Books International is grateful to the Drummond Trust, 3 Pitt Terrace,
Stirling, for financial assistance to make possible special purchase of copies of this
book for distribution in the Two-Thirds World.

Tradition has it that the Adinkra symbols at the chapter headings come from Gyaman,
now the Ivory Coast, and are often used on special funeral cloth to say farewell to the
departed: (chapters 1 and 8) *Gye Nyame*, symbol of the omnipotence and immortality
of God; (chapters 2 and 9) *Kra pa*, or good fortune and sanctity; (chapters 3 and 10)
Biribi wo soro, or hope; (chapters 4 and 11) *Nsoromma*, or star (literally 'child of the
heavens'); (chapters 5 and 12) *Osrane ne nsoromma*, or faithfulness; (chapters 6
and 13) *Akoma ntoaso*, or agreement; (chapters 7 and 14) *Afuntummereku denkyem-
merefunu*, symbolising the need for unity, particularly where there is one destiny.
(From a poster prepared by Ablade Glover, University of Science and Technology,
Kumasi, Ghana.)

Contents

1740

Contents

Preface

In July 1987, I was invited to be the Alexander Duff Visiting Lecturer in the Centre for the Study of Christianity in the Non-Western World, New College, University of Edinburgh. The Centre, first established in the University of Aberdeen, had just been transferred to Edinburgh in that year. The invitation to the Duff Fellowship also coincided with my assumption of the full-time directorship of the then newly established Akrofi-Christaller Memorial Centre for Mission Research and Applied Theology, in Akropong-Akuapem, Ghana.

It seemed to me that nothing could better serve to enhance the common interests which, from the start, linked Edinburgh and Akropong, than for me to accept the invitation from Edinburgh. By the new arrangements governing the Duff Fellowship, as decided by the Duff Trustees, I was required to spend three months of the year in Edinburgh, combining a programme of research and lectures within the regular activities of the Edinburgh Centre. Thus began for me several years which would be marked by truly enriching intellectual stimulation in a most congenial academic atmosphere.

The substance of this book, then, originated as the Duff Lectures I gave between 1989 and 1992. The initial series, delivered in the autumn term of the 1987-8 session, under the title 'The Roots of African Theology', formed part of a larger book which was eventually published as *Theology and Identity. The impact of culture upon Christian thought in the second century and modern Africa* (Oxford: Regnum Books, 1992).

I am more grateful than I can say for the warm and gracious hospitality that I enjoyed in New College on each of my visits throughout the entire five-year period that I held the Duff Fellowship. This time gave me the opportunity to explore some of the dimensions of the Christian presence in the modern world which struck me as indicating that it might be entering upon a new phase in its history. Among these was the realisation that the African continent now had a perhaps surprisingly important place in what was being increasingly recognised as a shift in the whole centre of gravity of Christianity as a world faith. David Barrett had written in 1970 that the phenomenal numerical surge of the faith in Africa could mean that 'African Christians might well tip the balance and transform Christianity permanently into a primarily non-Western religion'.[1]

But it was Andrew Walls who drew out the fullest implications of Barrett's observation by suggesting that 'what happens within the African Churches in the next generation will determine the whole shape of church history for centuries to come; what sort of theology is most characteristic of the Christianity of the twenty-first century may well depend on what has happened in the minds of African Christians in the interim'.[2] My intention, then, was to respond to Barrett's and Walls's suggestions. The crucial question, it seemed, was whether, and to what extent, this modern shift of the heartlands of the Christian faith has raised new religious and theological issues regarding the understanding of the faith itself.

The three parts of the book represent successive themes, and though each part was conceived separately, it is also possible to embrace them together. Part 1 treats some of the issues raised by this new pronounced role of Christianity in African life, discussing these from the specific perspective of Ghana so as to achieve greater interpretative depth. My concerns here are shaped by some of the critical intellectual and cultural problems which Christianity, it seems to me, will need to confront if it is adequately to establish its 'African' credentials. The rise of the Afrikania Mission, founded in the early 1980s by a Ghanaian ex-Roman Catholic priest, as a universal African Traditional Religion – an alternative to both Christianity and Islam – gives particular poignancy to these issues.

In Part 2, I broaden the field of discussion to embrace evidence drawn from elsewhere in the non-Western world. My concerns here relate particularly to ecumenical theological developments arising from the need to make specific Christian theological responses to specific non-Western realities. I am especially interested in exploring whether the realisation that 'primal religions are the most fertile soil for the Gospel' and 'underlie therefore the Christian faith of the vast

majority of Christians of all ages and all nations'[3] may give any indications as to how the faith itself may now be re-conceptualised and
re-formulated in terms of 'primal' apprehensions of reality.

To say 'primal', however, is not to suggest 'final'. Therefore, in Part 3
I return to the focus on Africa. On the understanding that the prospects for Christianity in Africa will continue to be high in the 1990s
and on into the twenty-first century, I attempt to identify some of
the challenges which a post-missionary Christian Africa may need to
face as an important flag-bearer of Christianity in the new century.

In view of an increasing perception of Africa as marginal to major
world affairs, it becomes important to appreciate what, on the other
hand, Africa's role may be as a privileged area of Christian religious,
cultural, social and political engagement in the world. In that respect,
Africa may not be so marginal after all in a changing world. Dietrich
Westermann, in his Duff Lectures of 1935,[4] took the view that the
transmission of Christianity in Africa ought to entail the complete
elimination of all that went to form the pre-Christian religious tradition. In short, 'giving the new means taking away the old'.[5] Thirty
years later, Kenneth Cragg countered Westermann's view, and suggested: 'On the contrary; it means harnessing its possibilities [i.e. of
the old] and setting up within it the revolution that will both fulfil
and transform it. For if the old is taken away, to whom is the new
given?'[6] The difference in viewpoint may owe less to Africa than to
the perspective which one adopts in relation to Christianity itself –
the one a 'Western' and the other a 'world' perspective. Given Africa's significant place in Christianity's resurgence in the present century, it would be difficult to avoid the conclusion that it has played a
major role in the renewal of Christianity as a non-Western religion,
and therefore as a world faith.

I have presented some of these chapters on other occasions,
following the completion of my Duff series in Edinburgh. Chapter 2
was read as my David Rigby Lecture at Northumbria Bible College,
Berwick-upon-Tweed, in March 1992, and Chapters 6, 9 and 11 were
read as my Henry Martyn Lectures at the Divinity School,
University of Cambridge, in March 1993. I am grateful for the warm
hospitality that I received in both institutions, as well as the responses
that the Lectures engendered, enabling me reflect further on the subject.

It remains for me to acknowledge the contributions by several

Preface

people. My grateful thanks are due to James P. Mackey, who as Dean of the Faculty of Divinity warmly welcomed me into the Fellowship of New College, Edinburgh, and who in the first place suggested that these lectures should be published in Edinburgh. With characteristic dedication and commitment, he initiated the conversation with Edinburgh University Press.

I also acknowledge gratefully the help of Stuart Roebuck, who keyboarded the entire typescript, and the role and encouragement of Vivian Bone, Jonathan Price, Alison Munro, Penny Clarke and Louise Hosking at Edinburgh University Press. They worked tirelessly, occasionally by fax and correspondence, to transform material which had a strong 'lecture feel' to being 'more book-like to read'.

My wife Gillian and our sons, Timothy Nana Yaw Nkansah and Daniel Kwabena Dakwa, have always participated in my every academic endeavour. Their support, spiritual fellowship and keen interest have been invaluable. Both Timothy and Daniel (twelve and nine years old, respectively) have always insisted on 'understanding' what I say or write. Submission to their exacting standards has often saved me from obscurities of expression.

There is one person whose shadow falls across much of the terrain covered in these chapters, namely Andrew F. Walls. My deepest appreciation and thanks go to him for his teaching, unstinting encouragement and warm friendship over the course of many years. I am more grateful than I can say that he agreed to write a Foreword and also accepted that this book be dedicated to him. It is an opportunity I have eagerly sought, and which I am glad to have and make use of on this occasion.

Akropong-Akuapem, Ghana
January 1995

Notes and References

1. David Barrett, 'AD 2000: 350 million Christians in Africa', *International Review of Mission*, vol. 59, no. 233, January 1970, pp. 39–54.
2. A. F. Walls, 'Towards an understanding of Africa's place in Christian history', in J. S. Pobee (ed.), *Religion in a Pluralistic Society*, Leiden: E. J. Brill, 1976, pp. 180–9.
3. A. F. Walls, 'Africa and Christian Identity', *Mission Focus*, vol. 4, no. 7, November 1978, pp. 11–13.
4. This was subsequently published as *Africa and Christianity*, London: Oxford University Press, 1937.
5. Ibid., p. 2.
6. K. Cragg, *Christianity in World Perspective*, London: Lutterworth Press, 1968, p. 57.

Foreword

This is a rich book, a treasury of good things. It is also (which does not always follow from rich books) an enriching book, one which opens up new visions, and prompts and hints and suggests, a book which invites its readers to explore new paths themselves. Its theme, the nature of African Christianity, might until recently have seemed recondite, and may still appear to be a matter of exotic or specialist interest. If there are still any who are mildly surprised at the existence of such an entity as African Christianity, or at least of such an entity as to furnish a book, Kwame Bediako will quickly disabuse them. Anyone who thinks the subject either peripheral to Africa or peripheral to Christianity will equally be led to reconsider. Dr Bediako demonstrates the extent to which the Christian tradition has, over the past two centuries in particular, become part of Africa, and indicates some of the distinctively African shapes that it is taking following its translation into African languages and cultural forms. But he goes far beyond this, showing how such processes are part of the consistent historical development of the Christian faith itself; Christian life and thought are developing from the interaction with the cultures and traditions of Africa as in past centuries they developed through interaction with those of the Greco-Roman and Western worlds. In other words, his story concerns a chapter in universal history, or, in Christian terms, in the history of redemption. This is a book bathed in the life and thought of Africa, and anyone who reads it is likely to learn more about both. But it is not just a book about Africa; it is also a book about Christianity. Dr Bediako invites us to consider the implications of a truly international Christian faith and a truly world church, of which the centre of gravity has moved decisively southwards so that African Christianity is the likely

representative Christianity of the twenty-first century. It is a plural-
ist Christianity in a plural religious situation, introducing a new era
of Christian thought as African cultural, social, political and above
all religious realities place unprecedented questions on the theological agenda. We catch glimpses of the dynamics of African church
life, the means by which thousands of ordinary Christians share in
making the decisions which give African Christianity its distinctive
shape. That Asia and Latin America share in providing the new
representative Christianity is not forgotten; nor is the relevance of all
this to the Western world, whose interactions with Africa provided
the matrix for the remarkable developments here described. Dr
Bediako's story is, as he puts it, ultimately about the 'renewal' of
Christianity itself, with Africa as its theatre.

'Tolle, lege' were the words the young Augustine, who became
the mightiest African theologian of the early centuries, heard in the
garden. I believe that those who 'take up and read' the present
volume are unlikely to be disappointed either.

Andrew Walls,
Centre for the Study of Christianiy in the Non-Western World,
The University of Edinburgh

PART I

Christianity in African Life
Some Concerns and Signs of Hope

I

'Is Christianity Suited to the African?'

The Legacy of Edward Wilmot Blyden and the Resurgence of a Nineteenth-century Intellectual Problem

African Christianity – a Note of Concern

In an age when we have become accustomed to speaking of a shift in Christianity's centre of gravity from the Northern continents to the South, with Africa having pride of place in this shift, it might seem paradoxical that a book on Christianity in African life should begin by asking if Christianity is in fact suited to the African. By all accounts, one could say, as indeed John Mbiti has asserted, that 'the Christian way of life is in Africa to stay, certainly within the foreseeable future'.[1] In view of the fact that the origins of the phenomenal presence of Christianity on African soil coincided with an intensified impact of the West on African life, one is compelled to recognise that the waning of Western dominance has not produced any general diminution in the influence of Christianity on the continent. On the contrary, the Christian churches of Africa, be they of missionary origin or the fruit of solely indigenous African initiative, whatever their varying fortunes in their diverse socio-political contexts, remain important religious and social institutions in their own right which cannot be ignored. In other words, Christian Baëta's evaluation of the place of Christianity in Tropical Africa, made thirty years ago following the International African Institute Seminar at Legon, Ghana, in 1965, has been more than sufficiently vindicated:

Intangible in many of its aspects, the Christian presence has

3

been, and remains, in the African scene, a massive and unavoidable fact and factor.[2]

Yet for all its 'massive and unavoidable' presence 'in the African scene', Christianity in Africa continues to carry a burden, a veritable incubus, which it has to come to terms with and, if possible, seek to overcome and lay to rest. African Christian leaders of thought cannot remain content with the unmistakable reality of the Christian faith in African life.

One of the most significant religious developments in Africa in the 1980s was undoubtedly the rise and establishment of Afrikania, founded by the ex-Catholic priest, Vincent Kwabena Damuah – later known as Osofo Okomfo Kwabena Damuah. Afrikania was more than another new religious movement, perhaps even more than a revitalisation of the traditional religion; it was, rather, a deliberate universalising of the traditional religion into an alternative to Christianity (and to Islam) in Ghana. It amounted to a fundamental challenge to Christianity offering an adequate interpretation of reality and providing a credible basis and satisfactory intellectual framework for African life.[3] I will return to Damuah and Afrikania in the next chapter.

In the 1980s, following three decades of reflection and writing on African Christian theology, a new task for African Christianity became apparent. There was intellectual criticism of the attempt made by some African Christian theologians to secure the roots of Christianity in the full African context by appropriating and integrating the pre-Christian primal cultural tradition.[4] However, the 'Christianising' of the pre-Christian tradition could also be seen as one of the most important achievements of African theology, most clearly evident in the writings of John Mbiti. The residual question now is this: will African Christianity be able to find viable *intellectual* grounds upon which to validate and secure its *African* credentials? In other words, following the 'Christianisation' of African tradition, African Christianity must achieve an *Africanisation* of its Christian experience, and this latter may well prove to be the more demanding task.

Perhaps it is important to clarify the Africanisation that is meant here. At stake is not the Africanisation or indigenisation of the Christian faith and Gospel. The emergence of such significant communities of African Christians as exist today must be reckoned a

4

valid witness to the degree to which the Christian message has been internalised. On the other hand, if the Christian way of life is to stay in Africa, then African Christianity should be brought to bear on the fundamental questions of African existence in such a way as to achieve a unified world-view which finally resolves the dilemma of an Africa uncertain of its identity, poised between the impact of the West and the pull of its indigenous tradition. If the Christianising of African tradition may be considered to have been largely concerned with resolving a basically *religious* problem – in that it had to do with making room in the African experience of religious powers for Christ and the salvation he brings – the Africanising of Christian experience can be seen as being concerned with resolving an essentially *intellectual* problem – how African Christianity, employing Christian tools, may set about mending the torn fabric of African identity and hopefully point a way towards the emergence of a fuller and unfettered African humanity and personality.

Twentieth-century African intellectual criticisms of Christianity – whether by Okot p'Bitek, Ali Mazrui or especially proponents of Afrikania in Ghana – share a persisting sense that Christianity can never become an adequate frame of reference for the full expression of African ideals of life because of the nature of its history in Africa.

African Identity – the Nineteenth-century Dilemma

These critiques share a particular intellectual perception of the problem of African identity which has its roots in the history of the contact of African peoples with the West. Whilst there were almost five centuries of near-regular contact, the problem with which we are concerned came to a head in the nineteenth century when increasing Western cultural and political penetration and dominance in Africa coincided with an equally massive Western missionary enterprise. It is the African reactions to that cumulative Western impact on African life and on African self-identity which have shaped and conditioned the twentieth-century perception of the problem.

It is important to recall that the image of Africa and of Africans as inherently inferior to Europe and Europeans that was prevalent in nineteenth-century Europe did not originate with the missionary movement. This image, as Philip Curtin has shown, 'was very largely drawn from Europe's first impressions taken during the earlier and formative decades'⁵ of contact with Africa. In any case, before 1800, as Kenneth Scott Latourette has pointed out, 'the chief contact of Negro Africa with European peoples was through the traffic in slaves for the white man's economic enterprises in the New World'.⁶ Together with theories of a racial hierarchy and a chain of being elaborated to explain social, cultural and economic diversities between the different groupings of mankind, perceived as races, this image ensured that 'consistently the Negro was relegated to the bottom of the scale'.⁷ Therefore, even though the missionary enterprise itself was part of a different, benevolent European involvement in Africa, wherever missionaries also treated Africa and Africans as savage, ignorant and superstitious, they were very often expressing something of this general European *Afrikaanschauung*.

In such circumstances, a thoughtful African who had come into contact with Europe, gained an insight into European attitudes and yet was concerned to establish a consistent African self-identity and integrity in the face of this image of Africa, could not avoid facing the question as to how the Christian peoples and nations of Europe had so long been the Africans' oppressors. The question would be further complicated if the African was also a Christian or attracted to Christianity. During the nineteenth century it was in West Africa that, as a result of a sustained contact with Europe and Christianity, the question of African identity received serious attention in African intellectual literature.

Edward Blyden and the Question of Identity

The one person whose response to the problem proved the most far-reaching and who has continued to influence some present African responses to the question of identity was a West Indian-born Liberian citizen, statesman, diplomat and educator: Edward Wilmot Blyden. It was Blyden who made his own the vindication of the African, or as he preferred to call him, the Negro and the Negro race.

Blyden was also an ordained Presbyterian churchman and, even though he later resigned from the Presbyterian Church, he remained a sort of non-denominational Christian and considered Christianity as the highest form of religious experience. Yet Blyden never constructed his solution to the African identity problem on Christian premises, for the humiliation of the Negro race had been largely at the hands of Christian people and had been inflicted in Christian lands. The treatment of the Negro in America, of which he had personal experience, and the works of American clergymen demonstrated to him how Christianity was used by upholders of slavery and racial discrimination to induce Negro submissiveness. Blyden commented:

> Such were the circumstances under which the Negro throughout the United States received Christianity. The Gospel of Christ was travestied and diluted before it came to him to suit the peculiar institution by which millions of human beings were converted into 'chattels'. The highest men in the South, magistrates, legislators, professors of religion, preachers of the Gospel, governors of states, gentlemen of property and standing, all united in upholding a system which every Negro felt was wrong. Yet these were the men from whom he got his religion, and whom he was obliged to regard as guides. Under such teaching and discipline, is it to be wondered at that his morality is awry, that his sense of the dignity of human nature is superficial – that his standard of family and social life is low and defective?
>
> Not so much by what Christianity said as by the way in which, through their teachers, it said it, were the Negroes influenced.[8]

With an evident sense of pain, Blyden would even pass comment on men he obviously otherwise respected:

> Some even of the most eminent divines were so far implicated with the error, that, with perfect ease of conscience, they held Negroes in bondage. The distinguished William Penn, the Rev. George Whitefield, of world-wide celebrity, and President [Jonathan] Edwards, author of several standard works in theology, were *slave-holders*. Good and conscientious men were led away by the plausible arguments of those who, while they were busy turning to pecuniary account the benighted Africans, alleged that they were thus being brought under the influence of the Gospel.[9]

Against this evidence of 'Christian' failure, who then were the Negro's friends and defenders, but those accounted heterodox?

> The defenders of the Negro during the days of his bondage, and the advocates of his full manhood and equality now that he is free, are, as a rule, found among those who are not regarded as orthodox in the Christian Church. Not the Evangelical churches in the United States, but the Unitarian, have furnished the ablest and most prominent defenders of the slave. The Channings, Theodore Parkers, Garrisons, Wendell Phillipses, Emersons, Longfellows, have preached the most celebrated sermons, written the most brilliant essays, delivered the most stirring lectures, and composed the most touching poems on behalf of the oppressed Negro. American Evangelicalism cannot show such an range of first-class literature in his favour.[10]

But as the fair-minded critic that he was, Blyden also acknowledged the Negro's champions among the orthodox:

> Nevertheless ... the annals of orthodox Christianity are graced with innumerable names of champions of the Negro. The names and brilliant efforts of the Wilberforces, Buxtons, Venns, Gurneys, in England; of the Beechers, Cheevers, Finneys, Whittiers, Stowes, in America, can never be forgotten. And if there could have been infused into their adherents and followers the lofty philanthropic spirit which actuated them – if they could have imparted more of their elevated and generous enthusiasm – the condition of the Christian Negro would be far different from what it is now.[11]

And yet, on balance, Christianity debilitated and demoralised the Negro in America; if so, then in Africa too, 'the constant effort of the missionaries ... to Europeanise [Africans] without reference to their race peculiarities or the climatic conditions of the country' led, in Blyden's view, to 'many serious drawbacks, preventing any healthy or permanent results'. In the final analysis,

> The thin varnish of European civilisation, which the native thus receives, is mistaken for a genuine mental metamorphosis, when as a rule, owing to the imprudent hurry by which the

converts' reformation has been brought about, his Christianity, instead of being pure is superstitious, instead of being genuine, is only nominal, instead of being deep is utterly superficial, and not having fairly taken root, it cannot flourish and become reproductive.[12]

For Blyden, therefore, the Christianity which the Negro encountered at the hands of Europeans could hardly provide a basis for re-establishing 'his sense of the dignity of human nature'. Since it was not Christianity in its essence, but the European racial characteristics of domination and control that had produced the lamentable results he saw in Negroes in Christian lands and under Christian tutelage, the Negro would achieve his 'sense of the dignity of human nature' only by keeping separate as far as possible from European contact, and that meant ideally in his native environment in Africa. It was this idea which motivated Blyden's ardent championing of schemes to repatriate Negros from America to Africa.

By the same logic, when Blyden proposed the establishment of a liberal education for Africans in Africa, in his inaugural address as President of Liberia College,[13] he 'excluded as subjects for study, at least in the earlier college years' the entire literature of modern Europe from the close of the medieval age to his own time. His justification was revealing. Despite his admiration for Shakespeare, Milton, Gibbon and other authors, that epoch of European literature was the product of the age of European racial dominance, and so could prove unhealthy for the African's intellectual growth. It was:

> the period that the transatlantic slave trade arose, and those theories – theological, social and political – [which] were invented for the degradation and proscription of the Negro ... It has produced that whole tribe of declamatory Negrophobists, whose views, inspite of their emptiness and impertinence, are having their effect on the ephemeral literature of the day – a literature which is shaping the life of the Negro in Christian lands.

In Blyden's view, 'these are not the works on which the mind of the youthful African should be trained'.[14] Instead, the emphasis was to be placed on the classics of ancient Greece and Rome, the study of African indigenous languages and customs, and on Arabic, this latter choice being an indication of the admiration that Blyden came to have for Islam and Islamic culture in Africa. Yet Blyden never excluded Christianity completely, for he proposed that 'In the religious work of the College, the Bible will be our textbook, the Bible without note or comment', and he insisted that, as far as possible, the Bible should be studied in its original languages.

Conditions in Liberia did not permit Blyden to implement fully his proposals for making Liberia College a major institution for, among other things, 'racial development'. But several years later, Blyden produced what could well be a college textbook for an appropriate liberal education for Africans.[15] According to Blyden, his motive was:

> the desire ... of unfolding the African, who has received unmixed European culture, to himself, through a study of the customs of his fathers, and also of assisting the European political overlord, ruling in Africa, to arrive at a proper appreciation of conditions.[16]

In what was perhaps the first important generalised study of African traditional customs and institutions, Blyden was clearly seeking to bolster the confidence of Africans in those institutions, social organisations and values which made the African unique in the human family. For, 'the African', wrote Blyden, 'has developed and organised a system useful to him for all the needs of life', a system as his 'environments have suggested – to be improved not changed by larger knowledge'.[17] It was such a valid and viable system that Blyden sought to portray in his descriptions of the African institutions of family – espousing plural marriage that made 'compulsory spinsterhood unknown in the African system' – African institutions of education for initiation into adulthood and African economic institutions of communalism and clan unity which acted both to minimise accumulation of wealth by a few and to mitigate destitution and crime. In each of these respects, Blyden was convinced, Africa was in advance of Europe with its pronounced individualism and egotism. From the standpoint of late twentieth-century views on African religion, his description of the African sense of religion is most interesting:

> The African believed that the great Being can be approached through every object which he has created, whether animate or

inanimate. He can conceive of nothing which is not instinct with the Creator. He is a Pantheist ... He never attempts to formulate any conception of the great Creator and hence he has no theology; but that he is a spiritual being all close observers of his condition admit.[18]

And still more provokingly:

From our standpoint, we do not believe that Africa needed the theological interference of Europe, for the theology of Europe is derived from the conceptions of Roman, Celt and Teuton, which have modified the Semitic ideas promulgated in the Bible. European Christianity is Western Christianity – that is to say, Christianity as taught at Nazareth, in Jerusalem and on the Mount of Beatitudes, modified to suit the European mind or idiosyncrasies.[19]

Africa may need help from Europe 'in the material development of the country. But for spiritual leadership in Africa, the events of a hundred years of effort do not justify her interference ...'.[20] And so Blyden could write with evident conviction, setting off African 'spirituality' against European 'secularity':

Owing to the intense and increasing materialism of Europe, especially Anglo-Saxondom, the people have lost touch with the spirit world. This is no reason why Africans should forget the privileges enjoyed by their fathers. The intercommunion between the people of the earth and those in the spiritual sphere is a cardinal belief of the African and will never be uprooted.[21]

Nearly thirty years earlier, Blyden had expressed similar sentiments:

Africa may yet prove to be the spiritual conservatory of the world. Just as in past times, Egypt proved the stronghold of Christianity after Jerusalem fell, and just as the noblest and greatest of the Fathers of the Christian Church came out of Egypt, so it may be, when the civilised nations, in consequence of their wonderful material development, shall have their spiritual perceptions darkened and their spiritual susceptibilities blunted through the agency of a captivating and absorbing materialism, it may be that they may have to resort to Africa to recover some of the simple elements of faith; for the promise of that land is that she shall stretch forth her hands unto God.[22]

Blyden was not necessarily setting the traditional religion of Africa off against Christianity. He believed that Africa needed Christianity, but a Christianity without the European distortions of it: 'The Bible without note or comment'. But the reference to Egypt was important to Blyden since he believed that the civilisation of ancient Egypt was the achievement of Negroes. On visiting the Pyramids in Egypt in 1866, he wrote:

> This … is the work of my African progenitors … Feelings came over me far different from those which I have felt when looking at the mighty works of European genius. I felt that I had a peculiar heritage in the Great Pyramid – … built by that branch of the descendants of Noah, the enterprising sons of Ham, from whom I am descended.

The visit to Egypt, for Blyden, was to the 'land of my fathers' sepulchres'.[23]

But in his views on African spirituality, Blyden was also expressing his belief that Africans possessed distinct qualities which they could offer to the world. Blyden believed these qualities formed an 'African Personality',[24] characterised by cheerfulness, a sense of harmony with nature, a religiousness and openness to the spiritual dimension of existence, as well as a capacity to suffer and to serve, which made Africa's 'lot not unlike that of the ancient people of God, the Hebrews'. Even more telling still, it made Africa's lot resemble 'also His who made Himself of no reputation, but took upon Himself the form of a servant and having been made perfect through suffering, became the "captain of our salvation"',[25] an evident reference to Christ.

Christianity in African Life – the Unresolved Problem

In spite of his linking the destiny of Africa and of African peoples with motifs derived from the Bible, Blyden seems to have been permanently troubled by his observation that 'since Christianity left the place of its birth, it has seemed to be the property exclusively of the European branch of the human family'.[26] He was fully convinced that Christianity was *not* a European religion, for then, that would have made it 'a local religion', which it was not: 'the teachings of Christianity are of universal application'.[27] He wrote further:

> Christianity is not only not a local religion, but it has adapted itself to the people wherever it has gone. No language or social existence has been any barrier to it; and I have often thought that in this country [Africa] it will acquire wider power, deeper influence and become instinct – with a higher vitality than anywhere else.[28]

But Blyden's problem lay in what he wrote next:

> When we look at the treatment which our own race and other so-called inferior races have received from Christian nations, we cannot but be struck with the amazing dissimilitude and disproportion between the original idea of Christianity, as expressed by Christ, and the practice of it by his professed followers.[29]

It was what 'Christianity in the hands of Europeans' had done to the Negro, Blyden himself having experienced that treatment, that caused Blyden to move towards the unusual conclusion that it was not Christianity which held greater promise for the enhancement of African life but Islam with its lack of racial prejudice towards the Negro. Islam's role was, however, to be only preliminary and preparatory: preparatory, that is, for the more authentic form of Christianity he hoped for in Africa. In a publication of 1875, 'Mohammedanism and the Negro Race', he concluded:

> We entertain the deliberate conviction – gathered not from reading at home, but from travels among the people – that whatever it may be in other lands, in Africa, the work of Islam is preliminary and preparatory. Just as Ishmael came before Isaac in the history of the great Semitic families, so here the descendant of Ishmael has come before the illustrious descendants of Isaac.[30]

In early 1891 in Lagos, Blyden proposed the establishment of a West African Church which 'should be an African, not an English production', and yet also one in which 'we may feel communion with all

God's saints of old – at present and to come. So that all His people we can embody in song, whether in English or Yoruba, in Ibo or Nupe ... beautiful sentiments'.[31] The only such church to be formed in his lifetime was the United Native African Church in Lagos which seceded from the Anglican Church. It is doubtful that Blyden foresaw the twentieth-century phenomenon of massive Christian Independency in Africa.

Therefore, whilst Blyden perceived most clearly and expressed most acutely the reality of an African identity problem as a result of the European impact on Africa, his own response to the problem never really resolved the question of the status and role of Christianity in African life. His solution hinged essentially on two elements: the adoption of a position of racial exclusiveness, even purity, and an equally vehement advocacy of a cultural nationalism and particularism based on a self-conscious cultivation of African indigenous values and attitudes. It is by this essential focus on 'race integrity', on 'African personality' and *Africanness* that Blyden's response to the problem of African identity has continued to hold an attraction, even if not by direct influence, for those African intellectuals of the twentieth century who, like Blyden, are troubled by a lingering sense that Christianity has an alienating effect on African life. Blyden's influence is all the more remarkable since, for the cultural nationalists of the twentieth century, the vindication of Africanness has come to focus on African traditional religion and the claim that traditional religion is the authentic repository of the African personality. Blyden himself was, however, rather dismissive of Africa's indigenous pre-Christian and pre-Islamic religion – describing it forthrightly as 'Paganism, with all its horrors and abominations' which he hoped to see 'forever abolished'.[32]

Thus, whilst the twentieth-century emulators of Blyden have inherited 'his' identity problem, they have taken his cultural nationalism to its extreme by jettisoning Christianity as he never did, and then fastening on to the one element in the heritage from the African past which he made the least use of – the traditional religion. A manifest example of this development was Osofo Okomfo Kwabena Damuah and his movement, Afrikania.

Notes and References

1. John Mbiti, *Bible and Theology in African Christianity*, Nairobi: Oxford University Press, 1986, p. 229.
2. C. G. Baëta (ed.), *Christianity in Tropical Africa – Studies Presented and Discussed at the Seventh International African Seminar, University of Ghana, April 1965*, London: Oxford University Press, 1968, p. xii.
3. I am glad to note that my estimation of Afrikania as an important event in modern African intellectual history is shared by Prof. Kofi Asare Opoku of the Institute of African Studies, University of Ghana, Legon, to whom I am grateful for access to his collection of Afrikania materials. The rather sudden death of Osofo Okomfo Kwabena Damuah on 13 August 1992 cut short the opportunity for pursuing with him the kinds of issues which he and his movement raised for Christianity in the modern African setting.
4. See Okot p'Biket, *African Religions in Western Scholarship*, Kampala: East African Literature Bureau, 1970, and Ali M. Mazrui, *The African Condition – A Political Diagnosis*, London: Faber and Faber, 1980, as representatives of an increasing number of African poets, novelists, playwrights, historians and other intellectuals who reject any Christian contribution to the solution of African problems as prima facie untenable, considering Christianity alien and alienating.
5. Philip Curtin, *The Image of Africa – British Ideas and Action 1780–1850*, Madison: University of Wisconsin Press, 1964.
6. Kenneth Scott Latourette, *A History of the Expansion of Christianity III, 1500–1800*, New York: Harper and Row, 1939, p. 240.
7. Robert July, *The Origins of Modern African Thought – Its Development in West Africa during the 19th and 20th Centuries*, London: Faber and Faber, 1968, p. 213.
8. Edward Blyden, 'Christianity and the negro race', in *Christianity, Islam and the Negro Race*, Edinburgh: Edinburgh University Press, 1967, pp. 31f.
9. Ibid., p. 28.
10. Ibid., p. 42.
11. Ibid., p. 44.
12. Edward Blyden, 'Christian missions in West Africa', in *Christianity, Islam and the Negro Race*, pp. 63–4.
13. In January 1881.
14. Edward Blyden, 'The aims and methods of a liberal education for Africans', in *Christianity, Islam and the Negro Race*, p. 82.
15. The work, published in 1908 in London under the title *African Life and Customs*, had begun as articles in the *Sierra Leone Weekly News*. It is quoted here as in Hollis R. Lynch (ed.), *Black Spokesman – Selected Published Writings of Edward Wilmot Blyden*, London: Frank Cass, 1971, pp. 163–81.
16. Ibid., p. 163.
17. Loc. cit.
18. Ibid., p. 178.
19. Loc. cit.
20. Ibid., pp. 178–9.
21. Ibid., p. 180.
22. Edward Blyden, 'Ethiopia stretching out her hands to God, or Africa's service to the World', in *Christianity, Islam and the Negro Race*, p. 124.
23. Hollis R. Lynch (ed.), *Black Spokesman*, pp. 150 and 157.
24. Ibid., p. 201.
25. Edward Blyden, 'Ethiopia stretching out her hands to God', op. cit., pp. 120–1.
26. Edward Blyden, 'Islam and race distinctions', in *Christianity, Islam and the Negro Race*, p. 241.

27. Edward Blyden, 'Liberal education for Africans', in *Christianity, Islam and the Negro Race*, p. 89.
28. Loc. cit.
29. Loc. cit.
30. Edward Blyden, *Christianity, Islam and the Negro Race*, p. 24.
31. Hollis R. Lynch (ed.), *Black Spokesman*, p. 194.
32. Edward Blyden, *Christianity, Islam and the Negro Race*, preface, p. vi.

2

African Identity
The Afrikania Challenge

Afrikania as a Force to be Reckoned With

Osofo Okomfo Kwabena Damuah and his Ghanaian movement, Afrikania, were significant in that they showed how the sort of questions that Edward Blyden raised in the nineteenth century regarding Christianity's impact on African life have continued to engage African attention in the twentieth century, Africa's Christian century. Afrikania established itself quickly as a literary movement because Damuah was a prolific and forceful writer. It is apparent from his writings – both academic and popular – that Damuah had read Blyden, had an affinity with some of Blyden's ideas and perhaps even considered himself to be in the tradition of Blyden.

There were no reliable figures regarding the number of Afrikania's adherents. The movement for a time had a regular weekly programme on national radio which indicated the sympathies it may have aroused in official circles, although Afrikania's access to the public media can also be interpreted as a simple acknowledgement that traditional religion, in its various ethnic manifestations, deserves due public recognition in a pluralistic modern state. Afrikania constitutes a vital component of the total religious situation in the country purporting to represent and manifest the religious beliefs, ideas and practices of pre-Christian and pre-Islamic times. The fact that an ex-Roman Catholic priest led this development is indicative of the seriousness of the challenge which Osofo Okomfo Damuah and Afrikania posed to the Christian churches in Ghana. This chapter should be seen as a preliminary and not exhaustive analysis of this challenge.

The Early Career of Damuah

Osofo Okomfo Kwabena Damuah, formerly Father Vincent Kwabena Damuah, born in April 1930, was a native of Wasa Amanfi Traditional Area in the Western Region, to the south-west of Ghana. After training for the Roman Catholic priesthood, he was ordained priest in 1957, at the age of 27. Four years later in 1961, he was placed in charge of a Preparatory Seminary at Saltpond in the Central Region, in the south of Ghana, and was also largely responsible for youth activities in both the Central and Western Regions, under the archdiocese of Cape Coast. An energetic man with a keen sense of social issues, Father Damuah wrote articles in the Catholic press which displeased the Convention People's Party government of the late Dr Kwame Nkrumah, and he experienced a brief six-day period of detention without trial. Then followed several years of study in the United States, beginning in 1964 at Canisius College, Buffalo, New York State, where he received a Bachelor of Arts (B.A.) in Sociology, and a Master of Science (M.Sc.) in Education. In 1967 he enrolled in Duquesne University, Pittsburgh, Pennsylvania, for a Master of Arts (M.A.) in Economic Development, graduating in 1968 with a dissertation on 'The role of the Ghanaian entrepreneur in Ghana's economic development' (which is unpublished). In 1971 he was awarded a Doctor of Philosophy (Ph.D.) by Howard University, Washington, D.C. for a thesis on 'The changing perspective of Wasa Amanfi traditional religion in contemporary Africa' (unpublished). He was at the University of the West Indies, Kingston, Jamaica, in 1972, pursuing post-doctoral studies on Pan-Africanism, after which he returned to the United States. He held various positions including that of Director of Black Studies at Delaware State University and Visiting Professor of Ancient History and African Politics at the University of Delaware and Wesley College, Dover, Delaware, and Consultant of Afro-American Affairs in the diocese of Pittsburgh, Pennsylvania, before finally returning to Ghana in 1976.

In 1980, Father Damuah was in charge of religious instruction in the Takoradi parish in the Western Region and President of the Ghanaian Catholic Diocesan Priests' Association. In 1982, twenty-five years after his ordination as a Roman Catholic priest, Rev. Dr Vincent Kwabena Damuah left the Roman Catholic Church, founded the Afrikania Mission and took the name of Osofo Okomfo Kwabena Damuah.

Damuah, Afrikania and the Political Scene

On 4 June 1979, Flight Lieutenant Jerry John Rawlings carried out his first coup, sweeping out of office virtually all the higher echelons of the corps of officers of the Ghana Armed Forces, and instituting the Armed Forces Revolutionary Council (AFRC). Rawlings's movement, populist and intended to rid the country of political corruption, managerial inertia and inefficiency, generated widespread popular enthusiasm. Damuah was among those who publicly welcomed Rawlings's appearance on the political scene.

In a booklet entitled *Let Your Light Shine – Father Damuah Series, Part I*, published in July 1980, in the name of the Ghana Humanitarian Association for National Advancement (GHANA), Damuah wrote about Flt Lt Rawlings:

> Rawlings ... that name rings like a bell. Now, whether we accept it nor not, he was sent by God to deliver a message to Ghanaians. And he did it. *As a prophet he is Ghana's John the Baptist; as a leader he is brave Moses.*
> He confirms the lesson that:
> You can fool all the people
> for some of the time,
> You can fool some of the people
> all the time,
> But you can't fool all the people
> all the time.
> Before the June 4th Revolution, we had given up hope for a better Ghana, but now through Rawlings and the AFRC, we realise that the time for our salvation is now. Here is a short prayer for action:
> 'Lord, I expect to pass through
> this world but once
> Any kindness that I can show my fellow man,
> or any goodness that I can do
> Let me not neglect
> nor defer it
> for I shall not pass this way again.'[1]

Throughout that booklet, with its miscellany of subjects, it emerges quite clearly that Father Damuah wished to see Rawlings's revolution

succeed, and that he was willing to make his contribution towards
that end, using Christian ideas and motifs to help to establish firmly
the new era that Flt Lt Rawlings was inaugurating. Thus Damuah
wrote in *Let Your Light Shine*:

> Christ was a revolutionary – Christ was the greatest non-
> violent revolutionary that ever lived. And that is not an academic
> phrase. By his word and example he transformed cultures and
> uplifted material and spiritual standards of life. He challenged
> the existing corrupt system. We, his followers, are expected to
> imitate his example.[2]

In the early days of Rawlings's revolution, his sense of commitment
to his revolutionary ideals and his ready availability to ordinary
people endeared him to large numbers of people, especially the
youth, who nicknamed him, following his initials, 'J. J.', 'Junior
Jesus'. For Fr Damuah at least, this was 'time for our salvation'. It is
not surprising therefore that at Rawlings's second intervention in
Ghana's politics, after 31 December 1981, Father Damuah was for a
time a member of the ruling Provisional National Defence Council,
the PNDC.

Nevertheless, there are two reasons why Osofo Okomfo
Damuah's political links with the PNDC government should not be
overstated. First, Afrikania itself could not be said to be political or a
state religion, being the work of Osofo Okomfo Damuah alone.
Furthermore, and more importantly, to be preoccupied with the
political connection would be to miss the real challenge that
Afrikania poses to the Christian churches, as a religious and intellectual movement in its own right, which may not need the support of
the government to survive.

A more accurate estimation of the link between Damuah and
Afrikania, on the one hand, and the PNDC government of Flt Lt J. J.
Rawlings, on the other – as no informed observer of the political
scene in Ghana, particularly in foreign policy, will fail to recognise –
is that not since the rule of Dr Kwame Nkrumah has Ghana been
more keenly concerned to affirm *Africanness*, to insist on and seek to
recover, in all dimensions of national life, her African and Ghanaian
'heritage of culture'.[3] There can perhaps be no more striking symbol
of this cultural orientation than the fact that visiting foreign

20

dignitaries and Heads of State – Christian or Muslim – are welcomed at the airport with libation. In their eagerness to regenerate the social and economic fortunes of the country, to rekindle a national sense of pride in Ghana's past achievements and to achieve a general sense of cultural equilibrium, it is unlikely that Rawlings and his associates would have been unmoved by the words of a man who could so persuasively popularise the idea that 'Africa was the cradle of civilisation' and that 'the light of ancient Africa did shine'.[4]

For the Ghanaian nation, Father Damuah believed, it was 'time to wake up'.[5] It is in ideas such as these and in the expression of sentiments such as:

> We have to think Afrocentrically (Ghanaianly)
> We have to decide Afrocentrically (Ghanaianly).
> We must act Afrocentrically (Ghanaianly),
> We must let our light shine now[6]

that one must locate the political link between Osofo Okomfo Damuah and the PNDC government. In 1980 when he wrote *Let Your Light Shine*, Damuah was still in the service of the Roman Catholic Church, seeking to use the Christian and ecclesiastical means at his disposal to further his concerns and his faith in the revolution. In pursuing those concerns and expressing those sentiments, Father Damuah was in fact, if not deliberately, helping to provide part, at least, of the intellectual and spiritual validation for the Ghana revolution as an *African* revolution, an outlook which would become explicit in his later Afrikania era.

Damuah and the Legacy of Edward Blyden

To appreciate this consistency and continuity in Osofo Okomfo Damuah's thought from his pre-Afrikania era into the Afrikania era, one must turn to the Ph.D. thesis he presented to Howard University in 1971.[7] This work is probably the prime indicator of the logical connection between Damuah's reading of Blyden's own cultural nationalism and his final repudiation of Christianity and the founding of Afrikania.

At the outset Damuah stated the purpose of his study, revealing also his motivation for it:

It is important to articulate the fact that despite the enormous literature dealing with descriptions of ceremonies, mystical tales and their eccentric interpretations, *no* study has as yet been made of the Traditional African Religion from *an ideological perspective within the framework of the African Personality*. We intend therefore to take a new look into this matter. I shall not lose sight of the fact that we are not only interested in an African Traditional Religion as such, but also the discovery of the man moulded by this religion.[8]

Damuah's insistence on 'an ideological perspective within the framework of the African Personality' is surely significant. He makes no explicit reference to Edward Blyden, but it is hard to miss the pervasive influence of Blyden's ideas about the African Personality. This is also discernible when Damuah elaborates further on his approach:

There is a definite effort to re-adjust concepts and practices which affect the African Traditional Religion. The main trend is to discover our own authentic native values and grow from those roots rather than trying to be an extension or offshoot of other traditions.[9]

This statement could well be a response to Blyden's sentiments expressed in his proposal for a liberal education for Africans in *Christianity, Islam and the Negro Race*:

The African must advance by methods of his own. He must possess a power distinct from that of the European. It has been proved that he knows how to take advantage of European cultures and that he can be benefited by it. This proof was perhaps necessary, but it is not sufficient. We must show that we are able to go alone, to carve out our own way. We must not be satisfied that in this nation [Liberia] European influence shapes our policy, makes our laws, rules our tribunals and impregnates our social atmosphere. We must not suppose that the Anglo-Saxon methods are final, that there is nothing for us to find for our own guidance, and that we have nothing to teach the world. There is inspiration for us also.[10]

An even clearer indication that Damuah had read Blyden's *Christianity, Islam and the Negro Race* is given in Damuah's criticism of

Dietrich Westermann, who in his *Africa and Christianity*[11] had expressed a totally negative verdict on African indigenous religions. After quoting Westermann's statement to the effect that the transmission of Christianity in Africa ought to entail the complete elimination of all that went to form the pre-Christian religious tradition, Damuah continued:

> He [Westermann] went on to say that Africans had no nations prior to European penetration.
>
> Well might the Martinique poet, Aimé Cesaire cry out in negative protest in 1939 on the eve of the Second World War to save civilisation – no letters, no books, no wheel, no plough before the white man came and now no nations! Eia pour ceux qui n'ont jamais rien inventé! Three cheers for those who never invented anything![12]

These words, except for slight modifications to the order of two of the sentences, are the comments of George Shepperson in his foreword to the 1967 edition of Blyden's *Christianity, Islam and the Negro Race*.[13] Blyden's book is actually listed in the bibliography of Damuah's thesis, though in the body of the thesis it is not acknowledged and referred to, nor is it explicitly quoted. Damuah might have misread Shepperson's foreword as Blyden's, though this is uncertain.

Blyden is, however, quoted in two places in the thesis: the first is a passage cited from Robert July's *The Origins of Modern African Thought*,[14] the second is a text from Blyden's *African Life and Customs*.[15] In both passages the dominant theme is race. Damuah's use of these passages is clearly conditioned by his own concern for a cultural nationalism, yet it is also clear that he draws on Blyden's ideas regarding the significance of an awareness of race and the importance of affirming an African racial character and constantly maintaining an African racial aspiration. It is upon these ideas that Damuah was to construct his 'ideological perspective within the framework of the African Personality'. Beyond seeing in Blyden 'the father of African Personality', as Damuah calls him,[16] Damuah apparently had no use for Blyden's profound questionings in *Christianity, Islam and the Negro Race* regarding the historical place and possible future role of Christianity in African life. It is hard to avoid the conclusion that in 1971, more than ten years before Afrikania, when he was still a priest in the Roman Catholic Church, Damuah's thought was already being unhinged from the Christian faith.

Blyden had urged his educated and Westernised Liberian audience to study African indigenous institutions and customs – 'we must study our brethren in the interior, who know better than we do the laws of growth for the race'[17] – while the focus for Damuah's study was his own native background in the Wasa Amanfi culture of Ghana, which he came to consider as a locus of divine self-disclosure through the traditional religion:

> Our analysis will entail a discernment of and a systematic reflection on God's ongoing self-communication and revelation in Wasa Amanfi culture.[18]

Damuah also linked his study to the modern African quest 'for independence from colonial rule', and to this end he sought to affirm what he called five 'leading ideas'. These were:

a) the profundity of Traditional African Religion and how it pervades every aspect of traditional Africa.

b) how this characteristic is ingrained even today in the twentieth century non-Westernised African.

c) how Christianity and Islam do not seem to satisfy adequately Africa's quest for identity and self-determination.

d) how a reconstructed Traditional African Religion may be considered as a likely answer to Africa's search for freedom and self-determination.

e) that Traditional African Religion can exist in its own right on equal terms with other religions within an ecumenical framework.[19]

The large middle portion of the thesis is taken up with affirming the first two leading ideas, drawing mainly on the theories of J. B. Danquah's *The Akan Doctrine of God*,[20] particularly his theory of God in Akan belief as Ancestor and its implications for the religious ordering of society and social relationships. Sometimes Damuah is content to use his sources with little or no comment apart from the odd necessary modifications to suit his focus on 'Wasa Amanfi culture'. Thus the whole of his two sections on *Abawo* (procreation) and *Mpaayie* (prayer) in African traditional understanding and practice are virtually lifted from Kofi Antubam's treatment of these two themes in his *Ghana's Heritage of Culture*. Essentially, his position is that what is held to be cultural is valid simply for being cultural. Culture itself becomes the measure of value, an out-working of his ideological commitment to 'the profundity of traditional religion'.

From the perspective of Damuah's own thought, the more important part of the thesis is the fourth and last substantive chapter entitled 'The Search for a New Synthesis'. Damuah states very early what he considered to be the problem:

> The conflict over the meaning of being African runs through all of African life today – religion, the arts and popular culture and education – so that it is in these areas that many of the crucial struggles over Africa's future in the world are being decided. When it comes to religious values, contemporary Africa is the battleground of four contending forces: Traditional Religion, Christianity, Islam and religiously indifferent materialism. The traditional religions seem to be everywhere in decline, in step with the dissolution of traditional society. There is no attempt to capitalise on any specific traditional religion. Nowhere in Africa is there anything parallel to the organised pressures for a return to Hindu theocracy found in India, State Shinto in Japan, or even to the politicisation of certain types of Buddhism in Southeast Asia. Attempts have been made to organise the Ifa cult along modern lines in Nigeria, and throughout the continent politicians take part in traditional religious rituals such as blood sacrifice of animals and ritual libations, but these are minor and superficial bows in the direction of the old ways.[21]

Obviously Damuah was not pleased with the decline of traditional religion, nor was he content with the 'minor and superficial bows in the direction of the old ways'. If the situation indicated religious change, the crucial factor was not what that meant for Christianity or Islam, but what it meant for traditional religion:

> It is not the rate of conversion to Islam or Christianity (however lasting they may or may not be) that is the crucial token of religious change, but the inability of traditional systems to come to terms with modern technological society.[22]

Having isolated traditional religion as the most crucial index of the critical state of African societies, Damuah then sought to show how both 'Christianity and Islam do not seem to satisfy adequately Africa's quest for identity and self-determination'.

Damuah acknowledged that though Christianity 'is increasingly regarded by nationalists throughout the continent as a "non-African religion"', it has nevertheless a long history of presence on African soil – a history which stretches back to Biblical times. Furthermore, despite being a religion which in the corporate African mind is connected with colonialism, Christian missionary enterprise has a paradoxical character, for 'the education they [missions] provided made nationalism possible as did their iteration of the idea of fundamental human equality'.[23] For Damuah, the fundamental problem with Christianity in African society, however, lies in what he mentioned next:

> Yet Christianity is generally viewed by Africans as not indigenously African, but rather a white man's religion, because as in other 'pagan' areas of the world, Christian missionaries often opposed or denigrated traditional local customs and institutions: veneration of ancestors, traditional tribal ceremonies and authority systems, and polygamy …

Therefore, even though

> many Christian churches have been rapidly Africanising their clergy and hierarchy and also incorporating traditional African musical and artistic forms into their services and religious edifices – *overall, Christianity's image in Africa is still that of a de-Africanising institution, whose educational and proselytising practices lead to the adoption of an alien culture and a turning away from African roots.*[24]

In a footnote, Damuah adds: 'This is the great dilemma facing Africans today'. Here I believe Damuah has expressed his deepest misgivings about Christianity in Africa.

Thus the numerical strength and even social importance of Christians in Africa, whether in the mission-related or independent churches, do not have much significance for Damuah. The strength in Africa of Christianity, a 'non-African' religion, simply goes to complicate further the crisis and the 'great dilemma' facing Africans today.

Set against Christianity, Damuah believed Islam has some distinctive advantages – for not being perceived as Western culture, nor being related to the colonial structure of Christianity's relationship with African societies. 'Islamic missionaries', therefore, 'swim in the wake of anti-colonial agitation, making what they can of the fact that colonial powers have been Christian'.[25] Islam displays a strength in Africa in being non-racial in its approach to Africans, and not insisting on a sudden break with the African past regarding some social practices, such as polygamy. But what Damuah left unsaid is equally significant here: Islam in Africa is *not* the Traditional Religion.

Damuah's Solution – A New Synthesis

Accordingly, when Damuah at last proposed his own solution of the 'great dilemma facing Africans today' in the form of a 'new synthesis', he completely set aside both Christianity and Islam. The new synthesis is a reconstruction of the traditional religion which he affirmed as being within the divine purpose for Africa and for the world:

> The time has come when the African intellectual must take a new look and help resuscitate Traditional African Religion so that she can take her rightful place in the struggle for liberation and self-determination. The fact that she has been able to survive despite the encroachments of Christianity and Islam, is an indication that there is something in the tradition which God wants preserved.[26]

At this point 'the father of African Personality', Edward Wilmot Blyden, became eminently useful to Damuah, as he quoted him:

> Each race sees from its own standpoint a different side of the Almighty ... It is by God in us, where we have freedom to act out ourselves, that we do each our several work, and live out into action, through our work, whatever we have within us of noble and wise and true. What we do is if we are able to be true to our nature, the representation of some phase of the Infinite Being ... As in every form of the inorganic universe, we see some noble variation of God's thought and beauty, so in each separate man, in each separate race, something of the absolute is incarnated.[27]

Here Blyden provides Damuah with his ultimate validation, that the world-view and the elemental realities of the Traditional Religion *can* form the basis for constructing a viable universal African alternative to the 'non-African' faiths – Christianity and Islam. Within this 'new synthesis', Damuah named first *God*, 'at the top of the hierarchy', but viewed as 'the Great Ancestor ... the direct object of our worship, not by abstraction but by actually caring for our neighbour'. Second, there are *Intermediaries*, namely, 'gods, spirit ancestors and other spirits', but these intermediaries are radically 'demythologised' so that 'their new role is honorific'. In the third place is the *Family*, as 'the centre of the African social system'. Chiefs and traditional priests belong within this category of family, but are given a 'new egalitarian role in partnership' with the rest of the community. Fourth, Damuah mentions the *Celebrations* of birth and naming of children, initiation, marriage, death and local events, presumably festivals, which provide the setting for social communality and the mutual enrichment of life. Fifth, Damuah proposed an *Ideology* of 'creative and spiritual humanism', as necessary to undergird and hold together all these elements. It is this new synthesis, also called 'Nanaism' or 'soul solidarity' with ancestors – essentially no different from J. B. Danquah's idea of Akan religion as 'the worship of the race'[28] – that was to become the foundation of Afrikania ten years after Damuah's thesis.

Thus, whilst still a Roman Catholic priest, Damuah had already made his break with Christianity. In a revealing discussion on religion as essentially 'conventionality', Damuah wrote:

> religious convictions and practices are held to be true and valid primarily because they were taught to be true and valid, either at home, at school, at church or in the religious milieu in which a person grew up and to which he has always belonged, and not because their truth and validity were grasped as a result of personal thought, personal experience and personal conscience.[29]

Damuah then commented in a footnote:

> The author grew up in traditional Catholicism, following the example of his parents. At present, however, he is more of a traditional African religionist than Catholic and sees no contradiction between the two. He believes that so-called conversion to a new faith is basically experiential contact, resulting in

accommodation with an element of intuitive or insightful personal reservation.

Conversion should always take into consideration a person's individual cultural baggage, which is anything but a *tabula rasa*.[30]

Effectively Damuah had no need for Christian conversion.

If Damuah's new synthesis may be taken to symbolise the intellectual aspect of the shift in his religious allegiance away from Christianity, perhaps the emotional dimension of that same shift is conveyed by the words of a poem, 'Black Religion: Folk or Christian?', which he quotes:

> What Christ is this
> Who guides the White ship
> From Africa across a deep Black sea
> To sell its human cargo?
> What Christ is this
> Who will sanction the bomb
> Over distant lands
> For freedom
> While denying it to these
> Who drop the bomb?
> He is White, he is American;
> But is he human?[31]

But Damuah did not seek a 'Black Christ'. For even a Black Christ, because he is a Christ, will remain an outsider in his conception of his African cultural identity. In the *Afrikania Handbook*, Damuah would be explicit:

> All of us have to serve God, and the best way to do so is through our culture. God is satisfied with the widow's mite and we do not need foreign exchange to fulfil this duty. The Afrikania Religion has a lot to offer the world. We can't neglect our heritage. This is our choice and a challenge.[32]

In Afrikania, cultural heritage – specifically traditional African culture with its religious world-view, and its elemental, spiritual and communal forces – has become not only the *locus* of divine revelation to the African, but also the *means* of the human response to the divine disclosure. In Afrikania, *Africanness* has achieved an apotheosis.

Afrikania – Some Leading Ideas

In Osofo Okomfo Damuah's distinctly Afrikania period, his most important literary work is clearly the *Afrikania Handbook*, a sixty-page work which describes the movement as 'Refined African Traditional Religion'. Included in the *Handbook* is a socio-political theme which had not been stated or hinted at elsewhere in his previous Roman Catholic period. The *Handbook* provides a further clarification and confirmation of earlier views and intuitions, but in its dedication Damuah states more explicitly his identification with the revolutionary process in Ghana and Africa:

> This Handbook is dedicated to God, our First Ancestor, and to the success of the total African Revolution and Reconstruction. It is meant to articulate the spiritual base of the Ghana Revolution and the total African Redemption Mission.

This socio-political orientation of Afrikania is further elaborated to explain its intended role in African politics:

> In order to succeed, the African Revolution must have a strong spiritual base, stretch her hand to God, the true and living God of Africa, the God of the whole universe (Ethiopia shall stretch forth her hand unto God) ... *Afrikania* has come to fill a vacuum, to quench the thirst of those looking for African religious culture.[33]

Furthermore, Afrikania's ideology which, in the new synthesis in 1971 was described as an 'Ideology of creative and spiritual humanism', is now elaborated as 'Afrocentrism':

> Afrocentrism is the philosophy and ideology of the New Africa. It teaches that Africans should know themselves and work hard for the development of Africa. This means, we must study, think, judge, evaluate and act from an African point of view. If we have to sign an agreement, it has to be in the interest of Africa. It follows that cheating, profiteering, exploitation and all kinds of dishonesty must be avoided. It is time for all of us to harness our resources and plan creatively for the development of Africa.[34]

When the *Handbook* describes libation as 'the climax of traditional worship, in which we pray to God, and through our ancestors, including Christ, Mohammed etc.'[35] it is not at all clear what significance Damuah gives to Christ and Mohammed. Not only are they not mentioned anywhere else in the work, but the origination of the Afrikania religion is also totally independent of Christ or Mohammed:

> The Almighty and Merciful God, by His divine providence chose His servant, KWABENA DAMUAH, to proclaim His message to mankind from an African perspective. He was assisted in no small measure by his Chief Spokesman, Osofo KWADWO OPOKU-POLU who is the general secretary of the Afrikania Mission. As a religion, it is the language of Africa and therefore has no founder. It is a gift of God and we must polish it up, refine it, animate it and live it. It is God's revelation to Africa that Osofo Damuah and his people the 'AFRIKANIANS' are preaching. They are messengers of God, not 'founders'. They are merely putting the pieces together.[36]

Nevertheless, it is clear that Afrikania feels the need not only for literary sources but also for historical roots. Unwilling to be outdone by other religions, Afrikania locates its historical roots in a revered antiquity. In answering the question, 'What is the basis of the Afrikania faith?', the *Handbook* states:

> First it is based on God. Second, it is based on the traditions of Africans especially the ancient black Egyptians who gave the world the first major civilisation in history ...[37]

Damuah drew the full implications of recognising black African origins for the religion and culture of ancient Egypt,[38] and claimed for Afrikania the Egyptian *Book of the Dead*. Yet the Egyptian *Book of the Dead* seemed to serve only the purpose of the historical argument, for neither in the guidelines for Sunday worship (for Afrikania does hold Sunday morning worship) nor on how to start a branch at school or in a town or village (if there can be a Christian fellowship in school, town or village, then there can be an Afrikania equivalent), nor in the daily spiritual exercises suggested is the *Book of the Dead* recommended for use. Instead the *Handbook* announces as being in preparation 'The Holy Afrikan Bible' (spelt with a 'k', not a 'c').[39] At this point, one can only speculate on the eventual contents of the 'The Holy Afrikan Bible', but from the present character of Afrikania worship, it is likely to include traditional maxims, proverbs and ritual prayers.

It is evident, then, that Afrikania seeks as much as possible to be uniquely African. In answer to the question, 'Why Afrikania?', the *Handbook* states:

> We live in Africa and the best way to serve God effectively and productively is through the expression of our unique identity. God is our Father, not a stranger. We must serve Him the way we know Him and understand Him. We should not be carbon copies of other people's experiments and styles. We should be ourselves and create our own forms of worship from our own perspective.[40]

But Afrikania also seeks to be a 'universal' religion, from Africa and from African tradition, reaching to the wider world with a universal vocation. To the question 'Is Afrikania a new religion?', the *Handbook* answers:

> It is not a new religion. It is traditional African religion 'come alive', reformed and updated. AFRIKANIA is here not to destroy but to fulfil the dream of the new Africa. It is Africa's religion of today's generation, but it is open to all, irrespective of race, creed, colour or ideological orientation.[41]

Thus we come full circle: what was rejected in connection with one missionary religion is now affirmed in connection with Afrikania, for this one too is a missionary religion seeking to convert the world, especially all Africans. To the prospect of someone converting from one religion to Afrikania, the *Handbook* declares:

> Yes, but it should spring from personal convictions, not from undue social pressure or influence. It means accepting new challenges, making new social relationships and breaking old ways. Conversion to AFRIKANIA is a kind of spiritual and mental liberation. It is actually being born again and again. Mental bondage is invisible violence. Spiritual bondage is a form of colonial bondage. The time to follow our own conscience is overdue.[42]

Afrikania – the Challenge to African Christianity

The challenge of Afrikania to the Christian churches of Ghana, and indeed of all black Africa, is, I believe, important and far-reaching. That challenge may be stated in Osofo Okomfo Kwabena Damuah's own words:

> Mental bondage is mental violence
> Religious bondage is invisible violence
> Cultural bondage is cultural suicide
> The time for liberation [is] now.[43]

When applied to Christianity and the Christian life in Africa, Damuah's words point to three interrelated challenges which his own personal career, as well as the emergence of Afrikania, pose to the churches and the Christian conscience in Africa.

There is little doubt that Christianity continues today as a 'massive fact and factor in the African scene'. Damuah and Afrikania compel the Christian scholar to ask whether this 'massive' Christianity in African life is instinctive religion or is reflective faith. Thirty years ago, the doyen of West African theologians, Bolaji Idowu, a Nigerian Methodist clergyman, indicted the Church in his own country, Nigeria, for having failed to develop 'a theology which bears the distinctive stamp of Nigerian thinking and meditation'. Instead, 'her theology is book theology; that is, what she reads in books written by European theologians, or what she is told by Europeans, is accepted uncritically and given out undigested in preaching or teaching'.[44] Idowu's criticism of the post-missionary church was echoed in virtually every part of the continent, and by the most eminent of the continent's Christian theologians. It is now believed that 'much of the theological activity in Christian Africa today is being done as oral theology ... from the living experiences of Christians ... in the open, from the pulpit, in the market place, in the home as people pray or read and discuss the Scriptures'[45] – an indication of a widespread *vernacular* appreciation of the faith. The presence of Osofo Okomfo Damuah and his movement, Afrikania, however, poses a challenge which recalls Idowu's query whether Christian Africa has adequately appropriated the faith that she professes.

Damuah and Afrikania also pose a challenge in connection with the nature of the Christian faith as religion. The problem is not limited to Africa but, coming from an African critic, it has a particular relevance to Christianity in African life. Is African profession of the Christian faith, even through European missionary instrumentality, mere 'conventionality', to be explained as the vestige of a 'colonial bondage'? There is little doubt that in the early encounters of African peoples with missionary Christianity, African converts believed that in responding to the Christian message they were accepting a total package – Christianity and European civilisation. This was also in large measure a response to the European value-setting for the Christian faith. Yet is African 'conversion' to Christianity little more than a response to sociological influence and pressures from the outside? Lamin Sanneh's *West African Christianity*[46] stresses the 'religious impact' of the Christian faith in African life by demonstrating the very real and preparatory religious role played by African traditional religions for the eventual assimilation of Christianity. On a broader scale, Sanneh's view recalls John Mbiti's affirmation that 'African [traditional] religion reflects ... God's witness among African peoples through the ages ... a valuable and indispensable lamp on the spiritual path ...'; but that 'it cannot be made a substitute for the eternal Gospel which is like the sun that brilliantly illuminates that path'.[47] Damuah and Afrikania raise the question as to why the transition from African religion to Christianity is at all necessary. In his Howard University thesis, Damuah quoted to advantage R. S. Rattray's observation on Ashanti religion:

> I sometimes like to think, had these people been left to work out their own salvation, perhaps some day, an African Messiah would have arisen and swept their Pantheon clean of the fetish (suman). West Africa might then have become the cradle of a new creed which acknowledged the Great Spirit who being One nevertheless manifested Himself in everything around Him and taught men to hear His voice in the flow of His waters and in the sound of His winds in the trees.[48]

Damuah and Afrikania challenge the claim of Christianity and Christian theology in Africa to be the authentic inheritor and therefore the true interpreter of the spiritual heritage of the past. The relationship of Christian faith to the religious traditions of African peoples may remain on the theological agenda for some time yet.

Perhaps the most fundamental challenge of Damuah and Afrikania to Christianity in Africa is the cultural question, the problem of identity: the problem of the identity of Christian Africa, and of African Christians themselves. Have Christian churches adequately indigenised the Christian Gospel when they have accepted 'traditional' drums, dance and dress into their practice? Does the Africanisation of church hierarchy, leadership and the ordained ministry amount to an adequate rooting of the faith in a community? Hans Debrunner, ending his account of *A History of Christianity in Ghana* in the year of Ghana's independence, wrote:

> Christianity, a Ghanaian religion – When Ghana became independent in 1957, an impressive Christian service was held in the Accra Stadium. Christianity has become a thoroughly Ghanaian religion, which is also in living connection with world Christianity. There (were) African Moderators, Chairmen and Bishops. Future history will show the part which Ghanaian Christianity will play in modern Ghana and in world Christianity.[49]

The eminent historian could not have been aware that the Presbyterian Church of Ghana had, for its part, never had other than African Moderators, even prior to Ghana's political independence.

How is indigenisation to be achieved. In 1955, two years before Ghana's political independence, at the important Conference of the Christian Council of the Gold Coast, which was called to discuss the theme of 'Christianity and African culture', Christian Baëta recalled the persisting attachment to traditional patterns of the extended family life and the continuing significance of the dead for many Ghanaians. What was the Christian response to be? His proposal was that the churches make a deliberate effort to identify with and fill every occasion of 'heightened feeling' with 'Christian content':

> The setting, the external framework of these observances should be taken directly from African culture and be plainly reminiscent of it. But the meaning, the content, especially as expressed in words, should serve Christian purposes and provide Christian nurture ... The important thing is that for every occasion of heightened feeling, there should be a custom combining African form and Christian content. For this reason

> I would suggest that these new customs be hitched principally, though not entirely, to the inevitable highlights of the common life, i.e. birth, puberty, marriage, death.[50]

I am not aware of any church in Ghana which is making the sort of 'deliberate effort' that Christian Baëta suggested over thirty years ago so that Christ may, for the Ghanaian, be truly revealed in the Ghanaian context of culture as the fullness that fills all things on every occasion of 'heightened feeling'. Osofo Okomfo Damuah's new synthesis in Afrikania, which is built around these 'inevitable highlights of the common life' that seem to be so vital for the definition of African cultural identity, may be perhaps the surest evidence that the most important challenge of Afrikania to Christianity in Africa concerns the problem of identity.

It is conceivable that Osofo Okomfo Damuah and Afrikania may not have any more permanence than other and earlier combative critics and opponents of Christianity have enjoyed. One recalls notably Celsus in the early Christian centuries. However, Celsus' challenge was no less real and serious; and the church very much needed Origen's response to Celsus. It is perhaps no exaggeration to suggest that the Afrikania challenge also requires an appropriate response.

Notes and References

1. Kwabena Damuah, *Let Your Light Shine*, Takoradi: Ghana Humanitarian Association for National Advancement (GHANA), 1980, pp. 13–14.
2. Ibid., p. 9.
3. This is the title of Kofi Antubam's intensely nationalistic presentation of Ghanaian cultural ideas and values. See his *Ghana's Heritage of Culture*, Leipzig: Koehler and Amelang, 1963.
4. 'For it is generally believed by scholars that the world's first civilisation was the work of Africans along the banks of the river Nile around 3500 BC, that Africans laid the foundations for scientific discovery. They were the first to discover and record scientific facts, for example, tools, vessels, metals, hieroglyphics or picture writing and writing materials.

   They established the foundation for medicine and surgery. The world's first medical doctor was a black Egyptian called Inhotep. He lived around 2340 BC. He was a first class genius and a man of many talents. In ancient Rome, he was 'worshipped' as the Prince of Peace in the form of a black man. He was the Prime Minister to King Zoser of Egypt and the most famous architect of his time.

   Yes our forefathers were the first to develop the science of agriculture along the Nile river.

   By a close study of the inundations of the Nile, they were able to provide a

satisfactory calendar and later laid the foundation of our modern clock system.
They were keen observers of nature, the moon and the stars, and developed the
science of astronomy and mathematics.' (Damuah, *Let Your Light Shine*, pp. 2–3)
5. Ibid., p. 3.
6. Ibid., p. 8.
7. Kwabena Damuah, 'The changing perspective of Wasa Amanfi Traditional Religion in contemporary Africa', Ph.D. dissertation submitted to Howard University, Washington, D.C., 1971. Unpublished.
8. Ibid., pp. 7–8 (my emphasis).
9. Ibid., p. 8.
10. Edward Blyden, *Christianity, Islam and the Negro Race*, Edinburgh: Edinburgh University Press, 1967, p. 7.
11. Dietrich Westermann, *Africa and Christianity* (Duff Lectures for 1935), London: Oxford University Press, 1937, p. 2.
12. Damuah, 'The changing perspective of Wasa Amanfi Traditional Religion', p. 10.
13. Edward Blyden, *Christianity, Islam and the Negro Race*, p. vi.
14. Robert July, *The Origins of Modern African Thought – Its Development in West Africa during the 19th and 20th Centuries*, London: Faber and Faber, 1968, p. 214.
15. Blyden's book *African Life and Customs*, published in 1908, was originally a series of articles in the *Sierra Leone Weekly News*. For edited extracts, see Hollis R. Lynch (ed.), *Black Spokesman – Selected Published Writings of Edward William Blyden*, London: Frank Cass, 1971, pp. 163–81.
16. Kwabena Damuah, 'The changing perspective of Wasa Amafi Traditional Religion', p. 153.
17. Edward Blyden, *Christianity, Islam and the Negro Race*, pp. 77–8.
18. Kwabena Damuah, 'The changing perspective of Wasa Amanfi Traditional Religion', p. 8.
19. Ibid., pp. 25–6.
20. See J. B. Danquah, *The Akan Doctrine of God – A Fragment of Gold Coast Ethics and Religion*, London: Frank Cass, 1944; 2nd edn, 1968.
21. Damuah, 'The changing perspective of Wasa Amanfi Traditional Religion', pp. 95ff.
22. Ibid., pp. 96f.
23. Ibid., p. 102.
24. Ibid., pp. 102f. (my emphasis).
25. Ibid., p. 123.
26. Ibid., p. 153.
27. Ibid., pp. 153f.; quoted from Robert July, *The Origins of Modern African Thought*, p. 214.
28. Danquah, *The Akan Doctrine of God*, p. 169.
29. Damuah, 'The changing perspective of Wasa Amanfi Traditional Religion', p. 140.
30. Loc. cit., n. 133.
31. Patricia Culverhouse in *Foundations: A Baptist Journal of History and Theology*, October–December 1970, p. 294. Quoted in Damuah, 'The changing perspective of Wasa Amanfi Traditional Religion', p. 158.
32. Kwabena Damuah, *Afrikania Handbook – Reformed African Traditional Religion*, Accra: Afrikania Mission, 1983, p. 1.
33. Ibid., p. 20, para. 38d.
34. Loc. cit., para. 44.
35. Loc. cit., para. 46.
36. Loc. cit., para. 35.

37. Loc. cit., para. 10.
38. See Henri Frankfort, *Kingship and the Gods – A Study of Ancient Near Eastern Religion as the Integration of Society and Nature*, Chicago: University of Chicago Press, 1948, and Eberhard Otto, 'Egyptian Religion', *Encyclopedia Britannica*, 1980, vol. 6, p. 508.
39. Damuah, *Afrikania Handbook*, appendix 7, p. 55.
40. Ibid., para. 38.
41. Ibid., para. 60.
42. Ibid., para. 40.
43. Ibid., back cover.
44. Bolaji Idowu, *Towards an Indigenous Church*, London: Oxford University Press, 1965, p. 23.
45. John Mbiti, *Bible and Theology in African Christianity*, Nairobi: Oxford University Press, 1986, p. 229.
46. Lamin Sanneh, *West African Christianity – The Religious Impact*, London: C. Hurst and Co., 1983.
47. John Mbiti, 'Christianity and African Religion', in Michael Cassidy and Luc Verlinden (eds), *Facing the New Challenges – The Message of PACLA (Pan-African Christian Leadership Assembly, 9–19 December, 1976, Nairobi)*, Kisumu: Evangel Publishing House, 1978, pp. 282–4.
48. R. S. Rattray, *Religion and Art in Ashanti*, Oxford: Clarendon Press, 1927, p. v; quoted in Damuah, 'The changing perspective of Wasa Amanfi Traditional Religion', p. 157.
49. Hans Debrunner, *A History of Christianity in Ghana*, Accra: Waterville Publishing House, 1967, p. 359.
50. C. G. Baëta, 'The challenge of African culture to the Church and the message of the Church to African Culture', in *Christianity and African Culture*, Accra: Christian Council of the Gold Coast, 1955, pp. 51–61; quoted in Noel Smith, *The Presbyterian Church of Ghana 1935–1960*, Accra: Ghana Universities Press, 1966, p. 174.

3

Christianity and African Liberation
Reaffirming a Heritage

Φ

A Gold Coast 'Bede' in the Nineteenth Century

As this book began by tracing the nineteenth-century roots of some twentieth-century problems, it may continue with another nineteenth-century topic: a contemporary picture of missionary activity and its achievement in the Gold Coast. The source is the pioneering historical work in the Gold Coast (now Ghana) by Rev. Carl Christian Reindorf, *History of the Gold Coast and Ashanti.*[1] Here Reindorf comments on the successes of the Basel Mission in the third quarter of the nineteenth century:

> We will now sketch the outward features of our progress during the last ten years. In 1868 we were able to assert that we had filled the regions of the Eastern Province of the Colony with the Gospel. Congregations had been gathered, schools founded, native assistants educated, the Bible translated into two languages, other books for school and church published in the native tongues, workshops opened, agriculture promoted. And as a step in the right direction, progress had been made towards building up a native church by several of the faithful catechists being ordained as pastors of congregations between 1868 and 1878. The report of 1879 says: 'It was a day of joy and gladness, when our dear brethren, the Revs. A[lexander] W. Clerk, Ch[ristian] Reindorf, and T[heophilus] Opoku, received this token of confidence and appreciation of faithful services by our Committee'. Four years later, Koranteng, Nath[aniel] Date, Jer[emias] Engmann and Ch[arles] Quist

were ordained. And we thank the Lord that he has blessed the labours of his servants the missionaries so that up to the present year (1891) we have 18 Native Pastors in active service, two of whom have been educated and ordained in Basel, viz: D[avid] Asante and N[icholas] Clerk.

The area of our mission field has extended over one half of the Gold Coast Colony. The country Okwahu has been occupied in the North, Western Akyem or Akyem Kotoku in the West and the Eastern boundary in the Volta with places beyond it.[2]

Reindorf was both a product and an agent of the progress he describes, having been ordained in 1872 after serving as a teacher-catechist and church planter since 1855, following education in the Basel Mission school which was founded by Johannes Zimmerman at Osu (Christiansborg), and at Abokobi after 1854. The Opoku, Koranteng and Engmann named in the lists of ordained men had also been his pupils at the Theological Seminary at Akropong where he taught between 1860 and 1862. Immediately after the passage quoted, Reindorf went on to describe the successes of the Wesleyan Missionary Society and the activities of the Bremen Mission east of the Volta, and gave shorter accounts of Roman Catholic and Anglican missionary efforts.

Yet Reindorf's work is not merely a history of missionary activity in the Gold Coast. As the title of the book suggests, the work is a study of the circumstances which brought the histories of the coastal peoples, notably the Fantes and his own people, the Gas, to be interwoven with the history of the then separate kingdom of Ashanti. It is interesting that Robert July includes Reindorf and his *History* in his study of nineteenth-century and twentieth-century intellectual developments in West Africa.[3] Robert July saw the significance of Reindorf's work as 'an African history for Africans and about Africans', and for good reason too: 'for the essential difference between his and other histories dealing with the same events is largely one of perspective. – they treating the subject from the European view and Reindorf treating it from the African'.[4] But Reindorf's work has more far-reaching significance from the standpoint of the impact of Christianity on African life. Reading sometimes like Bede's *History of the English Church and People* and occasionally more like Gregory of Tours' *History of the Franks*, particularly in his detailed descriptions of wars and battles and political intrigues, and akin to both in his sense of the role of Providence in the unfolding of the events of human history, Reindorf's *History* can be placed in the same category as Bede's and Gregory's histories – essentially national histories with, and arising from, Christian interest. Accordingly Reindorf's work is an important early example of the *Christian* interpretation of the histories and fortunes – past and to come – of the peoples he studied. In this sense it provides an important early view of the possible results of the impact of Christianity in an African society from an African perspective.

In the following passage Reindorf is ending his *History*, bringing his study to a close in 1860, ten years after Danish possessions on the Coast had been ceded to the English, whose power and influence were becoming ascendant; in 1874 the British dependencies were to become a British colony.

> Rule, supremely rule, Britannia, rule
> Thy newly acquired Colony on the Gold Coast!
> Protected from the tyrant and the destroyer
> By blood of thy noble sons shed on fields
> Let not thy treasures all be lost!
> Destined by Heaven to rule the land
> Let justice, love and peace prevail!
> For many years thou didst freely pour
> Blood and treasure on the land,
> With what return? The least.
> The Danes and Dutch, on profit bent alone
> Thy rivals were, with equal power.
> But now Britannia stands alone
> To bless and save!
> Two mighty foes impede her way,
> Ignorance and blood-stained superstition.
> To rule and not to fight such deadly foes
> Is not Britannia's way.
> To lift the nations which she rules:
> to educate, and leave the Gospel free;
> One word from her, and murderous customs died!
> Britannia's rule, then, blest by all

> Will superstition drive away,
> And Christianity and peace prevail.[5]

From this lyrical celebration of 'Britannia's rule' it is possible to form the impression that Reindorf was just a Westernised African who simply tied the destiny of the Gold Coast to the ascendancy of British rule or European civilisation – until, that is, one has read his analysis of what he saw as some of the social and economic weaknesses in his society, weaknesses which in turn led him to discern even more fundamental flaws. Reindorf's comment on the causes of economic decline in the Gold Coast are very revealing and have a strikingly late twentieth-century ring about them, testifying to an independence of outlook which is truly remarkable:

> The principal occupations of the former inhabitants of the Gold Coast were: agriculture, work in gold, iron and earthenware, fishery, salt-boiling, gold-digging and weaving. The new occupations introduced by Europeans were: brick-laying, carpentry, cooperage, clerkship, gold-taking, soldiery, tailoring, shoe-making, wheel-wrights work, stewardship, cookery, canoe-rowing, schoolmastership or teaching, sea-shell gathering. Sea-shell picking was a very profitable occupation for women at the time, because all the forts and tanks built by Europeans on the Coast were made with the lime obtained by burning the shells with wood and it was better than that obtained later from Europe. (Why did not our people continue making it? No, we desire to lead an easy life and to have everything manufactured in Europe instead of making for ourselves; sending everything we possess to foreign countries, which must result in making us slaves in the future).[6]

And, to critics who might argue that the Gold Coast could survive and prosper solely through the export of the available produce of the country, Reindorf had a well-thought-out answer:

> But the better classes among us, the educated part of the community, have given up agriculture as a means by which the riches of a country are augmented. Is not agriculture the mother of civilisation, the backbone of national wealth, the type of the various branches of human industry which have

sprung up in the civilised world? If our educated people abandon that work, is our civilisation on a sound basis? Can we speak of our civilisation when the real riches and resources of such a wonderfully rich country are buried in the ground? When the grass on thousands of acres of land is consumed by fire every year instead of being eaten by cattle? If our Government had all the native hands they require, and the merchants as many clerks as they want, and the missionaries too are well supplied, what would become of the rest of our educated community? If no attention is paid to other branches of industry, will not their future be miserable? Well dressed, fashionable, but without occupation, corruption must increase, and instead of our country improving, it will shamefully retrograde.[7]

In Reindorf's view, important lessons in this connection could be 'acquired from the most civilised nations, ancient and modern'.[8] Ancient Israel, the Greeks, the Romans, the Carthaginians, Egyptians, Persians ... all had a special regard for the 'tillage of the ground'.[9] 'Even distinguished statesmen, such as Gladstone and Prince Bismark were devoted to pursuits connected with agriculture.'[10] But the lessons from history pointed to only one conclusion: the key to the African's future lay not in emulating European habits, but in developing the skills and expertise which Africans already possessed:

When a farmer is enriched by his business and then instead of improving his trade by employing many more hands in extending his operations, he takes his profit and invests it in mercantile pursuits, about which he is quite ignorant ... When a fisherman becomes rich by his trade, ought he not to improve it by buying more boats and nets ... But if instead of this he becomes a general trader for which he was not trained ... When all the educated community are too fine to become farmers or fishermen, and all of them become traders and clerks ...[11]

they show that they have 'failed to grasp the essential quality of progress in civilisation',[12] wrote Robert July, commenting on Reindorf at this point. 'We have every facility to become respectable, well-to-do men, if we will only abandon our false ideas of civilisation and make up our minds to work with our hands.'[13] Then 'our educated ladies' whose only wish seemed to have been 'to dress as European ladies' would also seek to be 'hard-working' and have 'a desire for education'. Therefore Reindorf concluded:

> Let the better classes among ourselves impart to each other their best qualities Christian and moral, and then a decided change for the better will certainly take place in the Gold Coast; let us cultivate our own best qualities and not imitate badly those of Europeans ... and if there were more Young Men's Christian Associations and similar institutions here, agriculture, education and Christianity could be advanced.[14]

For Reindorf, Christianity had already become unhinged from European habits; it was simply a good thing and hence good for the African. And so 'Britannia's rule' was seen from this perspective, merely as a providential instrument for the progress and enhancement of Christianity in the Gold Coast.

History-writing as a Christian Concern in the Nineteenth-century Gold Coast

Carl Reindorf himself exemplified the virtues he was urging by devoting much energy to agriculture alongside his missionary activities as teacher, catechist and pastor, and acquired quite a reputation for his coffee plantation near Aburi on the Akuapim Hills. Reindorf was, however, urging these attitudes and virtues, not as a farmer, but as a historian, and his discussion of them was in fact a demonstration of his stated purpose in the composition of his *History*. For Reindorf, the study of history had become a truly Christian concern. Why was this so?

> A history is the methodical narration of events in the order in which they successively occurred, exhibiting the origin and progress, the causes and effects, and auxiliaries and tendencies of that which has occurred in connection with a nation. It is, as it were, the speculum and measure-tape of that nation, showing its true shape and stature. Hence a nation not possessing a history has no true representation of all the stages of its development, whether it is in a state of progress or in a state of retrogression.[15]

Reindorf was, of course, aware that Gold Coast peoples, like other societies, had had oral traditions which from antiquity served as 'a natural source of history'. But 'this important custom' has 'since the dawn of education, been gradually neglected and forgotten'.[16] Accordingly the need for a written history had become all the more urgent. Furthermore, such a national history brought the fortunes of one nation into contact with those of other nations and so opened the way for achieving a world perspective: '[Historical study provides] a means of judging our nation by others, so that we may gather instruction for our future guidance. When such is not the case with a nation, no hope can be entertained for better prospects.'[17]

Reindorf's study of the social, political and military events that linked the Gold Coast peoples and the Ashanti, and the European governments with whom they came into contact, was to show such value in the recording and understanding of history. It was also the basis of his confident hope in the future of a Christian Gold Coast.

An even more revealing indicator of Reindorf's overriding Christian concern is found in his elegy for the great Charles MacCarthy, Governor of Sierra Leone and the Gold Coast, following his death at the hands of the Ashanti at the battle of Nsamankaw in 1824:

> Hark to the ancient story of our forefathers' wars;
> Their battles and their victories;
> Their shouting and their deaths;
> Then let us turn our thoughts to praise of brave MacCarthy!
> But sad to say: the men he came to help,
> Deserted him, and he was left alone.
> Alone he stood, fighting with keen blade while life remained
> All round him lay the slain, the brave, the true,
> While cowards fled the field;
> But MacCarthy's spirit lived, at Katamansu it arose;
> A mighty force, he conquered Ashante,
> And made the Gold Coast free!
> Our liberty was gained by brave MacCarthy's loss;
> And Britain's loss was our dear gain!
> From bonds of sin and shame not man alone can set thee free
> To thy Redeemer Jesus turn,
> And then in truth be free![18]

It is as if he is saying to his compatriots: 'from bonds of sin and shame not man alone ... not even brave MacCarthy ... can set thee free. To thy Redeemer Jesus turn, and then in truth be free!' His all-consuming interest was that his people should become Christian, abandon their unhelpful attitudes and appreciate the values and virtues that he was urging upon them. Reindorf's study of history convinced him that there was no other or better way into the future for his people.

The Wider Significance of Reindorf's Work – a Truly Indigenous School of Christian Learning

The achievement of Reindorf gains even greater significance when it is set in the Christian and missionary context which produced him and in which he lived and worked. From his association with Johannes Zimmerman at Christiansborg and later at Abokobi, Reindorf came into contact with the peculiar integration of church planting, education and agriculture and other industrial training which became a hallmark of the Basel Mission's work in the Gold Coast and which he notes as among the successes of his time. But his years of teaching at the Akropong Theological Seminary brought him into contact with the meticulous study of language, culture and historical investigation and writing that grew up around Johannes Christaller and his African associates, David Asante and Jonathan Bekoe Palmer. Christaller liked to work in a team with his associates, having trained them to take note of and write up accounts of local religious events and historical traditions. It was from such material that Reindorf drew for the relevant portions of his *History* just as Christaller did for his *Dictionary of the Asante and Fante Language called Tshi (Twi)*.[19]

An indication of the aims of that 'Akropong school of Christian historiography' is given in an editorial policy statement printed in the Twi and Ga editions of the 1893 *Christian Reporter* (as the *Christian Messenger* was sometime called), and initialled by Johannes Christaller, its editor.[20]

Christaller himself had by then left the Gold Coast although his interest in mission in the Gold Coast continued until his death in 1895. In that editorial, Christaller stated his missionary aim as the formation of 'Christian nations' from the various Gold Coast peoples.

To that end, Christaller considered that 'A very effective help' to this 'will be that they become united by one common book language which must be ... cultivated, developed and refined' and so capable of serving as a means of communication among 'educated men'. His production of vernacular periodicals was intended to assist in the process of the emergence of such literary languages. Within the general aims of the development of such a vernacular literature, Christaller placed particular emphasis on history:

> A nation is on the path to civilisation when it tries to recollect its own history, when it begins to compare its former and its present state, to disapprove and reject bad observances, and to rejoice in real improvements, to learn from the past, and to progress towards what is better ... and so I hope that Ga and Twi Christians also in future days will be glad to read about the conditions and transactions of their ancestors.[21]

Result of the Impact of Missionary Christianity in Africa

In 1884, the first three volumes of *History of the Gold Coast – Native Reports in Tshi* (Twi), the fruit of the co-operative venture of Christaller and his associates in Akropong, were published. Five years later, in 1889, Reindorf's more systematic *History of the Gold Coast and Ashanti* was also published. Not only does Reindorf's *History* show that he and Christaller shared a common perspective on the aims and purpose of historical writing, but both Reindorf and the 'Akropong school' testify that in the mid-nineteenth century there did exist in the Gold Coast, as a result of the impact of missionary Christianity on African life, a number of educated Christians who had a clear self-consciousness as Africans and Christians and who were alive to their intellectual responsibility to their society. Reindorf's own influence must have been remarkable. This is indicated by the following comment by a contemporary missionary Inspector of Schools, J. A. Mader, on Reindorf's impact as a history teacher on his pupils at Christiansborg Middle Boarding School in the 1870s:

> Our Africans study history with great zeal and warmth. The study of world history helps this people to self-confidence.

> The class is one with the teacher, living the historical events ...
> We must expect a new generation on the Gold Coast after 10
> years: a nation, called to freedom and independence, able to
> give political expression to this and gaining its aim in due
> course.[22]

Mader could not have foreseen that in little over ten years the European scramble for Africa would begin and Africans would come into
closer contact with another kind of European: the colonial agent, as
well as the whole colonial and imperial apparatus! The impact of the
colonial experience on the increasing self-confidence of African
Christians is perhaps a subject which calls for special study.

Christian Education and the Making of the Independent African Christian

One explanation of the quite remarkable success of the Basel Mission
in some of its early converts must be traced to the Basel Mission
school system and its educational content. By the mid-nineteenth
century, the Basel Mission was already running a whole range of
educational institutions, comprising infant schools, primary and
middle schools and the Theological Seminary at Akropong, which
had been established in July 1848 to provide the kind of training
needed to equip church agents such as teachers and catechists, some
of whom would eventually become ordained pastors. These institutions were concentrated in a relatively small portion of the Gold
Coast, particularly the Ga, Krobo and Twi-speaking areas of the
south-eastern region; nor did every mission station have all levels of
educational institution. As a result, an individual might move
between a number of mission stations during the course of his education, ending up in Akropong if he were very able.

In the six years of primary education, foundations were laid in
literacy in the two main indigenous languages, Twi and Ga, in which
arithmetic was also taught. By the 1870s, Twi and Ga textbooks in
arithmetic had appeared. English was taught in the upper primary
classes, as were more general subjects such as the history and geography
of Africa and natural history. As would be expected, Scripture learning
was considered important, whilst singing also featured as a subject.

The middle schools were established late in the 1850s and

intended as an intermediary stage between primary education and the Seminary. Accordingly, the four years of middle-school education took on the character of preparation for the Seminary, even though not all pupils would eventually enter the Seminary. Reading and writing ability in the vernacular languages was intensified to include translations into and from English, as well as grammar and composition of texts. Natural history was continued and to arithmetic was added geometry, whilst the teaching of geography and history was taken to a still higher level, to encompass world geography and world history. According to S. K. Odamtten, this was done to give the pupils 'a true perspective'.[23] Scripture learning also took on a higher profile as Bible History. In the fourth and final year, Greek was taught, whereas it would seem that 'from 1872, Greek was taught even in the third year'.[24] For the purpose of hymn singing and teaching in church, it was considered useful to learn to play a musical instrument, often the accordion.

In the three years of Seminary training, itself modelled on the Missionshaus at Basel where the missionaries had had their own mission training, more advanced levels were achieved in studies of the vernacular languages, especially regarding translations of Biblical texts from and into English. One Twi source informs us that Christaller was particularly concerned with this aspect of the students' training.[25] English and Greek were continued whilst Hebrew was begun. Apart from the specifically theological subjects like church history, Christian doctrine and ethics, geometry and algebra, history and natural history were also taught as well as methodology of teaching and basic child psychology.[26]

Alongside the academic training that was given, the Basel Mission educational structure also provided training in manual skills in agriculture and some craft training – especially at the middle-school level. In this connection, Odamtten comments:

> The teaching of the art of writing and reading was only part of the missionary idea of education ... Indeed one of the greatest contributions the Basel Mission made towards education in the Gold Coast was the industrial training they gave. The carpenters, blacksmiths, etc., they trained not only improved their own circumstances, by selling their skills, they also gradually helped to improve the living standards of the peoples.[27]

And yet it might be asked how relevant the academic training given, particularly at the Seminary, was to African needs at the time. An indication of the Basel Mission's thinking on the question is given in the Memorandum that was presented by missionary Elias Schrenk to the House of Commons Select Committee appointed to investigate whether or not Britain was to abandon the Gold Coast following the second Ashanti invasion of the coastal regions in 1863. Schrenk's memorandum is discussed by Odamtten. When asked about the content of Basel Mission education, Schrenk

> Said Latin was not taught in their middle school but that Hebrew and Greek were because 'they [the Africans] must read the Bible in the original languages; we only teach it to those who will be missionaries and teachers'. Asked whether the teaching of the English language and literature would not be sufficient to develop the minds of the peoples, he said: 'It is our resolution to make the negroes independent and therefore we think that the native minister must be able to read the Bible in the original language if he would be independent'.[28]

Odamtten comments on this in his book:

> this is an indication that the policy of using the vernacular was based on the principle of helping the peoples to get a clear understanding of the teaching of the Bible. It is significant to note that they did not make attempts to teach their own language, German, in their schools. This shows that their refusal to use English as the sole medium of instruction did not spring from sheer sentiment.[29]

Whatever other factors might be adduced to explain the character of the Basel Mission's educational policy in the Gold Coast in the nineteenth century – including the tendency in German missionary practice to seek to produce a 'Volkskirche' (see for example, Bruno Gutmann in East Africa) – it is hard to ignore the influence of the Protestant Reformation tradition out of which a missionary society like the Basel Mission emerged. Believing so intensely that the Bible was the sole source of divine truth, the Mission would naturally insist that converts should be able to read and understand the Bible for themselves. The logical outcome of that conviction was a recognition of the importance of the vernacular language in much the same way that a vernacular Bible had affected their lives in Europe. Basel Mission instructions to its missionaries included the specific one that the 'vernacular of the people should never be suppressed by the English language' and, for the missionaries themselves, the learning of the vernacular was compulsory.[30] In the Gold Coast this meant, of course, the two 'mission' languages, so to speak, of Twi and Ga.

In view of the fact that education as conceived and practised by the Basel Mission in the Gold Coast was intended largely to serve the interests of mission and church – to enable congregations to read the Bible and to use the hymn-book; and to produce African collaborators, teachers, catechists and pastors, a feature which is sometimes seen as a weakness – its actual results were quite remarkable. It produced some of the most outstanding individuals of the period – people who were able to hold their own in relation to the wider world, as well as in their own society, like that 'Gold Coast Bede of the nineteenth century' mentioned above.

But it is in its wider impact on the social destiny of the communities it affected that the educational system of the Basel Mission achieved even more far-reaching results. The emphasis on the study and use of the vernacular, together with the exposure to the Biblical sources of Christian truth in their original languages, meant not only that Twi and Ga Christian congregations were being related in depth to a very vital aspect of their local cultures, but also that Twi and Ga Christian minds were being linked to universal horizons. To learn and understand in the vernacular had a significance within the universal relevance of the Christian faith: the sense of liberation – spiritual and intellectual – was tremendous. One Twi source for our knowledge of mid-nineteenth-century Christian scholarship in Akropong[31] gives a very revealing picture of how Johannes Christaller worked in his study, writing in Twi: Christaller insisted on finding, as far as possible, a Twi term for every item of thought and communication; whatever could be conceived of in Twi should find expression in Twi. He sought to arrive at this by painstaking interaction with students, chiefs and traditional language experts, the chief's spokesman visiting the king's palace regularly.[32] In this attitude, Christaller was simply working out the principle and conviction which he would later articulate in the editorial policy statement of the *Christian Reporter* of 1893 that was quoted earlier:

> A very effective help towards the formation of 'Christian nations' out of the peoples of the Gold Coast will be that they become united by one common *book* language ... cultivated, developed and refined ... means of communication between educated men (emphasis added).

The whole monumental achievement of Johannes Christaller in Twi – his Twi translations of the Bible, his Twi Grammar, his collection of 3,600 Twi proverbs, his Twi periodicals, his Twi translations of Christian doctrinal works, his Twi hymn-book and the similar, though perhaps less masterly, work by Johannes Zimmerman in Ga – all went to ensure that the formation of 'Christian nations' out of the peoples of the Gold Coast would have the necessary tools to be carried forward.

The Birth of a Vernacular Christian Scholarship

The important place which the study and use of the vernacular occupies in this concept of education persisted well into the Scottish Mission era. Thus in the Presbyterian Training College, the successor to the Seminary at Akropong, Scottish missionaries of the 1930s and 1940s – notably Douglas Menzies, John A. R. Watt, I. S. Beveridge, E. M. Beveridge and W. M. Beveridge – continued the development of vernacular literature, producing an irreplaceable series of school readers, *Kan me Hwe* (Twi) and *Kane mo mi okwe* (Ga). Ghanaian linguists on the College staff produced intensive studies of the language, the most outstanding being Dr C. A. Akrofi's *Twi Kasa Mmara* – a Twi Grammar in Twi (1937).

At about the same period, Ephraim Amu, who was later to be acknowledged and honoured as the nation's most eminent composer, was experimenting with tunes in African musical idiom. The researches in music of another African staff member, Otto Boateng, were eventually to lead to a doctorate degree in Music from the Martin Luther University of Halle-Wittenberg in 1963, for a thesis with the lyrical title: *Introduction to the Musical Culture of Africa through Ghana Gates*. In its studies of language and culture, the Akropong Seminary and teacher-training college functioned in a real sense as a research institution, rather than just a teaching college.

But in Akrofi's *Twi Kasa Mmara*, no less than in his revision of the Twi Bible, in *Twi Mmebusem*, Akrofi's own collection and explanation of 1,000 Twi proverbs, in the *Twi Spelling Book*, written in association with E. L. Rapp, in his more practical *English–Twi–Ga Dictionary* (jointly produced with the Ga linguist, G. L. Botchway), Clement Anderson Akrofi showed himself in every sense the intellectual heir of Johannes Gottlieb Christaller – 'the immortal Christaller', as Akrofi called him. For Akrofi produced what Christaller had not produced and perhaps could not produce, and yet for which he had paved the way, namely, the grammar of 'an African language interpreted by an African scholar writing in his own language', as Dietrich Westermann observed in his foreword to Akrofi's book.[33] Yet Twi was not Akrofi's mother tongue, any more than it was Christaller's. Akrofi was not an Akan but a Guan from Apirede, so that his achievement is all the more remarkable.

It is possible then to see the outcome in the twentieth century of the Basel Mission's educational policy during the nineteenth century as having surpassed by far its original narrowly-conceived intentions. It has resulted in a tradition of genuine scholarship; Dietrich Westermann was right to have noted, regarding Akrofi's *Twi Kasa Mmara*, that: 'It is always a proof of healthy self-consciousness and of a real education when a people shows an understanding interest in its own language and a desire to develop it'.[34]

Of note in this scholarly achievement in the Twi language was the fact that a Ghanaian Twi-speaking professor of Classics in the University of Ghana, Prof. Ofosu-Appiah, felt able to translate into Twi whole portions from the classics of ancient Greek literature – from Homer's *Iliad*, Herodotus' *History* and Sophocles' *Antigone*. If Hebrew and Greek provided the means for Africans to have access to the fullness of the divine truth in the Bible, now an African language served to mediate to Africans the literary treasures of another people. Twi has become, in the words of Christaller, a *'book* language'.[35] Twi-speaking culture has effectively ceased to be solely an oral culture; the seed for that development was sown in the educational vision of the Basel Mission in the nineteenth century. Of course, parallels to the Twi story are found in many other parts of the world, where Christianity has come into contact with other previously pre-literary cultures, as, say, in the history of the coming of Christianity to northern and central Europe. But whether it is in Anglo-Saxon

England, through the impact of Irish Celtic missionaries and eventually of Latin Roman missionaries too, or among Goths through the impact of a rather Arian form of Christianity, or in the Gold Coast through South German, Swiss and Scottish missionaries, the basic process is identical: a vision of Christian education, centred on the Bible, which, though intended for mission and congregation, in actual fact begets a tradition of Christian scholarship which comes to serve the community far beyond the church. The remarkable feature of the Twi story is how very early the specifically *vernacular* dimension of this development was established and how deeply rooted it became. Noel Smith's observation of Christaller's work is worth recalling here:

> Christaller's work achieved three things: it raised the Twi language to a literary level and provided the basis of all later work in the language: it gave the first real insight into Akan religious social and moral ideas; and it welded the expression of Akan Christian worship to the native tongue.[36]

There is thus a further sense in which this Christian achievement of literary scholarship in the vernacular languages, Twi and Ga, has produced a lasting impact on the social destinies of Akan and Ga Christians. This vernacular achievement, by its very character, also ensured that deep foundations were laid for a meaningful theological dialogue to take place between the Gospel and culture, meaningful in so far as the dialogue would be in terms of categories, not of a foreign language and an alien culture, but rather of the local language and the local culture. For all Christaller's concern to arrive at 'real insight into Akan religious, social and moral ideas', Christaller never lost sight of the *theological* – and we might say in our time, missiological – task that lay upon him and his associates. Thus his *Dictionary of the Asante and Fante language called Tshi* (Twi) shows itself in every respect as a theological work. Not only by his use of Twi proverbs and Biblical texts to illustrate his explanations, but also by his willingness to indicate the religious impact on the Akan mind as a result of the coming of Christianity, Christaller's work demonstrates how it is itself the fruit of dialogue as well as being an outstanding exemplar of the dialogue as a theological dialogue. Thus Christaller informs us that the pluralisation of the Akan name for God, *Onyame* into *Anyame,* was introduced by Europeans who assumed the local people to be polytheists, whilst the people themselves attribute the divine name to only one Being and none other. The impact of such intimations becomes significant in any modern enquiry into the relationship of the Biblical faith to Akan religious ideas in West Africa, as Patrick Ryan showed in his very illuminating article in *Journal of Religion in Africa.*[37] We now know from our closer study of African religions the reason why 'God' could not rise up against the 'gods' as He could do in the Semitic, Graeco-Roman and the northern European Teutonic contexts and phases of evangelisation. The God of the Bible turned out to be the God whose name has been hallowed in vernacular usage for generations. This did not happen in Europe. Christaller pointed in the right direction through his meticulous study of African language.

An Abiding Heritage ... Some Surprises

To re-affirm this vernacular heritage and expound on its genuine achievement of depth in local culture is, of course, not a comment on what the Christian communities concerned are actually doing with it now; rather, it is to indicate the *possibilities* which this heritage offers for meeting the challenges that currently face the church, some of which we have outlined in the earlier chapters. One of the signs of signs of hope for Christianity in Ghana is precisely the depth of the impact of this Christian heritage in the country and its ability from time to time to spring surprises, even upon the public scene.

One such event was the death in July 1988 of William Ofori-Atta at the age of seventy-eight. A veteran politician, Paa Willie, as he was affectionately known, had, in 1964, become a very keen Christian following a dramatic conversion whilst in detention under Nkrumah. His death revealed the great number of persons and sections of the community who believed that Paa Willie 'belonged' to them too – among them the government, the Bar Association, and obviously the Christian community because he was a much-loved and energetic Christian and Presbyterian layman. The Moderator of the Presbyterian Church of Ghana preached the sermon at his funeral, and a host of other associations paid tribute to him at his funeral. For our purposes, the most interesting and most significant one came from the Akyem-Abuakwa Traditional State Council (Okyeman Council) in a citation by which it awarded him a posthumous decoration, the traditional state's highest insignia, Okyeman Kanea (the light of Okyeman – the light of the Akyem-Abuakwa Kingdom).

The fact is, in the last twenty-four years of his life, Paa Willie's understanding of his conversion meant that the Christian faith could not merge with the religious aspects of traditional life and custom. In his own words: 'Christianity is a person. That person is Jesus Christ; the Son of God.'[38] So radical was his sense of his Christian identity the Okyeman Council could not have been unaware that they were honouring a Christian, for the citation ended with the words: 'Oheneba (Prince) Okyeman Kanea, fare thee well, and may you remain in the gracious keeping of *our* Lord Jesus Christ'.[36]

It is an open question as to how the terms of such a parting citation may be said to relate or not to the notion that in traditional Akan understanding, the dead – and the especially prominent dead – go to join ancestors bearing messages from the living. We are left to assume that this particular royal goes to Jesus Christ and that this is so is affirmed by the traditional state which had nurtured him but had had no influence on the faith in which he died. The impact of Christianity on African life – communal as well as individual – and at the specific level of cultural identity, may thus be more complex and perhaps more profound than those critics who allege Christianity's alienating effect may have recognised.

This chapter began with the 'Gold Coast Bede of the nineteenth century', Carl Christian Reindorf, product as well as promoter of Christianity and an ardent believer in its benefits to his people; we followed the story through the intellectual tradition that was thus inaugurated at Akropong and was centred on the missionary educational institution there, noting the achievement of Johannes Christaller and his successor in Clement Anderson Akrofi. While Akrofi achieved acclaim in his lifetime, Christaller, on the other hand, never received any special honours from his home country, Germany, for his work in Ghana. Moves to award him an honorary doctorate were blocked by academics who argued that the man had not earned a Masters degree!

Germany did, however, honour Akrofi. In 1960, he was awarded an honorary doctorate in Theology by the Johannes Gutenberg

University of Mainz for his Biblical and linguistic work. The actual award was made in Ghana since Akrofi had been afflicted at a very early age with a strange illness which left him partially paralysed; all his adult years he had worked from a wheelchair. In his acknowledgement of the award in the Great Hall of the University of Ghana, Legon, Akrofi spoke words which are a fitting conclusion to our story and a testimony to the liberating power which had come into Ghanaian tradition through the Gospel:

> I do not forget ... that I am receiving this honour primarily as a Servant of the Gospel, being at present engaged in the revision of the Twi Bible. I consider it a great privilege to have been allowed in my own generation to participate in this noble task of communicating the Gospel thus paving the way for the Kingdom of Christ. I must add that I enjoy this daily contact with the Word of God, and find it most rewarding. In this connection, and in view of the general tendency to regard Christianity as a foreign religion, I will remind my fellow Africans that although Christianity is Europe's greatest gift to Africa, it is not exclusively the white man's religion; it is not the religion of the imperialist. Christianity is a world religion because Jesus Christ is the Lord and King of the Universe.[40]

This was said seven years before Akrofi died and in the year in which the revision of the Twi Bible was completed.

Notes and References

1. Carl Christian Reindorf, *History of the Gold Coast and Ashanti*, 1889, reprinted Accra: Ghana Universities Press, 1966.
2. Ibid., pp. 224–5.
3. Robert July, *The Origins of Modern African Thought – Its Development in West Africa during the 19th and 20th Centuries*, London: Faber and Faber, 1968.
4. Ibid., pp. 257f.
5. Ibid., p. 335.
6. Ibid., p. 264.
7. Ibid., pp. 264–5.
8. Ibid., p. 265.
9. Loc. cit.
10. Loc. cit.
11. Ibid., p. 271.
12. Ibid., p. 261.

13. Carl Christian Reindorf, op. cit., p. 272.
14. Ibid., p. 274.
15. Ibid., p. viii.
16. Loc. cit.
17. Ibid., p. x.
18. Ibid., p. 188.
19. Johannes Christaller, *Dictionary of the Asante and Fante Language called Tshi (Twi)* (2 vols), Basel: Evangelical Missionary Society, 1881. See Hans W. Debrunner, *History of Christianity in Ghana*, Accra: Waterville Publishing House, 1967, p. 144.
20. The matter is discussed by the Basel Mission archivist Paul Jenkins in a stimulating article entitled 'A forgotten vernacular periodical', *Mitteilungen der Basler Afrika Bibliographien*, vol. 9, December 1973, pp. 27–33.
21. Ibid., p. 29.
22. *Jahresbericht der Basler Mission*, Basel: Evangelical Missionary Society, 1870, p. 69 quoted in Debrunner, *History of Christianity in Ghana*, p. 163.
23. S. K. Odamtten, *The Missionary Factor in Ghana's Development 1820–1880*, Accra: Waterville Publishing House, 1978, p. 210.
24. Debrunner, *History of Christianity in Ghana*, p. 151.
25. *Sikampoano Asafompanyimfo Asore asranna – 1932*, Basel: Evangelical Missionary Society, 1932, pp. 65–7.
26. On this whole section see Debrunner, *History of Christianity in Ghana*, p. 151 and also Noel Smith, *The Presbyterian Church of Ghana 1835–1960*, Accra: Ghana Universities Press, 1966, pp. 56–8.
27. S. K. Odamtten, *The Missionary Factor*, p. 124.
28. E. Schrenk, *What Shall Become of the Gold Coast*, cited in S. K. Odamtten, *The Missionary Factor*, pp. 119–20.
29. S. K. Odamtten, *The Missionary Factor*, p. 120.
30. Ibid., p. 118f.
31. *Sikampoana Asafompanyimfo Asore asranna – 1932*, op. cit.
32. Such visits were to listen to discussions in the palace, carried out in Twi.
33. Westermann, 'Foreword' to C. A. Akrofi, *Twi Kasa Mmara*, Accra: Presbyterian Book Depot; London: Longmans, Green and Co., 1937, p. vii.
34. Ibid.
35. Johannes Christaller, 'Editorial', *The Christian Reporter*, 1893. *The Christian Reporter* was Basel Mission's publication in the Gold Coast giving news of missionary work as well as containing short articles in both English and the local languages, Twi and Ga. It continues today as *The Christian Messenger*.
36. Noel Smith, *The History of the Presbyterian Church of Ghana 1835–1960*, p. 55.
37. Patrick Ryan, 'Arise, O God! – The problem of "Gods" in West Africa', *Journal of Religion in Africa*, vol. xi, fasc. 3, 1980, pp. 161–71.
38. William Ofori-Atta, 'The Uniqueness of Christianity', *Tribute to the late W.E.A. Ofori-Atta*, Accra, 1988, p. 29.
39. Ibid., p. 33.
40. Clement Anderson Akrofi, quoted from *Souvenir brochure on some Ghanaian Celebrities*, Cape Coast: University of Cape Coast, 30 November 1974, pp. 27–8.

4

'How Is It That We Hear in Our Own Languages the Wonders of God?'

Christianity as Africa's Religion

Christian Faith in Vernacular Apprehension – the Starting Point

He is the one
Who cooks his food in huge palmoil pots.
Thousands of people have eaten,
Yet the remnants fill twelve baskets.
If we leave all this, and go wandering off –
If we leave his great gift, where else shall we go?

But this text is a translation; in the original language, Twi, it says:

Ɔno na ɔnoa abɛsɛn mu aduan;
Nnipa mpempem di
ma no ka nkae;
asee mporoporowa nkɛntɛn dumien.
Se yegyaw eyi hɔ
na yekokyim a,
yegyaw adom yi hɔ,
na yerekɔ he?

These words are those of Madam Afua Kuma in her *Jesus of the Deep Forest – Prayers and Praises of Afua Kuma.*[1] I have sought previously to show how the sort of 'implicit' theology which is evident in her prayers and praises can become a liberating force for African academic theology and for the academic theologian.[2] Being an articulation of an apprehension of Jesus 'where the faith has to live' at 'the living roots of the church', this sort of grassroots or oral theology can deliver the academic theologian from the burden of imagining that it is his or her task 'to construct an African theology' unaided.

Madam Afua Kuma is an example of the importance of the vernacular in the apprehension of the Christian faith in Africa. Her book can be examined to understand how Christianity in African life is a genuine answer to African religiousness. Accordingly, we avoid speaking of Christianity as an African religion and speak instead, of Christianity as an African's religion; the point being, not that historical circumstances have made Christianity an unavoidable factor in African life, but rather that the African experience of the Christian faith can be seen to be fully coherent with the religious quests in African life.

Divine Speech as Vernacular

Once this point is granted, then it becomes evident that the happenings on the day of Pentecost, as recounted in the second chapter of the *Acts of the Apostles* which has provided the title for this chapter, give an important Biblical and theological warrant for taking seriously the vernacular languages in which people everywhere hear the wonders of God. The ability to hear in one's own language and to express in one's own language one's response to the message which one receives, must lie at the heart of all authentic religious encounter with the divine realm. Language itself becomes, then, not merely a social or a psychological phenomenon, but a theological one as well. Though every human language has its limitations in this connection, yet it is through language, and for each person, through their mother tongue, that the Spirit of God speaks to convey divine communication at its deepest to the human community. The significance of Pentecost, therefore, has to do with more than answering to the chaos of Babel and restoring harmony between God and humanity, and between human beings. Its deeper signficance is that God speaks to men and women – always in the vernacular. Divine communication is never in a sacred, esoteric, hermetic language; rather it is such that 'all of us hear ... in our own languages ... the wonders of God'.[3] Thus, at the specific level of perception which is the only level at which we can speak at all of this subject, divine speech or communication is always vernacular. In other words, theologically, Christianity, unlike say Islam, rejects the notion of a special, sacred language for its Scriptures; accordingly, the Christian faith becomes, in the words of Andrew F. Walls, 'culturally infinitely translatable'.[4]

The point being urged is not solely applicable to African languages, as if they were the only vernaculars. All human languages are vernacular languages in their appropriate contexts. In the history of the expansion of Christianity, the pivotal role of the vernacular was equally demonstrated in the Protestant Reformation in Europe in the sixteenth century. The Reformation and its subsequent flowering in renewed intellectual and spiritual life and activity in Europe can equally well be understood to be the result of the European rediscovery and repossession of the Gospel through the medium of European vernacular languages. The fact that Christianity in Africa has attained this vernacular status considerably more quickly constitutes, therefore, one of its most remarkable signs of hope in the twentieth century. Were the character of Christianity in African life more akin to Christianity in pre-Reformation Europe, one would be much less hopeful for it in the face of the sort of intellectual challenges that we outlined earlier.

The Value of a Vernacular Heritage in African Christianity

Accordingly, in the African Christianity of the post-missionary era, the extent to which a church can be said to possess a viable heritage of Christian tradition in its indigenous language is the extent of that church's ability to offer an adequate interpretation of reality and a satisfying intellectual framework for African life. In some churches this will mean repossessing a heritage from the missionary past in order to enhance and develop it; in others the task will be considerably more difficult, since no such heritage from the missionary past can be so easily called upon. Even in a church like the Presbyterian Church of Ghana, with such a heritage of indigenous Christian tradition in two of its major languages, that heritage has not been built upon with regard to the more recent expansion into new linguistic groups, which are also represented in it, particularly the languages of

61

Northern Ghana. The church cannot insist that its northern congregations come to terms with the South and receive the Gospel only in Twi and Ga; this would make it difficult for the northern congregations to hear the wonders of God in their own languages. The church needs to re-enact and take further its past missionary service in order that others too may perceive that God speaks their vernacular, so that they may in turn respond.

Obviously a mere abundance of translated literature originating from outside a church's own experience cannot by itself amount to a viable heritage of indigenous Christian tradition, for the simple reason that it does not represent local or indigenous reflection on the original sources of Christian revelation, as received in the local contexts. The single most important element for building such an indigenous Christian tradition is therefore the Scriptures in the vernacular language of a people. It is to the undying credit of the modern missionary enterprise from the West, and to the lasting benefit of the newer churches which have resulted, that the value of the vernacular Bible for converts was generally recognised quite early. There is probably no more important single explanation for the massive presence of Christianity on the African continent than the availability of the Scriptures in many African languages. By rejecting the notion of a sacred language for the Bible, Christianity makes every translation of its Scriptures substantially and equally the Word of God. Thus, the existence of vernacular Bibles not only facilitates access to the particular communities speaking those languages, but also creates the likelihood that the hearers of the Word in their own languages will make their own response to it and on their own terms. Probably nowhere else in the history of the expansion of Christianity has this occurred quite as widely as in modern Africa. The well-known diversities within African Christianity – between churches of missionary origin and independent or African instituted churches – may well be the best indicator that African peoples, as John Mbiti argues, have taken seriously to the message of the Gospel as they have heard it.[5] The phenomenon of African Christianity in the twentieth century, therefore, far from signifying an acute Westernisation of African life, may rather be the evidence of how much African peoples feel at home in the Gospel of Jesus Christ.

The Significance of the African Independent Churches

If hearers of the Word of God in their own languages may then be presumed to respond in their own terms, this is another way of saying that it is not others' but their own questions which they would bring to the Bible, taking from it what they would consider to be *its* answers to their questions. Some of the evident implications of this were seen early, understandably, in the so-called independent churches, since in the majority of cases, these churches, in their origin at least, were more self-consciously seeking to be African than the churches of missionary origin. In an early study of some of these independent churches in Ghana (or 'spiritual churches' as they are also called), Christian Baëta of Ghana attempted to account for the phenomenon of these churches and to place them within the changing religious scene in Ghana.[6] Baëta took the view that the traditional religion, its rituals and its remedies, were geared towards answering the questions and queries and solving the problems which were thrown up by African life: problems arising from a sense of enfeeblement and vulnerability – both physical and spiritual, in connection with 'ideas held regarding the role of spiritual agencies in human life'.[7] As a response to these omnipresent dangers, the resources of the traditional religion were sought in order 'to obtain, preserve, and increase what has been called "life-force", potency, vitality, élan, more vigorous, pulsating, prolific life'.[8] In the traditional religion, the resources for these benefits were 'the various divinities, semi-deified ancestors, spirits, demons, witches, fetishes, charms and spells'.[9]

Against these resources of the traditional religion, Baëta saw the 'spiritual' churches as having taken a great 'positive' step, the equivalent, in the apostle Paul's words, of 'turning to God from idols, to serve a living and true God ...'.[10] In Baëta's own words:

> The 'spiritual churches' represent a turning away from these traditional resources of supernatural succour in order that help may be sought for the same purposes, from the God proclaimed in the Christian evangel. As the needs, cravings and hopes remain unchanged, so also the basic ideas regarding the character of the universe, of its forces, their possibilities and the modes of their operation, have been preserved intact. In point of fact this turning away 'from idols to serve a living and true

God' does not appear to be essentially different from the usual practice in African religion whereby a god or fetish which has plainly failed to meet the requirements of its suppliants, is abandoned in order that another one, believed to be more effective, may be embraced. The 'spiritual churches' indeed have a very strong conviction that at long last the passage has been made from error to truth, from the wrong path to the right one, from darkness to light; and that, because this is so, the newly-found resource of helpful power cannot fail.[11]

Baëta then continues:

Thus I see them as engaged in a prodigious struggle to prove the reality of spiritual things in general and of the biblical promises in particular, taking these in a fully literal sense. They are in great earnest; with an intense concentration of all their energies and a glowing desire, they are knocking, so to speak, on the doors of the other-worldly world, with most urgently-felt needs of their followers, and in the keenest possible expect-ancy, are waiting for an answer.[12]

Baëta does not tell us his own view on the possible chances that these churches had of obtaining an answer to their earnest waiting. On the other hand he seemed to equate their resort to 'the God proclaimed in the Christian evangel' to a change of 'god or fetish' after the manner of the usual practice in the old religion. Yet, they have taken a positive step – indeed their 'greatest positive step' – in sweeping away the 'old' resources 'in order that help may be sought for the same purposes' from the Christian God. The really crucial question which Baëta left unanswered was whether in transposing 'the needs, cravings and hopes ... the basic ideas regarding the character of the universe ... its forces, their possibilities and the modes of their opera-tion' into the setting of the Christian evangel, these churches might not have been at least half right, and probably more than that. Might the world-view which had nurtured those perceived needs not have found an echo in their perception of the Biblical world of Moses, of Elijah, or Elisha, of Jesus, of Peter and Paul?

One of Baëta's conclusions was that: 'looked at closely, their religion is in essence a very different one from that of the historic churches though by the common use of the name of Christ the two appear superficially to be the same.'¹³ Baëta arrived at this conclusion by studying, among other things, the nature of the petitions which were presented in the 'spiritual' churches for prayer and intercession. Baëta's sample listing included items like the following: requests for healing and health (by far the largest single item), women concerned about their barrenness and eager to have babies, men concerned about their lack of employment, young people requesting assistance in school examinations and wisdom to succeed in life generally, a traveller requesting safety and protection against motor accidents, a businessman asking for success in his business ventures, a person seeking protection against the suspected ill-will of another, one person's requesting prayer for a sick relative at home.¹⁴ In relation to these petitions which he considered more characteristic of the 'spiritual' churches than the 'historical' churches, Baëta's comment was interesting: 'On the question of the types of requests entertained, most ministers of the "historical churches" would indeed have difficulty in including in their own lists of subjects for prayer, some of the items received by the others.'¹⁵ One is left to presume therefore that one could not rule out the possibility that similar requests could equally well be assembled from *members* of the historical churches, even if ministers, depending on their 'culturally conditioned taste and sense of propriety', would have difficulty in entertaining such requests. Baëta, of course, did not go on to investigate the question in connection with the *membership* of the historical churches. However, it is well known that many otherwise loyal Ghanaian Presbyterians and Methodists claim to find in these churches the spiritual help which they have looked for in vain in the historical churches to which they officially belong. In my own experience of healing services in the pastorate of a historical church – in both urban and rural congregations – the types of request that are presented can be matched in practically every respect with the petitions presumed to be characteristic of 'spiritual' churches. It all depends on people having the opportunity to express them.

I have made use of Baëta's book because it was an early study of the phenomenon of Christian independency in Ghana, at a time when the general view held about it in the churches of missionary origin was that 'they [the 'spiritual' churches] constitute a grave menace to the normal development of a healthy Christianity in the country'.[16] The distinctions between the historical churches, of missionary origin, and the independent or African instituted churches, have since become less meaningful, as features which were once thought to be characteristic of the latter have been found to be shared also by the former. The significance of the independents, therefore, has been that they pointed to the direction in which broad sections of African Christianity were moving, and so they testified to the existence of some generalised trends in the African response to the Christian faith in African terms.

The Vernacular as Bridge to the Traditional World-view

This leads us to look more closely at the question of world-view. Baëta was correct in suggesting that what the 'spiritual' churches he studied had done was, in effect, to bring the traditional world-view that underpinned the old religion into their allegiance to the Christian faith: the basic ideas regarding the character of the universe, of its forces, their possibilities and the modes of their operation, have been preserved intact. It is easy to assume that the spiritual churches are therefore syncretistic movements; however, the fact that they have simultaneously turned away from the 'traditional resources for supernatural succour' – 'the various divinities, semi-deified ancestors, spirits, demons, witches, fetishes, charms and spells' – means that any argument suggesting a residual 'paganism' becomes unconvincing. Rather, the clue to the persistence of the traditional world-view lies in the spiritual churches' vernacular hearing and perception of the Christian evangel through the vernacular Scriptures. The combination of this vernacular reading of the Bible with the earnest desire to arrive at African answers and solutions to *African* questions and problems, has the effect of making the living forces of the traditional world-view persist longer and with greater potency within the 'spiritual churches' than in the churches of missionary origin. The difference is, however, only minimal, relating largely to the extent to which in the latter the traditional world-view is allowed to influence outlook and practice.

The different attitudes to a purely social problem like polygamy are interesting. The Musama Disco Christo Church, one of the earlier important 'spiritual' churches, for instance, includes in its articles of faith and declaration: 'We believe that (as an African Church) polygamy is not a mortal sin: 1 Cor. 7:28, 36; Mat. 22:30; Gen. 16:23; 2 Sam. 12:8; Heb. 13:4; 1 Cor. 7:7-9; Matt. 19:10-11'.[17] It is hard to see how any of these Biblical texts offers a case for polygamy, and from the pronouncements of the church's leaders on the problem there is a sense of embarrassment at having to accommodate the practice. Yet there is also evidence that the church is seeking to wrestle with the problem of plural marriage as an African problem, but using the Bible to arrive at an answer. A historical church like the Presbyterian Church of Ghana, which has had a clearly-defined line of discipline on the matter, is still unable to offer any substantial help to its members on the problem of plural marriage simply because it has never adequately faced the problem as an African church confronting an African problem. Presbyterian pastors and elders, accordingly, continue to serve out the set menu from the church's *Regulations, Practice and Procedure*, one of the most revered legacies of the missionary administration of the church. In the meantime, plural marriage continues among church members and serves to exclude the 'guilty' from participation in Holy Communion. The spiritual churches are also known to be generally more supportive of their members than the historical churches, in connection with traditionally expensive events like marriages and funerals. In other words, being more alive to the importance of these aspects of traditional culture, they apply their sense of Christian fellowship more radically to recreate the traditional African clan solidarity in Christian terms. Baëta's observation on the social regulations between fathers and children within the Church of the Twelve Apostles inspired by the prophet Harris is very illuminating:

> For a religious group working almost exclusively among tribes which follow the rule of matrilineal descent, it is remarkable that this Church has laid down the rule that all fathers shall be responsible for the maintenance and upbringing of their children (nothing is said about nephews and nieces) up to marriage. Thereafter the children are at liberty to join their mother's clan for all social purposes, but they must in turn assume responsibility for their father in his old age. Any person contravening this rule is warned and if he or she persists, is expelled from the group.[18]

By moving and functioning more intensely within the African traditional world-view of their members and applying the Christian understandings which they gain from the vernacular Scriptures (they have little else by way of Christian tradition to fall upon), some of the independents arrive at solutions which tend more clearly towards a *Christian* direction while remaining also African. On the other hand, the historical churches, because they present 'Christian' solutions which have not been thought through from the standpoint of the persisting traditional world-view of their members, prove in the end less helpful. Accordingly, the phenomenon of 'living in two worlds', half-traditional and half-Christian, and not belonging fully to either, can be said to be more characteristic of members of the historical, so-called 'orthodox' churches than those of the 'spiritual' churches. Whilst the latter appear to be attempting to work out their salvation in Christ within the traditional religious milieu, the former, on the whole, are failing to do so. It is not surprising, therefore, that a good number of those in the 'spiritual' churches are ex-Presbyterians, ex-Methodists, ex-Anglicans and ex-Roman Catholics.

The Failures of the Vernacular Churches of Missionary Origin

The state of the churches in their relation to the traditional world-view presents a rather paradoxical picture: the churches which have a longer historical connection with the society, and a profound vernacular heritage, appear to be less effective in meeting the spiritual and psychological needs of their members for most of whom the traditional world-view continues as a potent element in their understanding of reality. The explanation for this paradox also lies partly in the failure of churches to avail themselves of their vernacular heritage and to enhance it in the interest of a continuing dialogue with their local cultures. S. G. Williamson's comment on the missionary failure to come to grips with traditional religion and its realities in the Akan culture of Ghana has become classic:

> The invitation to accept the Christian religion was also a call to participate in a western interpretation of reality. Thus converts were not merely required to abandon the worship of many gods for the worship of One God, but were taught to look

upon traditional religion as the worship of nonentities. The missionary enterprise was seeking to implant its Christianity by the method of substituting for the Akan world-view, what was a European world-view.[19]

Williamson's observation should be modified slightly. It was not so much a question of the 'worship of nonentities' but rather something more like this: the Christian faith possessed its own set of beliefs, quite distinct from the belief system of the traditional religion; accordingly, to accept the former was to reject the later. To fail to do this was to confuse Christianity with heathenism. And yet Williamson's overall judgement is, I believe, sound and its implications quite clear: if the Christian faith as it was transmitted failed to take serious account of the traditional beliefs held about 'gods many and lords many', ancestors, spirits and other spiritual agencies and their impact on human life, then it also failed to meet the Akan in his personally experienced religious need. Looked at from this perspective, missionary activity never amounted to a genuine encounter, and the Christian communities that have resulted have not really known how to relate to their traditional culture in terms other than those of denunciation or of separateness. Dialogue has been distinctively absent. The missionary enterprise of the nineteenth century did not see in African traditional religion and culture a partner for dialogue the way in which it viewed Buddhism and philosophical Hinduism in Asia. The 1910 World Missionary Conference in Edinburgh concluded that African traditional religions, which it roundly described as Animism, probably contained no preparation for Christianity. When more positive appreciations gained currency, it was too late: the mission churches were already in place, marked generally by their separateness from their cultures, rather than by their involvement in them. The Christian tradition as historically received through the missionary enterprise has, on the whole, been unable to sympathise with or relate to the spiritual realities of the traditional world-view. It is not so much a case of an unwillingness to relate to these realities, as of not having learnt to do so.

In addition, the various Christian communities of missionary origin, probably because of the nature of the missionary legacy outlined above, have in turn failed so far to make adequate use of their profound vernacular heritage in order to overcome the limitations of the received Christian tradition. This sounds rather strange on the face of it, yet the problem is quite simple: it is the failure to read the vernacular Scriptures from the standpoint of the traditional world-view and in the light of its realities.

Discoveries at the Grassroots

This fact has been brought to my attention quite vividly through our programmes in Applied Theology at the Akrofi–Christaller Memorial Centre in Akropong. Akropong is itself an ideal place to carry out this kind of work in Ghana, both because of its place in Ghanaian Christian history and because it is close to a still-vital Akan tradi-tional culture. This particular programme centres on a regular study of the Bible in the vernacular language, Twi, with a group of local Christians belonging largely, though not exclusively, to the Presby-terian Church, which is the oldest church in the town and the one with the deepest roots in the local culture. It is a purely voluntary group, averaging a dozen, but occasionally reaching twenty. Though the sessions are led by myself, all consider themselves to be learning together and seeking to hear together what the Word of God in the vernacular says, especially in relation to the realities of indigenous culture. The study text has been the *Epistle to the Hebrews*. Having worked on the Greek text, from time to time I bring some points from it to the attention of the group. The *Scriptural* text, however, is the Twi Bible.

The problem I referred to in connection with reading the Scrip-tures from the standpoint of the traditional culture came up in our study of *Hebrews* 1:3, particularly the middle section in which the Twi reads:

ɔde n'ankasa ne ho dwiraa yɛn bɔne no.

The New English Bible (NEB) renders it:

When he had brought about the purgation of sins

whilst the Bible Societies' Today's English Version reads:

After achieving forgiveness for the sins of mankind.

There is first of all a critical textual point to make about the Twi, which shows how such a language with a tendency to concreteness in expression can affect perception of the Word of God. It is obvious that the English versions cited translate the phrase as in the major edited Greek texts of this passage, namely, *katharismon tōn harmatiōn poiesamenos*. The Twi, however, tends in a direction of the variant rendering which adds *di' heautou* before the phrase, thus stressing beyond any shadow of doubt that Jesus, the subject of the sentence, was himself the instrument of the forgiveness which he achieved for mankind. To use the Twi verb, *dwiraa*, to render the thought of the passage requires the explicit declaration of the indirect object, the instrument through which the action of *dwiraa* is accomplished. Accordingly, 'ɔde *n'ankasa ne ho* dwiraa yɛn bɔne no ...' and the variant cannot be too easily set aside. Perhaps this is another way of saying that if the Word of God is always vernacular, then Biblical exegesis includes paying attention to how and in what terms the Word is heard and received in the process of its transmission in the vernacular.

The greater point of interest of the passage centred on the Twi verb *dwiraa*, for the time of year was *Odwira*, the traditional New Year festival which, because it marks the end of one year and the start of a new year, is above all, a festival of purification, reconciliation and renewal. As it happened, it was as we began to analyse the *Odwira* festival itself and its leading ideas that it seemed to have occurred to our group members that *Odwira* had something to do with Jesus, and that the atoning work of Jesus could be related to the traditional *Odwira* rituals and its anticipated benefits. This discovery amounted to their equivalent of the apostle Paul's declaration in *1 Corinthians* 10:4 that the rock which under the old covenant gave the Israelites water in the wilderness was Christ himself. The vernacular Scriptures became the means of gaining a further insight into the traditional culture, whilst the meaning of the Scriptures was also illuminated in a new way, in relation to a vital aspect of the traditional culture. It then became apparent that a genuine theological dialogue with traditional culture was not always likely to be irenical. For such a dialogue to be meaningful, there would necessarily also be a confrontation of experiences, sometimes alternative interpretations of reality and identity, and in the profound relating of Christ to the living forces of the traditional religion there would also be a power-encounter since the traditional religion, centred at its most vital points on ancestors, was at heart about power.

The programme's agenda was widening and deepening and probably also getting a little bewildering. But there was a shared awareness that the study, through the vernacular, had led to firm ground which was *within* the purview of the traditional culture: Christ had a stake in the spiritual universe of traditional religion.

Implications for Theology

I have recounted part of our learning process at the Akrofi–Christaller Centre to illustrate some of the possibilities for theological dialogue which the vernacular heritage of Christianity in Africa opens for the churches. But our attempt also illustrates some of the difficulties in the way of pursuing this kind of theological dialogue. The issue of power-encounter is probably the tip of the iceberg.

More urgent, perhaps, from the standpoint of the dialogue as intellectual activity, are the implications of the vernacular primacy, so to speak, of the Word of God for African academic theology. In a recent article I raised the question whether African theology can be expected to make much headway in the African context without taking more seriously than it has so far the vernacular languages in which the vast majority of the continent's Christians hear the Word of God at the living roots of the churches.[20] Indeed my fellow countryman, John Pobee, has suggested that 'ideally African theology must be in the vernacular' since he believes language has to do with more than communication: it is the means for 'assuming the weight of a culture'. Thus to write in a *lingua 'franca* like English, French, Portuguese or German is, for the African theologian, a second best even if it secures the writer a wider audience. Pobee goes some way in attempting to deal with the problem by making extensive use of Akan (Fante) proverbs and wise sayings in the exposition of Christian ideas.[21]

Traditional maxims and proverbs do not as a rule, however, arise from a vernacular Christian perception and experience. So in a sense, the problem remains. Perhaps the real challenge of the vernacular primacy of the Word of God is that African theology will make a deliberate attempt to relate theological reflection and construction to the actual vernacular articulation of faith in African Christian experience. Taking the vernacular seriously then, becomes not merely a cultural but also a theological necessity. For it is only through the vernacular that a genuine and lasting theological dialogue with culture can take place.

If it is adequately to reflect the experience of faith in Christ in African life, African theology will have to make greater use of the Scriptures in the vernacular, thus hearing and perceiving the Word of God in much the same way as the majority of Africa's Christians do. African theology should not set aside its academic concerns in relation to a wider ecumenical Christian scholarship, but the value of making the Scripture in African vernacular languages a major focus and point of reference is that African theology's methods, interests and goals will then be shaped and controlled by the genuine needs of Christianity in African life. As a result, African theology will be enabled to bring more effectively to African Christian life insights from other parts of the body of Christ without making them necessarily normative. It will also be in a stronger position to demonstrate the ecumenical significance of the African experience. African theology will therefore fulfil a crucial pastoral function: nurturing and equipping a people of God, who have heard in their own languages the wonders of God.

> Na ɛyɛɛ den na yɛn nyinaa te yɛn ankasa kasa a wɔwoo yɛn mu yi ... [na] yɛte sɛ wɔde yɛn kasa ka Onyankopɔn ade kɛse?[22]

Notes and References

1. Afua Kuma, *Jesus of the Deep Forest – Prayers and Praises of Afua Kuma* (English translation by Fr Jon Kirby, from the Twi original; see Afua Kuma, *Afua Kuma Ayeyi ne Mpaebo – Kwaebirentuw ase Yesu*), Accra: Asempa Publishers, 1981, p. 38.
2. See my 'Cry Jesus! Christian theology and presence in modern Africa', in *Vox Evangelica*, vol. 23, April 1993, pp. 7–25.
3. *Acts of the Apostles* 2:11.
4. Andrew F. Walls, 'The Gospel as the prisoner and liberator of culture', *Faith and Thought*, vol. 108, nos 1–2, 1981, p. 39.
5. John Mbiti, *Bible and Theology in African Christianity*, Nairobi: Oxford University Press, 1986.
6. C. G. Baëta, *Prophetism in Ghana – A Study of Some 'Spiritual' Churches*, London: SCM Press, 1962.
7. Ibid., p. 135.
8. Loc. cit.

9. Loc. cit.
10. *1 Thessalonians* 1:9.
11. Baëta, *Prophetism in Ghana*, p. 135.
12. Loc. cit.
13. Ibid., p. 145.
14. Ibid., pp. 136–41.
15. Ibid., p. 145.
16. Ibid., p. ix.
17. Ibid., p. 154.
18. Ibid., p. 18.
19. S. G. Williamson, *Akan Religion and the Christian Faith – A Comparative Study of the Impact of Two Religions*, Accra: Ghana Universities Press, 1965, p. 170.
20. Kwame Bediako, 'The roots of African theology', *International Bulletin of Missionary Research*, vol. 13, no. 2, April 1989, pp. 58–65.
21. John Pobee, *Toward an African Theology*, Nashville: Abingdon Press, 1979.
22. *Asomafo no nnwuma*, 2:7, 11 (*Acts of the Apostles* 2:7, 11: 'How is it that we all hear in our own languages the wonders of God'?).

5

'Here We Have no Abiding City'
The Perennial Challenge

The Two African Responses to Christianity

This book has so far sought to take a particular look at Christianity in African life. The demographic importance of Christianity in the African continent in the twentieth century is well known. I have not attempted to discuss its possible impact on the fortunes of world Christianity, although the place of Africa in the present shift in the centre of gravity of Christianity in the coming decades is bound to affect the way the Christian faith is understood, expressed and perhaps transmitted. At the very least this means that if the Christian religion in manifestation and practice is becoming increasingly the religion of black people and decreasingly the religion of white people, a reassessment of some long-standing attitudes is necessary. My interest, in this book, has centred on African attitudes.

The massive presence of Christianity on the African continent in the twentieth century cannot be separated from the modern missionary movement from the West. Yet the very circumstances in which the missionary enterprise was carried out, as well as some of its modes of operation, were enough to cause some African thinkers to raise questions about the eventual prospects for Christianity in African life. Not only had the Christian nations of Europe been the slaving nations of the previous four centuries, but also the era of repentance and reparation for the slave trade, one of the fruits of which was the missionary enterprise, came to be bedevilled by European colonialism and imperialism. The cumulative effect of the Western impact on Africa, therefore, was to produce an identity crisis which was to manifest itself in a variety of forms, one of which came to focus on the place and role of Christianity in African life.

... *The Early Theological Response: Christianising the Past*

Perhaps there was no more striking evidence of this than in the African Christian writing of the last three decades, following African independence in the 1960s. This period saw the first flowering of African theology in the post-missionary church. Virtually all theological writers – committed churchmen trained in the theological traditions of Western Christianity – expressed concern about the state of the faith as transmitted to the Christian community of Africa. The writings of Bolaji Idowu of Nigeria, Harry Sawyerr of Sierra Leone, John Mbiti of Kenya, to name only a few of the earliest and most prominent writers, all testify to the questioning that was going on regarding the Western planting of Christianity in Africa. The questioning was not so much about the missionary enterprise itself, rather it was about whether the churches as planted by the Western missionary effort could adequately come to terms with the realities of African life, especially the still potent realities of the traditional religions and their world-views. African theological writing came to focus on giving a more positive interpretation of the African religious past than the missionary assessment had done, and so demonstrated the continuity of the religious past with the Christian present. The essential thrust of this first flowering of African theological literature in the twentieth century has therefore been an effort towards indigenisation, a rooting of Christianity in African life by claiming for it a past in the spiritual harvests of the African pre-Christian religious heritage. In a curious way, it was indigenisation by Christianisation of the religious past, rather than by any serious adaptation or contextualisation and inculturation – to use two current words – of Christianity as such. The theological thought of Bolaji Idowu demonstrated this approach most clearly. Whilst Idowu argued a spirited defence of the necessity for indigenisation of Christianity in his book, *Towards an Indigenous Church*,[1] the 'fundamental question' of indigenisation was, in relation to his own native Nigeria,

Whether in the past pre-Christian history of Nigerians, God has ever in any way revealed Himself to them and they have apprehended His revelation in how-ever imperfect a way; whether what happens in the coming of Christianity and as a result of evangelism is that Nigerians have been introduced to a *completely* new God who is absolutely unrelated to their past history.

To decide the question one way or another, according to Idowu, African theologians were to study and interpret what he called 'the revelation contained in the heritage from the past'.[2] Thus the prime theological task in Africa – the indigenisation of the Christian faith as a vital element in African life – became a theological interpretation of African traditional religion, a living testimony to the sense that the religious past must be viewed as integral to the Christian present.

... *The Critical Response: Rejecting an Alien Religion*

There has been another set of African intellectual responses to the presence of Christianity in African life – the reaction of the anti-Christian critics. In Chapter 2 I attempted to show that Osofo Okomfo Damuah's Afrikania movement in Ghana represents one acute form of this African critical reaction which has also been expressed by others: notably, the late Ugandan, Okot p'Bitek and the Kenyan Ali Mazrui. Their critiques amount to a denial of Christianity's legitimacy of inhabiting the spiritual universe of the African religious past. For Damuah, in effect, the concept of an African theology that is Christian both in inspiration and orientation is intellectually unacceptable: African theology belongs exclusively to the realm of African traditional religion with its associated world-view, and is the coherent systematisation of it.

As I have attempted to show, however, this twentieth-century African critical reaction to Christianity in African life is the eventual hardening of a similarly critical and ambivalent African response to missionary Christianity in the nineteenth century. The most outstanding witness to this attitude was Edward Blyden. Blyden's criticisms of the failings and failures of a missionary Christianity, which he perceived as harmful and alienating in its effects on African peoples, have found renewed and more vigorous expression in a contemporary African theological rejection of Christianity as incapable of providing the intellectual frame of reference for a viable African self-identity.

Facing the New Challenge – the Value of the African Christian Tradition

This fundamental intellectual challenge to Christianity in African life has hitherto not been addressed in African theological writing. In Chapters 3 and 4 of this book, I have attempted to show from evidence drawn from Ghanaian Christian history that some of the elements for a response to this challenge can be found in the tradition of the existing churches. Accordingly the widespread view that Christianity, in a uniform manner, alienated African converts from their culture can be shown to be over-simplified. That Western missionaries, on the whole, took a negative view of African society and its values – religious and cultural – cannot be evaded. On the other hand, the early manifestation in Africa of the vernacular and therefore inherently universal character of Christianity as religion, meant that the very process of the transmission of the faith often acted *against* missionary cultural ethnocentrism and occasionally broke through in the achievement of a particular missionary.

An Unusual Tribute – Danquah on Christaller

The tribute by the Ghanaian philosopher, J. B. Danquah, to the Basel missionary, Rev. Johannes Christaller, for his work in the Gold Coast, is one vivid illustration of this feature of the missionary transmission of Christianity.[3] Danquah was not particularly in favour of the Christian missionary enterprise, nor did he believe that the 'new religion' from the West had any basis to claim superiority over Akan religious and ethical ideas. Indeed, he wrote his book to show that Akan thought (without the Christian component) was comparable to what Europe had attained through the impact of Christianity. Danquah recognised, however, that the foundations for his conclusions in his book lay in the achievement of Christaller. His words are worth recalling:

but for Christaller's foresight in recording in permanent and highly intelligible form the scattered elements of the beliefs and hopes and fears of the Akan people at the particular juncture in the nineteenth century when European ideas in the form of new learning, a new religion and a new economic life were sweeping the country, the Akan people of the Gold Coast of West Africa would today have failed to bring their indigenous contribution to the spiritual achievements of mankind.[4]

Yet Danquah saw in Christaller's achievement more than its ethnographic significance. Christaller had come to the conclusion, which he stated in his preface to his *Twi Proverbs*,[5] that from his case-study of Akan religious, cultural and moral ideas as enshrined in Akan/Twi proverbs, maxims and wise sayings, he had discovered 'sparks of truth entrusted to and preserved by their [Akans'] own people' which those Africans who are enjoying the benefit of Christian education 'should not despise'. This observation became important for Danquah, who used it as a basis for claiming that there did exist an 'Akan Testament', an 'old Testament of the Akan', which for Danquah was the palpable proof that 'the Spirit of God is abroad, even in the Akan of the Gold Coast'. Accordingly, Danquah saw his book as simply the literary testimony to the existence of such a divinely inspired 'Akan testament'. So highly did Danquah value Christaller's achievement that he postulated a *spiritual* link between himself and Christaller, under the Akan figure of the ancestor. Christaller thus became for Danquah:

> in the higher sense of that attribute, the *ancestor* of the thought that informs these pages with one lineal memory and imagination. In that sense, the spiritual sense, this book must be taken as having been written by him, or, not to be unnecessarily mysterious, with his spiritual co-operation.[6]

A Christian theologian may find it difficult to follow Danquah in his claim for an Old Testament of the Akan without qualification. But in his appraisal of Johannes Christaller, Danquah points to a way in which an African Christian theology in the Akan context may proceed to address the fundamental question of cultural alienation and to address the challenge of intellectual relevance for the shaping of a mature African self-identity.

Allowing for Danquah's predilection for hyperbole and the striking phrase, nonetheless there seems no reason to doubt that Danquah's designation of Christaller as *ancestor* is a serious one. Danquah was a competent exponent and advocate of Akan religious and moral ideas and when he ascribed *spiritual* ancestorhood to Christaller, he meant it. Within the range of Akan notions regarding ancestors, even though ancestors are essentially lineage elders and so are primarily *natural* ancestors, yet not all the dead are ancestors. This fact opens a way into Danquah's understanding of Christaller's achievement and how Danquah would come to consider him an ancestor. For ancestors become so not solely by association in blood lineage, but also by quality of life, by the social significance and impact of their work; in other words, the dead become ancestors by achievement in life and not solely for having lived in the community. One may even say then that the dead are pronounced ancestors by virtue, not of their physical kinship alone, but also for their *spiritual* qualities, seen in their lives and their achievement. From this perspective, therefore, the significance of Christaller for Danquah consisted in Danquah's intuition that Christaller's work and his insight into Akan tradition – all accomplished with outstanding devotion and sympathy – was of such a character that they marked him out as one who *spiritually* belonged within Akan tradition.

If this was Danquah's thought regarding Christaller, it would not have been purely individual speculation. For the Akan, like several other African societies, have a custom of honouring foreigners in their midst who distinguish themselves in ways that enhance the life of the community and nation, sometimes by enstooling them as chiefs with all the appropriate royal titles and dignity. For Danquah, Christaller would have qualified for such a singular honour; his elevation to ancestorhood, therefore, would be in that 'higher sense of the attribute' which related not to physical association by blood allegiance alone, but to those spiritual and moral qualities which truly make the dead ancestors.

Danquah's thought is, I believe, an important indicator of how Christian achievement can find an entry into the spiritual world of African tradition and become highly relevant intellectually in shaping a fully *African* self-consciousness. It is evident that Christaller enters the world of ancestors with all the designations which

Danquah ascribes to him: 'missionary, philologist, anthropologist, scientist, philosopher, moralist and a man of genius'.[7] Christaller assumes his elevated status, in other words, not by shedding the faith by which he lived and worked; on the contrary, his elevation magnifies that faith; Christaller enters the world of the ancestors as a *Christian* ancestor.

African Christian Theology as a New Christian Idiom

It is not clear how far Danquah would have pursued these ideas had he returned to them in subsequent writing. However, I believe he has left us enough to enable us to appreciate the coherence of the concept since one can argue that within Akan tradition the only basis for the meeting of religious ideas and religious forces is in the realm of the spirit. The insistence on ethnicity as an unassailable principle for the affirmation of culture as the ultimate measure of value and significance, as advanced by Osofo Okomfo Damuah of Afrikania, therefore becomes an inadequate basis for a full appreciation of the truly human. It is an unacceptable particularism, in that it shrinks the notion of Africanness and the African personality into less than its full human proportions and potential.

Once this is granted, then the real challenge to Christianity in African life, in terms of its cultural and intellectual relevance, becomes a challenge to Christianity to demonstrate its spiritual credentials for what they are and to show how efficacious these spiritual credentials are to provide a unified world of meaning to meet African needs.

In my remarks on the early flowering of African theology in the decades of the 1960s and 1970s, I noted that the African theological quest then resolved itself into an 'indigenisation' of Christianity and the church which was achieved by a process of Christianisation of the pre-Christian past. The process was as much about rehabilitating African identity as it was about affirming a Christian commitment. It is curious indeed that whilst that early era of African theology was obviously seeking to achieve Christian ends, that is, the indigenisation of the church, it seemed to be doing so with rather scant attention to what might be described as 'areas of traditional Christian doctrine', which, as Adrian Hastings commented in 1976, disappeared or were

81

marginalised for not being 'reflected in the African past'.[8] The bibliographies of those authors are indeed revealing of the priorities of African theology of that era.[9]

I speak of an 'era' here because I believe we have entered upon a new era in African theology marked by a greater realisation among African theologians themselves that, in the words, of John Mbiti, 'the Christian way of life is in Africa to stay, certainly within the foreseeable future'.[10] This confidence is revealed in the formation of bodies like the Ecumenical Association of African Theologians, within the wider Ecumenical Association of Third World Theologians in the late 1970s and the emergence of a Fellowship of Mission Theologians from the Two-Thirds World (with continental manifestations in Africa, Asia and Latin America as the African Theological Fraternity Partnership in Mission Asia and the Latin American Theological Fraternity). These bodies have a clear commitment to seek the contextual relevance of the Gospel in the Christian communities of the former mission-fields of the Western Churches and missionary societies and are confident that the Gospel of Jesus Christ can be the basis for guiding and defining the pathways of human destiny – transcendent as well as immanent, individual as well as collective. This activity comes at a time when Western churches do not seem, on the whole, to have such confidence in the Gospel anymore. Perhaps this is evidence that the shift in the centre of gravity of Christianity from the Western to the non-Western world has begun to register, if not in the textbooks, at least in the contexts where the centre of gravity now lies. Black Theology in South Africa and in North America has vindicated that faith in Jesus is a meaningful option for a hard-pressed people, even when oppressed by 'Christian' governments. Liberation Theology in Latin America has also raised the question whether Jesus can be on both sides at once.

Thus the task of theology in Africa has altered. The struggle for the indigenisation of the church by the Christianisation of the pre-Christian heritage is past. Obviously this topic will continue to be discussed in some places and also written about, but as a trend in theological reflection, it is over. The African theology of the earlier era has had no small part to play in ensuring that the debate should now rage over the abiding relevance of the old religions in the transition to the new in Christianity. African Traditional Religion has been a serious preparation for the Gospel in Africa and forms the major religious substratum for the idiom and existential experience of Christianity in African life.

Furthermore, through the scholarship associated with the Centre for the Study of Christianity in the Non-Western World, both in its earlier incarnation in Aberdeen and through its continuing influence in the field of the history of religions, the primal religions of Africa and elsewhere in the world have entered upon a new career in Christian scholarship. Not only have we learnt to understand these primal religious traditions as the background of the Christian profession of the vast majority of all Christians of all generations and all nations in the twenty centuries of Christian history, and therefore as the most fertile ground for Christian conversions, but also this peculiar historical connection between the primal religions of the world and Christianity may have implications for understanding possible affinities between them.[11] The impact of such insights is far-reaching in the shaping of the mind of the new African theology.

In 1976 Adrian Hastings observed that one of the areas of traditional Christian doctrine which was marginalised in African theology was *Christology*.[12] Between 1979 and 1984, three studies by African theologians were published which treated the subject of the meaning of Christ in relation to African religious life. Interestingly, each study treated the doctrine of Christ under the figure of Ancestor.[13]

This treatment was, I believe, significant and indicative of a trend. The new African theology would necessarily seek a new idiom, its own idiom – its own *'discours théologique'* as Bimwenyi-Kweshi, a francophone scholar of Zaire, puts it – in relation to an African reading of the Scriptures. Such a reading of the Scriptures will take seriously the African religious apprehension of Christ in the African world that is going to inform this new African theology, answering to the challenge to show the relevance of faith in Jesus Christ at the roots of African existence and humanity.

What shape is the new African theology likely to take? Danquah's attitude to Christaller gives us helpful clues as to the challenges that are likely to confront the new African theology. In my treatment of the subject of Christology in the context of African traditional religions,[14] I attempted to confront three areas of religious meaning in

African traditional life in Ghanaian society: the practice of sacrifice, priestly mediation and ancestral function. Drawing mainly upon the *Epistle to the Hebrews*, I argued that in relation to each of these areas of religious meaning for traditional society, Jesus, by the incarnation and by his atoning self-offering, provides a sufficient frame of reference for the fulfilment and attainment of full human potential – communal as well as individual – and that this can be related to the intentions of traditional society in each of the three specific areas of meaning.

I shall not rehearse here the details of the argument. I refer to it only in order to point to some of the inescapable questions that I see as facing any attempt at a relevant theology in the context of Christianity in African life at the living roots of the church. It seems that the new African theology will have to attempt what the writer of the *Epistle to the Hebrews* did: that is, to make room, within an inherited body of tradition, for new ideas, for new realities which, though seemingly entering from the outside, come in to fulfil aspirations within the tradition, and then to alter quite significantly the basis of self-understanding within that tradition.

For, in a profound sense, the Jesus of the *Epistle to the Hebrews* comes in as an 'outsider' to Jewish tradition at the specific point at which his significance and his relevance are urged in the main argument of the epistle. For 'If he were on earth, he would not be a priest at all, since there are priests who offer the gifts required by Jewish Law'.[15] And how can he be a priest when: 'It is well known that he was born a member of the tribe of Judah, and Moses did not mention this tribe when he spoke of priests'?[16] And yet the whole point of the Christological argument in *Hebrews* is that we have a priest, and more than a priest: 'a High Priest who sits at the right hand of the throne of the Divine Majesty in heaven. He serves as High Priest in the Most High Place, that is, in the real tent which was put up by the Lord, not by man.'[17] The earthly link is through one whom the tradition had glimpsed only fleetingly in the past with some fascination, not only an 'outsider' but also greater than the father of the nation. Melchizedek is the pattern, not Aaron. 'Jesus is the High Priest that meets our needs',[18] meeting and fulfilling all the aspirations and yearnings expressed and anticipated in all the rituals of atonement and redemption presided over by Aaron and his successors. So Jesus attains his singular position not by legal succession, but by divine designation, not by physical descent, but by spiritual achievement – by a quality of life that triumphed over evil, by an inimitable passion and death, and the power of an indestructible life in resurrection – in short, in the realm of power, in the realm of spirit. On that basis He becomes significant for all, and available to all. 'In the higher sense of the attribute, in the spiritual sense' Jesus becomes *the Ancestor* of all.

So, if Johannes Christaller can by spiritual achievement become an Akan ancestor, how much more can Jesus ... and so also Abraham ... Joseph ... Moses ... David ... Isaiah ... Peter ... Paul of Tarsus.

The challenge that now faces the new African theology in the age of Africa's faith and confidence in the Gospel of Jesus Christ, is how to make clear in the religious world which men and women inhabit and by whose spiritual realities they make sense of their existence, that Jesus Christ, the Supreme *Ancestor*, belongs there as Incarnate and Risen Saviour, as Redeemer and Lord, as *Nana*, as Ancestor. The challenge also will be to achieve this clarification without losing Jesus' uniqueness in that world.

To choose to stay within easy reach of the safe shores of the dogmas and conclusions of other periods and climes in the history of the church may seem expedient and have the appearance of fighting for the faith which once and for all God has given to His people. But the divine giving of that faith is also re-enacted for every generation, and in every place, not in pre-set formulations.to be handed on, but in a disclosure to be received, obeyed and 'fleshed-out' afresh, just as that disclosure itself was a fleshing-out in the context of contending religious and social forces.

In short, the challenge is that of relevance without syncretism. Perhaps, paradoxically, the resources for achieving this end will not lie solely with the academic theology which may, nevertheless, be charged with the task. Rather, the larger resources will lie within the variegated communities of Christians throughout tropical Africa who, having heard in their own languages the wonders of God, in turn, in their own languages, in worship and adoration, in celebration and in prayer, in present joy as in anticipated hope, testify that Jesus Christ, Iesu Kristo, by whatever name he is known, has come, and become a reality within the universe of their religious ideas, forces, powers and spiritual agencies.

I have argued in Chapter 4 that the extent to which a Christian community avails itself of and develops its heritage of Christian thought and tradition in the vernacular is the extent to which that community will be in a position to meet the challenge of showing the relevance and significance of Jesus. This is also another way of saying that I see African academic theology as being challenged to be in close contact with the vernacular apprehension of the Christian faith and with its roots in the continuing realities of the traditional primal world-view.

Every Christmas Day the Christians of Akropong in Ghana sing this hymn:[19]

> Iesu awoda
> yɛ me fɛ koraa;
> Iesu Kristo ne m'agyenkwa.
>
> Sɛ wɔanwo Iesu a,
> anka yɛbɛyera;
> Iesu Kristo, meda w'ase.
>
> (Jesus' birthday
> Fills me with joy;
> Jesus Christ is my saviour
>
> If Jesus had not been born,
> We would for ever be lost;
> Jesus Christ, I thank you.)

They sing this hymn without any awareness that Christmas itself was originally a Christian substitute for a pre-Christian New Year religious festival in northern Europe. One may hope that they will one day sing it at the traditional New Year festival of *Odwira* to welcome and worship the One who achieved once and for all purification for their sins, their Great Ancestor, Iesu Kristo (Jesus Christ).

Notes and References

1. Bolaji Idowu, *Towards an Indigenous Church*, London: Oxford University Press, 1965, pp. 24–5.
2. Ibid., p. 26.
3. J. B. Danquah, *The Akan Doctrine of God – A Fragment of Gold Coast Ethics and Religion*, London: Frank Cass, 1944 (2nd edn, 1968).

4. Ibid., p. 186.
5. Johannes Christaller, *Twi Proverbs*, Basel: Evangelical Missionary Society, 1879.
6. Danquah, *The Akan Doctrine of God*, p. 185.
7. Loc. cit.
8. Adrian Hastings, *African Christianity – An Essay in Interpretation*, London: Geoffrey Chapman, 1976, p. 52.
9. On this subject, see my *Theology and Identity: The Impact of Culture upon Christian Thought in the Second Century and Modern Africa*, Oxford: Regnum Books, 1992.
10. John Mbiti, *Bible and Theology in African Christianity*, Nairobi: Oxford University Press, 1986, p. 229.
11. Andrew F. Walls, 'Africa and Christian identity', *Mission Focus*, vol. VI, no. 7, 1978, pp. 11–13; Harold W. Turner, 'The primal religions of the world and their study', in Victor Hayes (ed.), *Australian Essays in World Religions*, Bedford Park: Australian Association of World Religions, 1977, pp. 27–37.
12. Adrian Hastings, *African Christianity*, p. 52.
13. John Pobee, *Toward an African Theology*, Nashville, Tenn.: Abingdon Press, 1979; Charles Nyamiti, *Christ as our Ancestor – Christology from an African Perspective*, Gweru: Mambo Press, 1984; Kwame Bediako, 'Biblical Christologies in the context of African traditional religions', in Vinay Samuel and Chris Sugden (eds), *Sharing Jesus in the Two-Thirds World*, Bangalore: PIM-Asia, 1983; Grand Rapids: Eerdmans, 1984, pp. 81–121.
14. My earlier study has since been reissued in a modified form in Ghana as *Jesus in African Culture – A Ghanaian Perspective*, Accra: Asempa Publishers, 1990.
15. *Hebrews* 8:4.
16. Ibid., 7:14.
17. Ibid., 8:1–2.
18. Ibid., 7:26.
19. *Atwifo Kristofo Asore ne Dwom (Liturgy and Hymns for the Use of the Christian Churches in Ghana Speaking the Twi Language)*, Accra: Presbyterian Book Depot, 1965, hymn no 57.

PART 2

Christianity as a Non-Western Religion

Issues Arising in a Post-missionary Setting

s

6

The Primal Imagination and the Opportunity for a New Theological Idiom

Prophet Harris

> One man preached the Gospel in West Africa for nine years and only converted 52. But another man preached the same Gospel just for two years and 120,000 adult West Africans believed and were baptised into Christianity.[1]

So runs the first sentence of an article in the weekly publication, *West Africa*. This sentence itself raises several questions. For instance, did the different socio-economic and political conditions in which the two men preached the Gospel have any effect on the varying results achieved? Indeed, did they preach the 'same Gospel'? The author did not deal with either of these questions. He seemed much more impressed by the fact that the second man 'depended far less on Western missionary finance and control' than the first.

The two men whose careers are being compared are Philip Quaque (1741–1816) of Ghana (then Gold Coast), the first African ordained into the priesthood of the Anglican Communion in 1765 in Exeter and London and then sent to the Gold Coast as missionary and catechist in 1766, and William Wade Harris (1865–1929) of Liberia, a trail-blazer and a new kind of religious personage on the African scene, the first independent African Christian prophet.

1989 marked the sixtieth anniversary of the death of Prophet Harris, which occasioned the article evaluating his work in the last issue of *West Africa* for that year. In this chapter, the first on the theme: 'Christianity as a non-Western religion – issues arising in a post-missionary setting', I wish to regard Prophet Harris as a paradigm both of a non-Western and essentially *primal* apprehension of the Gospel and also of a settled self-consciousness as African Christian, which is uncluttered by Western missionary controls. Even though Prophet Harris has not been alone in demonstrating these qualities, it seems that he exemplifies them to a very high degree. He is reported to have told a missionary who interrogated him, 'I am prophet. Above all religion and freed from the control of men, I am under God only through the intermediary of the Angel Gabriel.'²

My reason for evoking the achievement of Harris is not to make a fresh study of his work. Both Gordon Haliburton³ and David Shank have served us well here. Rather, it is simply that in his personality and career, Prophet Harris foreshadowed so powerfully some of the new insights into the Gospel which can emerge from the non-Western world in the changed situations of our time.

According to Prophet Harris's own account, while he was in prison in 1910 on a charge of instigating anti-government revolt, certain events changed the course of his life and made him a prophet of God and Christ. These events included a trance-visitation in which he said the Angel Gabriel called him into the preaching ministry. In subsequent trance-visitations during his ministry, Harris also 'saw' Moses, Elijah and Jesus: 'Moses, Angel Gabriel, Elijah, these three great prophets come and I alone speak with them'.⁴ Prophet Harris's message was quite simple: essentially based on the Bible as the Word of God, he taught that God was One and good, and that people were to repent of their sins, that the cult objects of the old religion – amulets and charms – were to be destroyed, that people were to believe in Jesus, to be baptised and to join churches (he did not establish a church of his own), and that those baptised were to live a new life and to prepare for the return of Christ. In other words, Prophet Harris appeared to function in a spiritual universe which was both simple and complex, and yet which he seemed able to embrace as a totality. It is this outlook that makes him, in my view, a paradigm of what I term 'the primal imagination'.⁵

What Harris typified we find in another African Christian personage of our own time, Cardinal Milingo, the former Roman Catholic archbishop of Lusaka, Zambia. It is quite clear from Cardinal Milingo's ministry and writings⁶ that he develops his theological ideas on healing, exorcism and pastoral care consciously in relation to the thought-patterns, perceptions of reality and the concepts of identity and community which prevail within the primal world-view of African societies. He does this, however, not as a mere practical convenience, but because he considers that the spiritual universe of the African primal world does offer valid perspectives for articulating Christian theological commitments.

It is important to recognise that both Harris and Milingo are deeply committed and convinced Christians. They demonstrate how the primal imagination can transcend primal religions as distinctive religious systems. As stated at the 1973 Ibadan Consultation:

> A primal world view operates in varying degrees within the continuing primal religious traditions, within neo-primal forms, within those who have abandoned the primal inheritance of their fathers and found no new faith, and within those who have adopted some form of the Christian or any other religion without shedding their own culture.[7]

It is this abiding presence of the primal world-view 'across a wide front ranging from worshippers in a continuing primal religious system to Christian believers' which I wish to convey by the use of the term 'primal imagination'. It is evident, nonetheless, that a starting point for appreciating the primal imagination must be in primal religions themselves.

The Nature of the Primal World-view – H. W. Turner's Six-feature Analysis

In 1977 Harold Turner, a sure guide into the phenomenology of the world's primal religions, proposed a six-feature framework for understanding primal religions as authentically religious, rather than as merely epiphenomena of the social organisation of simple or pre-literate societies.[8] Turner listed these six features as follows.

First, a sense of kinship with nature, in which animals and plants, no less than human beings, had 'their own spiritual existence and place in the universe' as interdependent parts of a whole. Accordingly, 'any object of the natural environment may enter into a totemic spiritual relationship with human beings or become tutelary and guardian spirits' whilst the environment itself is used realistically and unsentimentally but with profound respect and reverence and without exploitation. This 'ecological aspect' of primal religions, Turner considered to be 'a profoundly religious attitude to man's natural setting in the world'.

He described the *second* feature as 'the deep sense that man is finite, weak and impure or sinful and stands in need of a power not his own'. Turner linked this feature to the notion in Rudolf Otto's *The Idea of the Holy*, that 'man's basic reaction to the Holy is in terms of a sense of creaturehood'.[9] Here too, Turner saw 'an authentic religious sensitivity, coupled with a realistic assessment of man's condition, a sensibility and an assessment that have been hidden from people like ourselves [Westerners] by the proliferation of our technical and socio-political power'.

The *third* feature, which he described as 'complementary to the second', was 'the conviction that man is not alone in the universe, for there is a spiritual world of powers or beings more powerful and ultimate than himself'. The universe of primal religions is thus a *personalised* universe, in which the appropriate question is not 'What caused this or that?' but '*Who* did it?' Man therefore lives with an awareness of the presence of transcendent powers which, however, are ambivalent. 'Not only is there the hierarchy of benevolent ancestors, and of spirits, divinities and high gods, but there is also the range of evil spirits, of demons and malevolent divinities and the lesser, more earth-born occult powers of wizards and witches.'

The *fourth* feature which in turn completes the third, is 'the belief that man can enter into relationship with the benevolent spirit-world and so share in its powers and blessings and receive protection from evil forces by these transcendent helpers'. For Turner, this feature which reveals 'the profound emphasis on the transcendent source of true life and practical salvation' goes 'contrary to all the neat projectionist theories that explain religions away' as 'man-made' and 'ignore the primary testimony of so much of the data about religions'.

The *fifth* feature, which Turner saw as an extension of the fourth, relates to the acute sense of the reality of the afterlife, a conviction which explains the important place of ancestors or the 'living dead' in many primal religions: 'In the majority of these religions, the ancestors, the "living dead", remain united in affection and in mutual obligations with the "living living". Indeed, the ancestors figure so prominently in the first level or region of the spirit world that they seem to create an ancestor cult and to obscure the spirit beings before whom they otherwise serve as mediators between the transcendent and the human.'

The *sixth* feature is the conviction that man lives 'in a sacramental universe where there is no sharp dichotomy between the physical and the spiritual'. Accordingly, the 'physical' acts as vehicle for 'spiritual' power 'whilst the physical realm is held to be patterned on the model of the spiritual world beyond ...'. Even where there is a clear ethical dualism with respect to good and evil, nevertheless, 'one set of powers, principles and patterns runs through all things on earth and in the heavens and welds them into a unified cosmic system'.[10]

Following this general structural analysis of primal religions, Turner then made a number of comments which I consider important for our present discussion. In the *first* place, he noted that his proposal 'may be used for the understanding of other kinds of religion besides the primal and will be found readily applicable to the Christian tradition'.[11] *Then*, going on to argue for the educational importance of primal religions in religious studies 'within ... the Christian tradition', he drew attention to a 'special relationship' of primal religions with Christianity, which arises from the fact that 'in the history of the spread of the Christian faith ... its major extensions have been solely into the societies with primal religious systems'. These societies were, according to Turner, the Mediterranean world of the early Christian centuries, and tribal peoples of Northern and Western Europe and finally the primal societies of Africa, the Pacific and parts of Asia. This meant that 'the form of religion that might seem farthest removed from the Christian [i.e. from the standpoint of nineteenth- and early twentieth-century Western missionary estimations of 'non-Christian religions'] has in fact had a closer relationship with it than any other'.

Therefore it came as no surprise to Turner that 'it is the people of the primal religions who have made the greatest response' to the Christian faith. To him:

> There seem to be affinities between the Christian and the primal traditions, an affinity that perhaps appears in the common reactions when Christian missions first arrive ('this is what we have been waiting for') and that is further evident in the vast

range of new religious movements born from the interaction between the primal religions and Christianity and in no comparable degree in the reaction of primal religions to their meeting with the other universal religions.[12]

My own response to Turner's very stimulating analysis is twofold. In the first place, whilst affirming the six-feature structure he outlined, it seems important to state that it is the sixth and final feature, conveying the primal conception of the universe as a unified cosmic system, essentially spiritual, which provides the real key to the entire structure. But in the second place I am rather surprised that, having drawn attention to the special relationship of primal religions with Christianity, a relationship which is not only historical but may also be phenomenological, Turner saw the future for primal religions as merely 'a component within the folk religions of all cultures, or in a wider sense as part of the permanent religious heritage of all mankind'. The most precise point in his conclusion was that:

> more specifically, the primal religions will continue as one of the components in the new syncretistic and neo-primal religious movements [born from the interaction of primal religions with Christianity].[13]

What he did not state was that this special relationship of primal religions with Christianity and the existence of 'affinities' between the primal and Christian traditions could have far-reaching significance for our understanding of the nature of the Christian faith itself. If there is only a minimal 'paradigm-shift' as we pass from the spiritual universe of primal religions into the spiritual environment of the Christian faith ('this *is* what we have been waiting for'), then one would want to pursue the matter by asking how the primal imagination might bring its own peculiar gifts to the shaping of Christian affirmation. This issue becomes even more pressing if Christian thought has hitherto been moulded by a world-view from which the living forces of the primal imagination seem to have been expelled.

The African World and the Problem of Unresolved Multiplicity

African Christian scholars who have examined the spiritual universe of African primal religions, have, to my mind, done less than full justice to the complexity of the African primal world. Keen to show the relationship of continuity between the pre-Christian religions and Christian belief, they have stressed, particularly and rightly so, the continuity of God. This must be reckoned an important achievement by African theology and is validated by the fact that in virtually every Christian community in Africa, the Christian name for God is usually a divine name hallowed in the pre-Christian religious tradition for the Supreme God. By stressing the centrality and uniqueness of God in African tradition, African theology has, however, left the wider spirit world of African primal religions – divinities, ancestors, natural forces – unaccounted for. In other words, it has answered to only part of what has been described as the 'unity and multiplicity of Divinity'[14] in African primal religion, which I would prefer to call the unity and multiplicity of the Transcendent.

To take just two representative figures who have written extensively on the subject, Bolaji Idowu (of Nigeria) and John Mbiti (of Kenya), there is the distinct impression that these writers wish the multiplicity were not there. Because of his fundamental commitment to the vindication of an African monotheism, Idowu was definitely uncomfortable with the actual situation in Yoruba religion, in which the multiplicity of divinities so 'predominate that it is difficult for the casual observer to notice that under them there is one vital cultic basis'.[15] Yoruba religion is a diffused monotheism with the divinities functioning as ministers of the Supreme God, and Idowu was even prepared to countenance their eventual disappearance:

> to those who worship the divinities and derive succour from belief in their existence, to such they are real; but to those who have outgrown them, all reality is concentrated in the Deity.[16]

According to Idowu, the supreme service that the coming of Christianity has rendered to his own people, the Yoruba, was to give to their 'diffused monotheism' a sharper focus and to direct attention more intently to the 'one essential Factor by which the life and belief of the

Yoruba cohere and have sustenance', namely the Supreme God, Olódùmarè.[17]

John Mbiti, in his discussion of the place of divinities within the African primal universe, came to similar conclusions:

> Most, if not all, of these attributive divinities are the creation of man's imagination. This does not, however, cancel their reality: the divinities are *real beings* for the people concerned. With increasing scientific knowledge, no doubt, most of the divinities will be explained away and the major divinity of science will take over.[18]

In fairness to our two eminent authors, it needs to be recognised that whilst divinities and ancestors may be found together within a particular religious structure in the African primal world, as in the Akan tradition, they nevertheless belong to two quite distinct categories of spiritual reality. Divinities are inherited, can be acquired and also dropped, should they prove ineffectual. Ancestors, on the other hand, being lineage personages, are irreplaceable. Consequently, in Africa, ancestors represent a more enduring problem theologically than divinities, and the intuition of Idowu and Mbiti may well have been correct, that the divinities of primal religions would eventually fade away through the Christian impact. Yet it has also to be pointed out that wherever this has happened in the spread of the Christian faith, it has been through a process of the demonisation of these divinities in the Christian religious consciousness. This is, in fact, the case in the more radically Christian African independent churches which have then reinstituted a new and this time 'Christian' and Biblical multiplicity, incorporating angels, Gabriel and Michael and others, with Abraham, Elijah … Jesus. The great Harris is paradigmatic of this development.

If this latter trend is an indicator, it shows that the 'multiplicity' within the primal world-view cannot be ignored.

There is undoubtedly a positive gain in the near-unanimous affirmation through African scholarship that much in the primal religious experience and heritage is genuinely contiguous with Christian understanding and religious experience.[19] What is less satisfying is the way this indication of a religious and spiritual continuity has been used to buttress a presumed African monotheism. A misreading of the spiritual realities of the African primal world has often resulted from this process, for example the failure to engage adequately with the dimension of multiplicity.

This situation has arisen largely because the theological effort has been aimed at drawing together the total African religious experience into a coherent and meaningful pattern and has focused unduly on the African sense of God, making it continuous with the received Western account of God in terms of monotheism. To look at the whole process in reverse, African theology, by establishing its link with its African world in terms of the One Supreme, Ultimate God of Africa, has answered to only part of the total spiritual universe of African primal religions. What goes on in actual daily religious life and practice – in the company of divinities, ubiquitous spirits, ancestors – has been left virtually untouched. Thus, whilst the affirmation of continuity has been made on the properly religious grounds of the 'unity' of God and is supported by the evidence of African religious thought, African theology has failed to wrestle adequately with the 'multiplicity' of the Transcendent and has undercut the contribution which it can make towards a fresh Christian account of the Transcendent, drawing on its background in the primal imagination of African primal religions.

Towards a Fresh Approach

Neither Idowu nor Mbiti has fully acknowledged 'the unity and multiplicity of divinity' (or the Transcendent) in African primal religion or regarded it as a positive element in a creative Christian engagement with the primal world-view. Idowu's irritation with the multiplicity of divinities which swarm all over the place must be noted and, rather than reducing divinities into attributes or manifestations of God, recognise them as they are actually treated in normal religious practice, as entities which operate as ends in themselves. It would then be acknowledged that the spiritual universe of African primal religions is not without *hiatus*. It is not a neat hierarchy of divine beings and spirit-forces held in unitary harmony. The African primal world can be conceived of as a universe of distributed power, perhaps even of fragmented power; it is as much a universe of conflict as the rest of the fallen world in that it is a world not of one

Centre, God, but many centres; the unity and multiplicity of the Transcendent in the African world also reveals a deep ambivalence. It is this ambivalence to which a creative Christian engagement must answer and do so in terms of the primal imagination itself.

Hitherto the mainstream of Christian theology, as a legacy of the Western philosophical approach, has tended to treat the question of the Transcendent by postulating a transcendent God. African theology too, seeking to respond to the Western interpretation (or misinterpretation) of African tradition, has fastened upon the African Transcendent God. But in 1963, John V. Taylor, himself a non-African, sought to demonstrate how little the African primal world needs a transcendent God.[20] It is *this* life, *this* existence and its concerns, its cares, its joys which are the focus of African primal religions.

I suggest that both views were correct; only that there was no dialogue between them. Most African primal religions do have a transcendent God, but a transcendent God is also part of the religious structure that yields the problem of ambivalence that was mentioned earlier. However, this essential point has been made by two African francophone scholars, the Rwandan philosopher Alexis Kagame and the Zairean theologian Mulago. In two studies on 'The place of God and man in Bantu religion' published in *Cahiers des Religions Africaines*,[21] Kagame has shown that man is the centre of the universe, and therefore the heart of religion; but this means man not as individual but rather as humanity, the goal of man's centrality being the perpetuation of humankind, and he concluded:

> Bantu primal religion assembles its fundamental beliefs around two vital centres: God and man. The high place that God occupies is however seen as the basic presupposition which underlies the purpose of the Creator who has oriented everything towards the perpetuation of the summit of his work: humankind.[22]

Writing on the same subject in his *La religion traditionnelle des Bantus et leur vision du monde* (a definitive work which brings together all his research on African primal religions), Mulago actually referred to Kagame's articles, agreeing that Bantu religion was essentially anthropocentric. Mulago's concern, however, was to draw out the implications for affirming a specifically African religious and theological viewpoint:

To gain a proper understanding of African primal world view, we must set aside the dualistic dialectic which characterises Western thought whereby the exaltation of man would entail the rejection of God. On the contrary, African primal religious viewpoint has as its two fundamental notions and vital centres: God and man.[23]

Two key ideas emerge from these studies: first, that the stress in the primal religious world-view is decidedly *this-worldly*; second, there is the notion that this *this-worldliness* encompasses God and man in an abiding relationship which is the divine destiny of humankind, and the purpose and goal of the universe.

Here we need to recall the sixth and final feature in Harold Turner's analysis, namely that the primal understanding discloses a universe conceived as a unified cosmic system, essentially spiritual, in which the 'physical' acts as sacrament for 'spiritual' power. In such a universe or in such a conception of the universe, the Transcendent is not a so-called 'spiritual' world separate from the realm of regular human existence, since human existence itself participates in the constant interplay of the divine–human encounter. Consequently, the conclusion of Kagame and Mulago that at the heart of the universe and of religion is a divine–human relationship for the fulfilment of man's divine destiny, constitutes a real advance and lies at the heart of the contribution which African theology from a primal perspective can make to a fresh Christian account of the Transcendent. This insight signifies in Christian terms that the revelation of God in Christ is the disclosure that God is abidingly involved in a relationship with man, and for man; God has never left man and never been far removed from man, as St Paul declared on Mars Hill, in *Acts* 17:27, in another time and place where a Christian account of the Transcendent was being forged in an encounter with a primal world-view, the Hellenistic world-view being essentially primal. Most African primal myths of origins, being structurally anthropocentric, thus depict God as departing from human company, from centre-stage, so to speak. The Biblical account sharpens the ethical focus of that alienation and indicates in more precise outline the divine commitment to reconciliation, which was already embedded in the primal myth.

This same understanding was expressed by the Ecumenical Association of African Theologians at Accra in 1977, speaking of an

African view of the *human* as an important element in African Christian theological thought.

> For Africans there is unity and continuity between the destiny of human persons and the destiny of the cosmos ... The victory of life in the human person is also the victory of life in the cosmos. The salvation of the human person in African theology is the salvation of the universe. In the mystery of the incarnation, Christ assumes the totality of the human and the totality of the cosmos.[24]

To this whole subject John Mbiti has made a most illuminating and seminal contribution which shows a depth of primal understanding. Yet it is one which, so far as I am aware, he has never followed up. It is found in a little-known article on 'Christianity and East African culture and religion'[25] and was originally an address delivered to the Christian Union of Makerere University, Kampala. Recalling the six-fold categories of what he called 'African ontology' in which God, Spirits, Man, Animals, Plants and Inanimate creation exist in a 'unity, so that to break up that unity is to destroy one or more of these modes of existence, and to destroy one is in effect to destroy them all', Mbiti sought to show how the divine invasion of the world of man in the Incarnation, far from upsetting that unity, in fact retained it 'in equilibrium'. For though 'God ... in our traditional concepts lives in another mode of existence, separated from ours, He became one of us, and we can become one with Him'. The mystery of the Incarnation is therefore illuminated as the mystery of the mutual indwelling of God and Man in which 'no department of Man is segregated or left out'. It is no surprise that Mbiti felt confident to conclude that if the 'man of Africa' understood the Gospel in these terms, 'he will not have very far to go before he begins to walk on familiar ground'.[26]

The revelation of God in Christ is therefore the revelation of transcendence. The process is, however, not so much that of God *coming* to mankind, but rather, as the primal imagination perceives it, it is like the rending of the veil, so that the nature of the whole universe as instinct with the divine presence may be made manifest, as also the divine destiny of man as an abiding divine–human relationship. On this point, the New Testament speaks in the idiom of the primal imagination when it declares that 'Now God's home is with mankind. He will live with them, and they shall be His people. God Himself will be with them, and He will be their God.'[27] Even though the consummation of this divine destiny has to be allowed to lie 'at the end' yet its reality in present existence must also be granted. The primal imagination is able to grasp this reality and we see evidence for it in the bold expectation with which Christian churches that are alive to their primal world-view anticipate and *do* experience 'transcendent' happenings like visions, prophecies and healings.

This is another way of saying that the community that is open to the manifestations of the transcendent comes to participate in the transcendent. For the Christ-event has now resulted in God's presence in actual history in the community of His believers. Ideally, then, the Church which has come into existence through the death and resurrection of Christ, and is the household of God,[28] participates, through the Holy Spirit, in transcendence.

But is the experience of transcendence limited only to the knowledge of the love of the Father mediated through the redemptive work of the Son and actualised through the indwelling Holy Spirit? The primal imagination suggests that there is more. The clue lies in what Mulago has mostly written about, namely the notion of 'vital participation' as a fundamental category for understanding communal life.[29] The basic idea here is that it is participation in a common life and in its resources and powers that constitutes community. Applied to the experience of transcendence, 'vital participation' in Christ then opens the way for a participation equally in the resources and powers of all those who are also brought within the community. Since this is a community constituted in Christ and actualised through the Spirit, that is, in terms of spirit, it includes both living and dead. The divine presence in the community of believers constitutes it into a 'transcendent' community in which the human components experience and share in divine life and nature.

These are quite clearly Biblical categories which are applied to Christian faith and experience, as in *1 Corinthians* 10:14–22 and *2 Peter* 1:4. It is interesting to find therefore that it was this notion of 'vital participation' which David Shank, himself a non-African, used to explain how Prophet Harris came to speak of his direct involvement with Moses, Elijah, Angel Gabriel and Jesus Christ.

Harris, through vital participation had been 'grafted in' to the 'holy root' of Israel's life and faith to such an extent as to 'partake of the root and fatness of the olive tree', to use the apostle Paul's expression (Romans 11:16–24). In so doing he was indeed participating in the life of the living dead and their God, of whom Jesus Himself had said, 'He is not a God of the dead but of the living, for all live unto Him' (Luke 20:33ff and parallels). Harris had earlier cut himself off from his Glebo life and family in a radical conversion; yet he was not now without living ancestors. He had simply changed family connections, now based on faith in Christ as known though Scriptures, but by means of a spirituality of vital participation totally indigenous to his African way of being.[30]

Prophet Harris's appropriation of the Bible as truth

was in ways that were no longer simple patterns of 'belief in' the truth as he had known previously, but an African pattern of 'participation in' the truth. It was no longer a question of what Moses saw, or what Elijah did, or the words and works of Jesus as reported in the Bible. It became a question of involvement – as with the ancestors, the living dead – with Moses, with Elijah, with the Archangel Gabriel, and supremely with Jesus Christ.[31]

When we are able to reformulate the Christian faith drawing on aspects of the primal imagination in the ways indicated – although only some aspects have been dealt with – it seems that we can achieve a unified and organic view of the knowledge of truth, and so avoid the destructive dichotomies in epistemology which, since the European Enlightenment, have gradually drained the vital power out of Christian theology by shunting its affirmations into the siding of mere opinion. Bishop Lesslie Newbigin wrestles with this problem facing the modern church, particularly in the context of the religious pluralism of our time.[32] Perhaps it may be necessary to recognise afresh that, after all, the real encounter with alternative viewpoints and interpretations of reality takes place not in words alone, but in the realm of spirit and in the things of spirit.

There may therefore be an even more fundamental service which the primal imagination renders to Christian theology. Curiously, modern theology in the West seems to have pursued a course of development which divorces the Christian Gospel and the issues it raises from religion and the mainsprings of human religious quests and questions. Consequently, this modern theology appears to have lost touch with, and to be incapable of answering to, the crucial issues which lie at the heart of human existence, issues which are essentially religious: questions of human identity, community, ecological equilibrium and justice. Because primal world-views are fundamentally religious, the primal imagination restores to theology the crucial dimension of living religiously for which the theologian needs make no apology. The primal imagination may help us restore the ancient unity of theology and spirituality.

Perhaps a final observation on primal world-views and primal religions is in order. Even though I have related my argument almost solely to evidence and literature drawn from the African field, yet primal religions cannot be adequately described as 'ethnic' religions. If in the history and phenomenology of religions, primal religions are in fact 'both primary and prior', in that they are 'the most basic or fundamental religious forms in the overall history of mankind' and 'have preceded and contributed to the other religious systems', and so 'represent a common religious heritage of humanity',[33] then the primal imagination cannot be the ethnic possession of some portions alone of the human race. The primal imagination can surface anywhere. Furthermore, if as the history of Christian expansion shows, 'it is primal religions which underlie the Christian faith of the vast majority of Christians of all ages and all nations',[34] then can Christians treat such considerations lightly? What do we make of the possibility of 'affinities between the primal and Christian traditions'?

At the 1973 Ibadan Consultation on Christian Dialogue with Primal Religions, the Greek Orthodox Bishop Anastasios Yannoulatos, from Athens, spoke on 'Growing into an awareness of primal world views' out of a Christian tradition which retains perhaps the deepest feelings for Christian origins. He wondered whether Christianity in the twentieth century had lost touch with its primal heritage, particularly from 'the first centuries when Christians lived in a comparable climate of primal world views' and so were able to develop a Christian tradition which incorporated vital elements of primal religious experience:

such as the sense of total devotion, of being cut to the heart, of deep symbolism, or of participation of the whole person in worship ... Or have missionaries only tried to transplant the Christianity and the problems of the Western Europe of the 16th century onwards?[35]

Lesslie Newbigin has indicated what he thinks is needed to overcome the destructive dichotomies which weaken the impact of Christian affirmations, making them into private opinion rather than public truth within a 'unified view of things'. For Bishop Newbigin:

this calls for a more radical kind of conversion than has often been thought, a conversion not only of the will, but of the mind, a transformation by the renewing of the mind so as not to be conformed to this world, not to see things as our culture sees them, but – with new lenses – to see things in a radically different way.[36]

The 'our culture' he spoke of was modern Western culture. If Bishop Yannoulatos was right in saying that a rediscovery of 'primal elements' is what may be needed, this may also mean growing into a primal awareness of the Christian Gospel as religion. Primal religions generally conceive of religion as a system of power and of living religiously as being in touch with the source and channels of power in the universe; Christian theology in the West seems, on the whole, to understand the Christian Gospel as a system of ideas. And yet, when the apostle Paul described the Gospel, that is what he wrote: 'I have complete confidence in the Gospel; it is the power of God to save all who believe ...'.[37] Surely, this calls for a new idiom.

Notes and References

1. Kweku Howard, 'First West African Prophet', *West Africa*, no. 3776, 25 December 1989 to 7 January 1990, pp. 2149–51.
2. David Shank, *A Prophet for Modern Times – The Thought of William Wade Harris, West African Precursor of the Reign of Christ* (2 vols), unpublished Ph.D. Thesis, Aberdeen, 1980; vol. 1, p. 354.
3. G. M. Haliburton, *The Prophet Harris – A Study of an African Prophet and his Movement in the Ivory Coast and the Gold Coast, 1913–1915*, London: Longman, 1971.
4. As reported in David Shank, *A Prophet for Modern Times*, vol. 1, p. 338.
5. I use 'primal imagination' in much the same way and with much the same

connotation as the term 'primal world-view' was used in the 1973 Consultation in Ibadan, Nigeria on Christian dialogue with traditional thought forms. This recognised that:

> It is possible ... that religious systems as such may decline, disappear from public view, or even vanish altogether, while much of the religious culture with which they have been associated may continue. In particular, many of the beliefs and values, the views about reality, man and the world, that prevailed in a primal society may survive the loss of its overt religious system and continue to provide at least part of its terms of reference in a new and more complex situation, indeed even within a new religious faith and practice. It is this structure of beliefs and values, this way of life, that may be called a primal world view. (John B. Taylor (ed.), *Primal World Views – Christian Involvement in Dialogue with Traditional Thought-forms*, Ibadan: Daystar Press, 1976, pp. 4–5)

6. See, particularly, E. Milingo, *The World in Between*, London: C. Hurst and Co., 1984.
7. John B. Taylor (ed.), *Primal World Views*, p. 5.
8. This framework, which has come to be seen as a major advance in the study of primal religions, first appeared in Harold W. Turner, 'The primal religions of the world and their study', in Victor Hayes (ed.), *Australian Essays in World Religions*, Bedford Park: Australian Association for World Religions, 1977.
9. Rudolf Otto, *The Idea of the Holy: An Inquiry into the Non-rational Factor in the Idea of the Divine and its Relation to the Rational* (transl. John Harvey), London: Oxford University Press, 1950 (2nd edn).
10. Harold W. Turner, 'The primal religions of the world', pp. 27–37, especially pp. 30–2.
11. Ibid., p. 32.
12. Ibid., p. 37.
13. Ibid., p. 35.
14. See G. Lienhardt, *Divinity and Experience – the Religion of the Dinka*, Oxford: Clarendon Press, 1961.
15. Bolaji Idowu, *Olódùmarè – God in Yoruba Belief*, London: Longman, 1962, p. 141.
16. Ibid., p. 63.
17. Ibid., p. 202.
18. John Mbiti, *African Religions and Philosophy*, London: Heinemann, 1969, p. 77.
19. It is extraordinary, for instance, how the African names for God in African indigenous languages have made an easy transition into Christian vocabulary to designate the God of the Bible – a feature which was lacking in the earlier missionary history of Europe.
20. John V. Taylor, *The Primal Vision – Christian Presence amid African Religion*, London: SCM Press, 1963.
21. Alexis Kagame, 'La place de Dieu et de l'homme dans la religion des Bantu', *Cahiers des Religions Africaines*, vol. 2, no. 4, July 1968, pp. 213–22; and vol. 3, no. 5, January 1969, pp. 5–11.
22. Alexis Kagame, 'La place de Dieu et de l'homme dans la religion des Bantu', *Cahiers des Religions Africaines*, vol. 3, no. 5, January 1969, p. 1.
23. Gwa Cikala M. Mulago, *La Religion Traditionelle des Bantu et leur vision du monde*, Kinshasa: Faculté de Théologie Catholique, 1980, p. 166.
24. Quoted in K. Appiah-Kubi and Sergio Torres (eds), *African Theology en route*, New York: Orbis Books, 1979, p. 193.
25. John Mbiti, 'Christianity and East African culture and religion', *Dini na Mila (Revealed Religion and Traditional Custom)*, vol. 3, no. 1, May 1968, pp. 1–6.
26. Ibid., p. 4.

27. *Revelation* 21:3.
28. 1 *Timothy* 3:15.
29. See V. Mulago, *Un visage africain du Christianisme – L'union vitale bantu face à l'unité vitale ecclésiale*, Présence Africaine, Paris, 1962; also Mulago, 'Vital Participation', in Kwesi Dickson and Paul Ellingworth (eds), *Biblical Revelation and African Beliefs*, London: Lutterworth Press, 1969, pp. 137–58.
30. David A. Shank, *A Prophet for Modern Times*, vol. 1, p. 467.
31. Ibid., p. 466.
32. Lesslie Newbigin, *The Gospel in a Pluralistic Society*, Grand Rapids: Eerdmans and Geneva: World Council of Churches, 1989.
33. Harold W. Turner, 'The primal religions of the world', p. 28.
34. Andrew F. Walls, 'Africa and Christian Identity', *Mission Focus*, vol. v, no. 7, November 1978, p. 11.
35. Anastasios Yannoulatos, 'Growing into an awareness of primal worldviews', in Taylor, *Primal World Views*, p. 75.
36. Newbigin, *The Gospel in a Pluralistic Society*, p. 38.
37. *Romans* 1:16.

7

Translatability and the Cultural Incarnations of the Faith

Translatability as Universality

Andrew Walls has taught us to recognise the Christian religion as 'culturally infinitely translatable'.[1] From this perspective it becomes possible to see Christianity's various cycles of expansion into different cultural contexts in its history as so many cultural manifestations or incarnations of the faith. Each incarnation has been different and yet each has managed to preserve elements which unite them all as sharing in a common reality, elements like worship of the God of Israel, attribution of ultimate significance to Jesus Christ, a sense of belonging to a people of God extending beyond the local context and in the midst of whom God's activity is recognised, reading of common Scriptures, and sacramental use of bread and wine and water.[2]

Translatability is also another way of saying universality. Hence the translatability of the Christian religion signifies its fundamental relevance and accessibility to persons in any culture within which the Christian faith is transmitted and assimilated. Nowhere is this character of Christianity more evident than in the Christian view of Scripture. Unlike, say, Islam, in which the effectual hearing of the Word of Allah occurs essentially only through the medium of the Arabic language, Christian doctrine rejects the notion of a special, sacred language for its Scriptures and makes God speak in the vernacular so that 'all of us hear ... in our own languages ... the wonders of God'.[3] Accordingly, the Bible translated into whatever language remains essentially and substantially what it is believed to be in its original autographs.

But behind the Christian doctrine of the substantial equality of the Scriptures in all languages, there lies the even profounder doctrine of the Incarnation, by which the fullest divine communication has reached beyond the forms of human words into the human form itself. 'The Word [of God] became flesh and dwelt among us.'[4] Translatability, therefore, may be said to be in-built into the nature of the Christian religion and capable of subverting any cultural possessiveness of the Faith in the process of its transmission.

I do not intend to pursue these ideas in the manner of a theoretical discussion, but rather to show how, in our post-missionary setting, such considerations truly come into their own, and also to point out how it is only by an adequate and firm grasp of this principle of the translatability of the Christian religion that we can appreciate the true character of continuing Christian witness and enhance the genuine development of new indigenous traditions of Christian thought. The discussion will relate mostly to a body of literature and developments in the African field.

Non-Western Christianity and Western Value-setting – the Seventh International African Seminar

It is appropriate to begin this discussion by recalling an event which indicates the extent to which Western value-setting for Christianity was still exerting an impact on the interpretation of non-Western Christianity even in the post-missionary era, and was therefore having a distorting effect on indigenous developments in Christian thought. The principle of translatability is not necessarily one which is most readily recognised in the process of the transmission of Christianity.

In April 1965, an international gathering of academics and scholars representing various intellectual disciplines with interest in the missionary transmission of Christianity in Africa met in the University of Ghana, Legon, near Accra, under the auspices of the International African Institute, to discuss and assess the place of Christianity in sub-Saharan Africa. The proceedings of that seminar, edited by Christian Baëta of Ghana, were published under the title *Christianity in Tropical Africa.*[5] When one reads the papers presented and the account of the discussions, one gets a distinct impression that the gathering took a positive but not triumphalist view of the fortunes of Christianity on the African continent. Clearly, not all issues were considered to have been resolved, yet *Christianity in Tropical Africa* gives every indication that there was a feeling that the Christian presence in Africa represented the most significant spread and advance of the Faith in history since the penetration of the early Roman Empire and of Europe. The phenomenon of Christianity in Africa was therefore an important subject to study. An observation by Baëta sums up the mood of the gathering and the state of understanding reached: 'Intangible in many of its aspects, the Christian presence has been and remains, in the African scene, a massive and unavoidable fact and factor'.[6] Africa seemed to be a success story of the missionary endeavour. Adrian Hastings, writing in the 1970s and looking back to the two previous decades, could comment: 'Certainly, if one looked around Africa in 1950, the achievement of the missionary enterprise could not but appear considerable'.[7] And yet it also seems that there was some measure of surprise, with not a little perplexity, at this rich African harvest. In the mind of the missionary movement, there had been a general hesitancy about ascribing to Africa's pre-Christian religious traditions and socio-cultural forms of life any substantial theological status. Not many had been convinced that African societies gave evidence of any 'preparation for Christianity'. Furthermore, the entanglement of the missionary histories of African peoples with European colonial ventures served to complicate the outcome all the more. How successfully could the one be dissociated from the other?

On the specifically religious plane, it was not the great and high religious cultures of Asia – on which considerable missionary resources and personnel had been expended – but the 'animistic' world of Africa, to use the language of the Edinburgh World Missionary Conference of 1910,[8] which now became the test case of the missionary enterprise, and probably of Christianity generally, in the new era that was beginning.

One area of the discussions at the Accra seminar in which this perplexity seemed particularly acute was that relating to African conversion. The seminar seemed to give a variety of interpretations of the 'massive and unavoidable fact and factor of the Christian presence' in Africa. The explanations ranged from those which were broadly sociological and political to those which sought to be specifically religious. The British theologian, F. B. Welbourn who had worked in Uganda, for example, wondered whether a missionary (Protestant) preaching of salvation from the standpoint of guilt could be understood by traditional African societies which, in his view, were conditioned more by a shame-culture.[9] He saw conversion to Christianity in Uganda as providing a 'phantasy structure' for an African identity within the new political structure that was emerging.[10] On the other hand, the Kenyan theologian, John Mbiti, then working in Makerere University College, Kampala, Uganda, called for greater attention to be given to religious considerations in their own terms, and asked whether sociological or political considerations alone provided an adequate explanation of the facts. Mbiti cited the testimonies of converts who gave as reasons for their conversion a positive demonstration of love by missionaries and the impact of some Christian doctrines, particularly the resurrection and the nature of the Christian afterlife. 'Did they not have an inner religiosity which found fulfilment in Christianity?'[11] Perhaps it is not surprising that the need was felt for a study comparable to the work of Arthur Darby Nock on conversion in the Hellenistic world of the early Roman Empire, another time and place which recorded a massive response to Christianity as it crossed cultural frontiers.[12] The feeling was that 'the spread of Christianity in Africa is a topic of far greater importance in Christian history than is generally recognised',[13] that there was a need to explore 'fundamental questions', and that at issue was really the question of Christian identity, a study of which was made even more urgent by the wind of political nationalism then sweeping across the continent:

> The search must continue for an identity which ensures to all African Christians ... a satisfying self-consciousness and dignity in social and inter-racial relations. If the definition of this identity has so far been predominantly in nationalistic terms, ... this must be supplemented by the reflection that a Christian comes from God and goes to God; [his citizenship is in heaven, i.e. his total and final value system extend well beyond those of his own culture]. Full realisation of the potentialities of genuine Christian culture within the African context will involve both the working out of a clear Christian mind regarding this

context and an equally clear African mind concerning Christian values and ideas.[14]

The Accra seminar of 1965 is important for an understanding of what was happening to Christianity in Africa, at least in the minds of its most influential scholars, interpreters and advocates, at the critical time of the heyday of African nationalism, and also in the period when African Christian intellectuals were themselves beginning to make serious efforts to come to terms with the Christian presence in African life.

The seminar is also important in a rather disturbing way, in that, in at least some of its aspects, it is a pointer to the hurdles which still had to be overcome, if the Christian religion in Africa was to be seen as a truly African experience and reality. For despite the recognition in some of the papers presented, that there was a valid African contribution,[15] an appreciation of the full dimensions of their contribution was only just beginning to be recognised. It still seemed as if the whole matter of the planting of Christianity in Africa was little more than the religious equivalent of the political and cultural impact of the West. The difficulties in the interpretation of African conversion are an indicator of the inhibiting effects of such a frame of reference.

Furthermore, African independent churches had become a significant element of the Christian presence on the continent. Yet despite George Shepperson's argument in his paper, 'Ethiopianism: past and present' that these African initiatives in Christianity had a 'rightful place in the history of the Church'[16] and David Barrett's analysis from 200 different societies across Africa, showing that independency was 'playing an increasing part in the expansion of Christianity in Africa',[17] the seminar's treatment of the phenomenon of the independent churches was less than positive, seeing them rather as 'separatist' movements. Academic orthodoxy was still far from recognising that it was the independent churches which were in fact indicating the trend and direction of African Christianity. In a later trenchant criticism of the seminar on this point, two African historians with an interest in African Christian history have asked why the convenors failed to 'invite participation by these African Churches, or to recognise their existence as propagators of Christianity in Africa'.[18]

A False Start for African Theology? – the Indigenisation Crusade of Idowu

Perhaps it was the whole conception of the nature of African church history which was the problem in 1965. In some 'polemical thoughts on African Church History', Paul Jenkins wrote a few years ago: 'An African church history that begins with missionary institutions – and especially one that begins with missionary initiatives – is almost bound to stress the foreign nature of the faith and its practices'.[19] This was the dominant frame of reference for understanding Christianity in Africa at the time, as can be seen in the early direction that the then emergent movement of African theology took. This direction reveals the skewing effect of that frame of reference on the development of theological thought and agenda.

All who were concerned with the fortunes of Christianity in Africa at the time naturally felt the urgency to demonstrate the African credentials of the faith but, understandably, it was African Christian scholars and churchmen themselves upon whom that burden fell most heavily. Apart from Christian Baëta, there were three other African churchmen and theological academics who presented papers at the Accra seminar, and who were destined to become influential in the growth of African theology in the subsequent decades. These were Bolaji Idowu (of Nigeria), John Mbiti (of Kenya) and Vincent Mulago (as he was then called) of Zaire. Idowu's paper, under the title 'The Predicament of the Church in Africa', presented a disturbing picture of the church in Africa as 'still dependent, ... looking to missionaries from outside for manpower and material resources, dependent in its theology, its liturgy and its church discipline, in fact in its whole expression of the Christian life'.[20] For Idowu, 'the Church in Africa came into being with prefabricated theology, liturgies and traditions'.[21] Mbiti presented a paper on 'Ways and Means of Communicating the Gospel' to ensure effectiveness and relevance,[22] whilst Mulago, in his paper entitled 'Christianity and African Culture: the African Contribution to Theology',[23] made a case for an African theology which would make use of African categories of experience and thought.

This is, perhaps, not the place for a detailed exposition of those papers. All these men were, however, testifying to what they, together with others, perceived to be the 'predicament of the

church', to use Idowu's language, and were also showing an awareness of the intense pressure which this perceived predicament was
exerting upon African churchmen, compelling them to find (one
might even say, almost invent) a theological identity, a theological
idiom and a Christian *modus vivendi* that would be more appropriate
to the African context and reality. They seemed united in the concern
that the 'massive and unavoidable fact and factor' of the Christian
presence still needed deeper rooting in the African scene, at least to
the extent that it should cease to be and be seen as a foreign plant, and
to become instead, a home-grown and indigenous reality.

Not surprisingly, therefore, in the subsequent few years, the major
concern became the 'indigenisation' – of Christianity, church and
theology. Idowu quickly earned a status as a 'doyen' among African
theologians, certainly in the West African region, and took up the
challenge of indigenisation in a spirited publication of 1965, *Towards
an Indigenous Church*,[24] though some of the material had been
developed for three radio talks as far back as 1961, on the 'problem of
indigenisation of the Church in Nigeria'. This was probably the first
and clearest statement by a leading African theologian, setting forth
specific proposals that an African Church might consider in order to
transform itself into an authentic African Christian community, if it
found itself 'heavily tinged with Western culture'. For Idowu, Christianity was in Africa, but not of Africa ... not yet. In other words, for
Idowu, the 'foreignness' of Christianity in Africa was a fundamental
datum and the starting point of the discussion. Indigenisation was as
much about discarding 'foreignness' as it was about rooting the faith
in local realities. Accordingly Idowu specified five areas which, in his
view, needed attention:

1. the Bible in Nigerian languages,
2. the language of evangelisation,
3. theology,
4. liturgy,
5. dress and vestments.

It may seem odd that for all his insistence on the church in Nigeria
bearing 'the stamp of originality', Idowu decided that ministers'
vestments was one area in which 'the Church in Nigeria must
preserve something as token of her being part and presence of the

Universal Church'. On the other hand, it could also be argued that Idowu was seeking a far more fundamental indigenisation than merely external features. Whatever the merits of Idowu's arguments, the reason for replacing, in his words, 'the European complexion of the Church' with an indigenous complexion was that 'Christian Nigerians cease to see Jesus Christ as an imported divinity from a European pantheon' and that they come to see Him as 'God's Messiah to Nigerians, their own personal Saviour and Lord'.[25]

The really important question to ask for our present purposes is why this spirited apologia for indigenisation has not been followed through in the theological and intellectual career of Idowu; why, eight years later, in his *African Traditional Religion – A Definition* Idowu concluded that:

> African traditional religion is *the* religion practised by the majority of Africans, nakedly [i.e. overtly] in most cases, but also in some cases under the veneers supplied by Westernism and Arabism.[26]

Why, when Idowu quoted the Biblical text of *1 John* 3:2: 'It does not yet appear what we shall be', did he apply it not to the church in Nigeria, but to the prospect of African traditional religion? The task of vindicating and establishing 'a satisfying African self-consciousness and dignity' which in *Towards an Indigenous Church* was laid upon the Christian church, later came to be confidently entrusted to the old traditional religion, now revitalised with its 'God-given heritage and indigenous spiritual treasures'.[27] Through the years, it seems, Idowu remained haunted by the 'foreignness' of Christianity, and having started from that foreignness, was never able to arrive at indigeneity.

Translatability Seen in Mbiti's Writings

Like Idowu, Mbiti was early to deplore the lack of sufficient and positive engagement by Western missions with African cultural and religious values. He saw the result of this in an African church which had 'come of age *evangelistically*, but not *theologically*': 'a church without theology, without theologians and without theological concern' as he was writing in 1967 and also in 1969.[28]

Mbiti, however, soon came to make a distinction between 'Christianity' which 'results from the encounter of the Gospel with any given local society' and so is always indigenous and culture-bound, on the one hand, and the Gospel, which is 'God-given, eternal and does not change' on the other. In 1970 he wrote: 'We can add nothing to the Gospel, for this is an eternal gift of God; but Christianity is always a beggar seeking food and drink, cover and shelter from the cultures it encounters in its never-ending journeys and wanderings'.[29] Mbiti had already given an indication of this trend of thought in his paper at the Accra seminar of 1965, when he stated: 'We cannot artificially create an "African theology" or even plan it; it must evolve spontaneously as the Church teaches and lives *her* Faith and in response to the extremely complex situation in Africa'.[30] But the definitive break came later, when Mbiti rejected the very idea of the quest for indigenisation of Christianity or of theology in Africa. In a response to a study of his theology by John Kinney,[31] Mbiti wrote:

> To speak of 'indigenising Christianity' is to give the impression that Christianity is a ready-made commodity which has to be transplanted to a local area. Of course, this has been the assumption followed by many missionaries and local theologians. I do not accept it any more.[32]

It may be of interest also to compare the attitudes of our two representative thinkers to the African independent churches. Idowu found no place for them in his drive for indigenisation. He saw them instead as 'syncretistic sects which have spread all over the country like the seed of contagion …, the product of syncretising Christianity with some dominant practices of the national cults'. He saw no positive contribution coming through the ministries of these churches:

> The end product of this syncretism is a church whose characteristics are frothy, ecstatic ritual, seeing of visions and dreaming of dreams, making predications and prescriptions, mass hysteria which gives birth to babbling of incoherent things as symptoms of possession by the Spirit. All these naturally make them popular with the mass who like neglected hungry sheep flock where they find promises of nourishment.[33]

Mbiti, on the other hand, though not an uncritical admirer of the independents, nevertheless saw in them an African Christian consciousness and experience having its own integrity. They represented not only a massive rejection of imported forms of the Christian life; they also bore witness to the fact that 'African peoples have taken seriously to Christianity'. Through them and their distinctive styles of ministry and community, God was speaking to the world church and to the world. Mbiti looked forward to a time when they would not be 'as far apart from the historical churches as they are at present'.[34]

For Mbiti, therefore, the Gospel is genuinely at home in Africa, is capable of being apprehended by Africans at the specific level of their religious experience and in fact has been so received through the missionary transmission of it. The Western missionary enterprise, from this perspective, has a place within a religious history which properly belongs to African tradition. Since God is One, Mbiti maintains, 'God, the Father of our Lord Jesus Christ is the same God who has been known and worshipped in various ways within the religious life of African peoples' and who therefore, was 'not a stranger in Africa prior to the coming of missionaries'. They did not bring God; rather God brought them, so that by the proclamation of the Gospel through the missionary activity, Jesus Christ might be known, for 'without Him [Jesus Christ] the meaning of our religiosity is incomplete'.

> The Gospel enabled people to utter the name of Jesus Christ ... that final and completing element that crowns their traditional religiosity and brings its flickering light to full brilliance.[35]

By this approach, Mbiti in effect 'exorcises' the 'Westernism' and 'foreignness' in the Western transmission of the Gospel, and internalises whatever was of the Gospel. By the same process, he affirms the missionary endeavour, but without making the missionary central; for the whole operation began with God and was carried through by God. The encounter was, at its deepest levels, not the meeting of Western ideas and African traditions; rather it was the meeting of African man in his religiosity with Jesus Christ, whose 'presence in the world is not a historical [i.e. chronological] but a geographical presence in the world made by Him and through Him'.[36]

The theological principle we see operating in Mbiti's thought is that of translatability – the capacity of the essential impulses of the

Christian religion to be transmitted and assimilated in a different culture so that these impulses create dynamically equivalent responses in the course of such a transmission. Given this principle, it is possible to say that the earlier concern to seek an 'indigenisation' of Christianity in Africa, as though one were dealing with an essentially 'Western' and 'foreign' religion was, in effect, misguided because the task was conceived as the correlation of two entities thought to be unrelated. Such an effort was bound to lead to a dead end, as we have noted in Idowu's case, precisely because it fastened too intently on the 'foreignness' of the Western modes of the transmission of the Faith, and correspondingly paid too little attention to actual achievement 'on the ground'. The achievement meant here is not to be measured in terms of Western missionary transmission, but rather by African assimilation of the Faith. Evangelisation is not simply the 'communication of foreign ideas to passive recipients who have to swallow every bit whether or not they approve',[37] it was therefore misguided to assume that African converts to Christianity assimilated the missionary message in Western terms rather than in terms of their own African religious understanding and background.

Translatability and an Appropriate Historical Framework

Since the subject of Western missions will continue to provide part, at least, of our understanding of Christianity in the non-Western world, it is important that we pursue the question of an appropriate frame of reference for appreciating their role from the perspective of the principle of the translatability of the Christian religion. A most stimulating contribution to the subject has been made by Lamin Sanneh.[38] Since Sanneh's treatment is important to the present discussion, I shall summarise its salient points.

Sanneh states his concern as follows: 'The subject of Western missions needs to be unhinged from the narrow colonial context and placed in the much wider setting of African culture, including the religious background of African societies.'[39] For Sanneh this is crucial because it is what African converts did (and do) with the Gospel received through the Western missionary transmission which really counts, certainly more than the mere transmission itself. He asks:

'The question with which we are faced fundamentally is this: Of the two processes at work, the historical transmission and the indigenous assimilation, which one is more significant?'[40] Sanneh has no doubt, and he expects his readers to agree with him, that 'without hesitation it is the latter. For it is within that that the historical process itself becomes meaningful.'

To put this shift of emphasis firmly into the context of the assimilation of the missionary message, Sanneh adds the crucial role that Bible translation has played in Western missions. For Sanneh, the importance of Bible translation and its priority in missionary work are an indication that 'God was not disdainful of Africans as to be incommunicable in their languages'.[41] This carried two far-reaching consequences for how one may view the African cultural world. First: 'This imbued local cultures with eternal significance and endowed African languages with a transcendent range.' And second, it also 'presumed that the God of the Bible had preceded the missionary into the receptor-culture – so the missionary needs to discover Him in the new culture'. Therefore, according to Sanneh: 'It is the hidden reality of this divine presence that both validates external mission and requires translation as a *sine qua non* of witness'.[42] Through the very process of Scripture translation, 'the central categories of Christian theology – God, creation, Jesus Christ, history – are transposed into their local equivalents, suggesting that Christianity had been adequately anticipated'.[43] But, as we noted earlier, Sanneh is concerned to show not only that the crucial factors involved in the Gospel communication do not require the Western missionary transmitter to be at the centre of the picture, but also that African pre-Christian religions have had a theological significance in the whole process. The centrality of Scripture translation points to the significance of local religions for providing the idiom for Christian apprehension:

> The enterprise of Scriptural translation, with its far-reaching assumptions about traditional religious categories and ideas as a valid carriage for the revelation and divine initiative that precedes and anticipates historical mission, concedes the salvific value of local religions.[44]

Accordingly, the popular notion of Christianity as 'the white man's religion' or Western religion, is effectively set aside, for African Christianity is no less Christian for being mediated through African languages, whilst Western Christianity does not enshrine universal standards. On the contrary, the very possibility of Scripture translation, as well as the elements that come into play through it, demonstrate that an African 'incarnation' of the Faith is valid too:

> Translation assumed that the abstract Word of God would find its true destiny when embodied in concrete local idiom, lending credence to the theological insight that the Word of God had always carried the burden of the incarnation, and that its historical manifestation in Jesus Christ concentrated and made visible a process that is occurring throughout history.[45]

Sanneh's description of this whole process is the comprehensive term, *Missio Dei*, encompassing the divine initiative through the pre-Christian tradition, the historical missionary transmission and the indigenous assimilation:

> *Missio Dei* sustained traditional religious enterprise by bringing about a convergence with Christianity ... so that *Missio Dei* activated by the stimulus of historical contact with the West, has fused with local religious enterprise and acquired a concrete reality.[46]

But the 'concrete reality' is a local reality, achieved by indigenous assimilation and African religious agency through the critical role of the Scriptures in African languages. Observing this phenomenon at its highest in the independent churches – the 'African Charismatics' as he calls them – Sanneh finds the evidence to vindicate the claim that 'local adaptation held incomparably greater prospects for the future of the religion in Africa than external agency did'.[47]

Then Sanneh finally comes full circle: once we have subordinated Western missionary transmission to local assimilation and adaptation under African agency, then 'we cannot continue to appropriate Christianity as an ideological theme and annex it as a subplot to the history of Western imperialism'.[48] If we wish to maintain the principle of the translatability of the Christian religion as well as the proper religious perspective on the process of its transmission, then we must admit that Sanneh is right.

A large portion of Sanneh's argument is also that 'the historical experience of Africa is a demonstration of the salvific value of religion',[49] by which he means African primal religions. One would wish that he pursued the question as to why his statement could not be made equally with regard to areas which are 'highly Islamised'. The phenomenological relationship of primal religions to the Christian religion may need to be taken seriously here too.[50]

But the major contribution which Sanneh's article makes is the historical frame of reference that it gives for understanding issues which lie beyond the missionary enterprise itself. By placing the whole exercise of missionary transmission and indigenous assimilation under the overarching concept of *Missio Dei*, Sanneh shifts the discussion away from considerations of the impact of the West upon the non-Western world. The Christian religion is rescued from a Western possessiveness of it, whilst at the same time the true proportions of the missionary endeavour are seen for what they really were, that is, the extent to which it stimulated the emergence of a genuine indigenous Christian tradition in terms of *Missio Dei* in the local setting; a fresh cultural incarnation of the Faith.

If it is translatability which produces indigeneity, then a truly indigenous church should also be a translating church, reaching continually to the heart of the culture of its context and incarnating the translating Word. For the Word who took flesh and dwelt among us, not only exegetes (and so translates) God (*John* 1:18), but also exegetes the human predicament (*John* 4:29), bringing the two together in a mutually intelligible communication. This makes it all the more important to pay attention to what happens at the level of indigenous assimilation. To agree with another of Paul Jenkins's 'polemical thoughts' on African Church history:

> African Church history must be concerned with the free dialogue that is already taking place between questions and problems as formulated in the different traditional cultures and the answers and solutions latent in the Christian message.[51]

It is by doing this that we come to recognise the extent of indigenisation that is already present in the very process of indigenous assimilation. Sustained by *Missio Dei*, the indigenous and translating church becomes a catalyst for newer assimilations, hence further manifestations and incarnations of the Faith.

Accordingly, translatability is the only true basis and starting point for seeking indigeneity. From this perspective, however, indigeneity does not lie at the *end* of a quest. Rather it is presumed within the very translatability of the Christian religion. Indigeneity is as much a matter of recognition within the Gospel as it is an achievement of actual Christian witness. Thus, universality, translatability, incarnation and indigeneity belong in a continuum and are integral to the warp and woof of the Christian religion. It is only by a serious misconception then that we can call it a Western religion.

There is an interesting comment by E. A. Ayandele (the Nigerian historian) reported by Walbert Buhlmann in his book, *The Coming of the Third Church*.[52] At the first international congress of the International Association for Mission Studies held in Driebergen, The Netherlands, in 1972, after many Western scholars had expressed views which he considered too critical of the missionary enterprise from the West, Ayandele intervened: 'Even if *you* came to us within the framework of colonialism, and did not preach the Gospel in all its purity, that has not prevented *us* from receiving the Gospel and genuinely living it'.[53] For Ayandele and others like him, Christianity had already become disentangled from any Western possessiveness of it; it is a non-Western religion.

Notes and References

1. Andrew F. Walls, 'The Gospel as prisoner and liberator of culture', *Faith and Thought*, 108 (1–2), 1981, pp. 39–52; also in *Missionalia*, vol. 10, no. 3, November 1982, pp. 93–105.
2. Andrew F. Walls, 'Christian tradition in today's world', in F. D. Whaling (ed.), *Religion in Today's World*, Edinburgh: T. and T. Clark, 1987, pp. 76–109.
3. *Acts of the Apostles* 2:11.
4. *John* 1:14.
5. C. G. Baëta (ed.), *Christianity in Tropical Africa* (Studies presented and discussed at the seventh International African Seminar, University of Ghana, April 1965), London: Oxford University Press, 1968.
6. Ibid., p. xii.
7. Adrian Hastings, *A History of African Christianity 1950–75*, Cambridge: Cambridge University Press, 1979, p. 43.
8. C. G. Baëta (ed.), *Christianity in Tropical Africa*, p. 129. At the Accra seminar too it was stated that Africa has never had a general high culture of its own. See also *World Missionary Conference 1910: Report of Commission IV – The Missionary Message in Relation to Non-Christian Religions*, Edinburgh and London: Oliphant Anderson and Ferrier, 1910, p. 24.

9. Ibid., pp. 182–99.
10. Ibid., p. 125.
11. Ibid., p. 126.
12. Ibid., p. 3. (See also A. D. Nock, *Conversion: The Old and the New in Religions from Alexander to Augustine*, Oxford: Clarenden Press, 1933.)
13. Ibid., p. 123.
14. Ibid., pp. 129–30.
15. For example, Richard Gray, 'Problems of historical perspective: the planting of Christianity in Africa in the 19th and 20th centuries', in Baëta, *Christianity in Tropical Africa*, pp. 18–30.
16. C. G. Baëta (ed.), *Christianity in Tropical Africa*, p. 363.
17. Ibid., p. 284.
18. Ade Ajayi and E. A. Ayandele, 'Writing African church history' in P. Beyerhaus and C. Hallencreutz (eds), *The Church Crossing Frontiers – Essays on the Nature of Mission* (in honour of Bengt Sundkler), Gleerup: Studia Missionalia Upsaliensa XI, 1969, pp. 90–108.
19. Paul Jenkins, 'The roots of African church history: some polemical thoughts', *International Bulletin of Missionary Research*, vol. 10, no. 2, April 1986, pp. 67–71.
20. C. G. Baëta (ed.), *Christianity in Tropical Africa*, p. 353.
21. Ibid., p. 426.
22. Ibid., pp. 329–50.
23. Ibid., pp. 308–28.
24. Bolaji Idowu, *Towards an Indigenous Church*, London: Oxford University Press, 1965.
25. Ibid., pp. 22–4, 49.
26. Bolaji Idowu, *African Traditional Religion – A Definition*, London: SCM Press, 1973, p. 208.
27. Ibid., p. 205.
28. John Mbiti, 'Some African concepts of Christology', in G. F. Vicedom (ed.), *Christ and the Younger Churches*, London: SPCK, 1972, pp. 51–62; published earlier in German in P. Beyerhaus et al., *Theologische Stimmen aus Afrika, Asien und Lateinamerika III*, München, 1968; also *African Religions and Philosophy*, London: Heinemann, 1969, pp. 232 and 233.
29. John Mbiti, 'Christianity and traditional religions in Africa', *International Review of Mission*, vol. 59, no. 236, October 1970, p. 438.
30. C. G. Baëta (ed.), *Christianity in Tropical Africa*, p. 332.
31. John Kinney, 'The theology of John Mbiti – his sources, norms and method', *Occasional Bulletin of Missionary Research*, vol. 3, no. 2, April 1979, pp. 65–7.
32. John Mbiti, 'Response to the article of John Kinney', *Occasional Bulletin of Missionary Research*, vol. 3, no. 2, April 1979, p. 68.
33. Bolaji Idowu, *Olódùmarè – God in Yoruba Belief*, London: Longman, 1962, pp. 211–12.
34. John Mbiti, 'The future of Christianity in Africa 1970–2000', *Communio Viatorum XIII*, nos. 1–2, 1970, pp. 34f.
35. John Mbiti, 'Response to the article of John Kinney', p. 68.
36. Loc. cit.
37. Ajayi and Ayandele, 'Writing African church history', p. 91.
38. Lamin Sanneh, 'The horizontal and the vertical in mission: an African perspective', *International Bulletin of Missionary Research*, vol. 7, no. 4, October 1983, pp. 165–71.
39. Ibid., p. 165.
40. Ibid., p. 166.
41. Loc. cit.

42. Loc. cit.
43. Loc. cit.
44. Ibid., p. 170.
45. Loc. cit.
46. Loc. cit.
47. Loc. cit.
48. Loc. cit.
49. Loc. cit.
50. Sanneh has since developed this theme more fully in his *Translating the Message – The Missionary Impact on Culture,* New York: Orbis Books, 1989.
51. Paul Jenkins, 'The roots of African Church history', p. 68.
52. Walbert Buhlmann, *The Coming of the Third Church* (English translation), Slough: St. Paul Publication, 1976. (First published in German as *Es kommt die dritte Kirche – Eine Analyse der kirchlichen Gegenwart und Zukunft,* 1974.)
53. Ibid., p. 171.

8

Christianity as the Religion of the Poor of the Earth

'The Coming of the Third Church'

In this chapter the aim is not, to paraphrase the words of Sanneh quoted in the last chapter, to appropriate the subject of the poor as an ideological theme and annex it as a subplot to bash the rich! In other words, I do not intend to assume the role of a theological Robin Hood and conjure up a corresponding Sheriff of Nottingham and a Prince John among the rich of the earth. On the other hand, the presence of Friar Tuck among the gang in the forest does raise the distinct possibility of some interesting correlations, and perhaps there might be more theological significance to the Robin Hood stories than we would probably allow.

The aim instead is simply this: starting from the recognition of a demographic fact of the church in our time, I wish to offer some reflections on how this fact has affected the nature of Christian understanding, and points to new tasks in world mission in our changed situation.

When Andrew Walls's observation about the shift in the centre of gravity of Christianity to the southern continents of Africa, Asia, Oceania and Latin America in the wake of the missionary enterprise from the West was published in his essay 'Towards Understanding Africa's place in Christian History',[1] that reality had not yet found its way into the general textbooks on Western missions and missiology. Around the same period, the Swiss Roman Catholic Capuchin missionary scholar, Walbert Buhlmann, made the same point, in rather dramatic style, by speaking, according to the title of his book, of *The Coming of the Third Church – An Analysis of the Present and Future of the Church.*[2] Buhlmann explained his choice of 'the third church' as follows:

I make the point that Third Church has no derogatory connotation in the sense of 'Church of the third rank'! It simply expresses the fact that, alongside the Western and Oriental Church, there has arisen a new entity which, by its special characteristics and future expectation, deserves to be denoted and appreciated by its own special name. 'In the third place' means not 'at the end' or 'in conclusion', but rather a new reality alongside what existed before, a fresh peak reached.[3]

Since then, these observations, anticipations and expectations concerning the demographic reality of the church world-wide in this latter part of the twentieth century have been documented in the authoritative *World Christian Encyclopaedia – A Comparative Study of Churches and Religions in the Modern World* AD *1900–2000*, edited by David B. Barrett.[4] In other words, we may assume that this fundamental shift of Christianity's centre of gravity to what Western economists and political scientists have long called 'the Third World' has finally entered the textbooks.

What is still perhaps not so easily finding its way into the textbooks and probably the general Christian consciousness is the extent to which this 'coming of the Third Church' has influenced the perception of the crucial issues for the church and Christian discipleship in this post-missionary setting.

In Buhlmann's view, 'the migration of the Church towards the southern hemisphere' meant that the Church was turning:

1. 'towards the peoples of antiquity' and realising in the process that 'world history did not begin in Europe, that Latin America, Africa and Asia are more ancient and more interesting ... from the point of view of the history of culture and the origins of man, than the West',
2. to 'dynamic' peoples in newly independent nations,
3. to the youth, that is to nations with relatively higher proportions of youth in their populations, but, most importantly of all for Buhlmann, the Church was gravitating
4. 'towards the poorer peoples' of the earth and there to find 'the opportunity not only to be in a real sense the Church of the poor', but also to have 'some experience of the goodness, humanity, simplicity and integrity of poor peoples'.

It was this complex reality of the 'third church' which constituted for Buhlmann 'the Church of the future as well as the future of the Church'.[5]

The Third Church – the Church of the Two-Thirds World

It is not necessary to pledge unqualified agreement with all that Walbert Buhlmann wrote twenty years ago to recognise that it is the reality of poverty in 'the South' and the view of 'the Third Church' as 'the Church of the poor' which have proved most influential in shaping Christian thinking and action in the period. This is seen not only in the substantial increase in the number, and the high profile, of Christian and church agencies devoted to aid and development in the Third World, but also in the seriousness with which theological education in the West, in some institutions at least, now seeks to integrate what has become known as 'development studies', focusing on Africa, Asia and Latin America.

The important thing to note in relation to this whole subject is, however, that whilst the economic gap between the richer nations of the North and the poorer nations of the South has progressively widened, at the same time the Christian churches of the South have generally continued to register growth, whilst those of the North, particularly in the older heartlands of the Faith in Western Europe, have declined, with the result that the majority of Christians in the world are now found living in contexts of poverty, even if all of them do not share in personal poverty. Curiously, therefore, the poor, 'underdeveloped' or 'developing' nations of the South, which in an earlier missionary age were the lands of the 'non-Christian religions', have become the lands where the Christians are, the two-thirds of the world, 'Two-Thirds World' being a term preferred by residents of these new lands of the Christians, which are marked by economic poverty, political powerlessness, but also religious pluralism. The coming of the Third Church, therefore, has also been the emergence of the Two-Thirds World churches. The significance of this event lies in more than the weight of numbers: it has to do also with what has happened to the Gospel in the minds of Christians of the Two-Thirds World, since they have received the Gospel and sought to appropriate it in their contexts of poverty, powerlessness and religious pluralism.

Momentous changes have taken place in Christian thinking and action in the last twenty to thirty years in relation to mission. There has been the recognition that the Gospel is essentially holistic and directed at the whole person – physical as well as spiritual, corporate as well as individual – and therefore requires a corresponding holistic missionary engagement. There has come about the recognition that there is a valid cultural plurality in the ways that we apprehend and express the Christian faith and that there is a plurality of theologies within the world-wide body of the church. It would be an exaggeration to say that these have all been due solely to the strivings of Christians in the Two-Thirds World. Nevertheless, insofar as these have become accepted and recognised in the period, they have been the agenda of the Two-Thirds World. In several instances, it is Christians of the Two-Thirds World who have initiated and charted new directions in Christian thought and action, responding to issues and realities at their sharpest end, because those have been the issues and realities of their contexts needing to be addressed by the Gospel. The view that has become generally accepted – that all theology, wherever it is produced, is contextual and therefore provisional rather than universal, and that theology itself is always a struggle with culturally-related questions – is a contribution of the Two-Thirds World. In that sense, the theologies of the Two-Thirds World – African theology, Black theology, Liberation theology, Indian Christian theology in relation to indigenous Indian religions, Minjung theology from Korea, and all the other expressions of contextual theology in the Two-Thirds World – are essentially missionary theologies. They arise out of efforts to let the Gospel encounter the reality of the Two-Thirds World in all its complexities. The comment of Dutch missiologist, Johannes Verkuyl, about African theology can equally be applied to all Two-Thirds World theologies:

> African theology does all the things which theology in general does, but in African theology (as in Asian) all these other functions are embraced in the missionary or communicative function. It is not primarily an intra-ecclesiastical exercise, but a discipline whose practitioners keep one question central: How can we best do our theology so that the Gospel will touch Africans most deeply?[26]

The Post-colonial 'Crisis in Mission' – an Alternative View

It is customary to refer to the early post-colonial period of the present century as an 'era of crisis' for the Christian world mission, at least for Protestant missions. It would seem as if the catastrophic effects of two wars which had opposed the Christian nations of Europe, the Chinese Communist revolution and the rise of nationalist movements of liberation in Asia and Africa, had produced a crisis not only for missionary activity, but also in the theology that undergirded it. In the oft-quoted words of the leading Protestant missionary statesman of the period, Walter Freytag, 'mission itself has become a problem'.[7]

Attempts at a theological analysis of the crisis have tended to focus on a progressive 'diluting' and 'weakening' of the international missionary zeal and motivation through the impact of forces and trends which eventually led to the merger of the World Council of Churches (WCC) (formed in 1948), with the International Missionary Council at the third General Assembly of the WCC at New Delhi in 1961. By this process, it is argued, the truly missionary and evangelistic motivation inherited from the missionary movement of the nineteenth century was displaced by other concerns, namely the demands for political freedom and socio-economic justice which began to be raised, in Africa and Asia in particular , in response to Western colonial domination. In theological terms, the 'vertical' dimensions of spiritual salvation and redemption became overshadowed by the 'horizontal' demands for socio-political liberation and the 'humanisation' of social structures. This trend reached its peak at the 4th General Assembly of the WCC in Uppsala in 1968, and continued to influence and shape the missionary theology of the WCC into the 1970s and beyond.

Perhaps the best-known exponent of this view of the 'crisis' is the German Lutheran missiologist, Peter Beyerhaus of the University of Tübingen. In the words of the title of his book, in which he stated and analysed the 'crisis', the subject is reduced to a choice: *Missions: Which Way? Humanisation or Redemption*.[8] The title of the original German version focused on that aspect of the antinomy at which his criticism was particularly directed, 'Humanisation' in the form of a question, which was for him inescapable, *Humanisierung – Einzige Hoffnung der Welt?* 'Humanisation – the World's Only Hope?'

It seems that without minimising the importance of the genuine theological issues that would have been at stake in the 'crisis', it is possible to interpret the 'crisis' in mission from a different perspective. It is possible, that is, to see it also as the process of adjustment whereby the Western church was coming to terms with the emergence of the non-Western church; in other words, the Second church, ill-prepared perhaps, but nonetheless learning to make room for the coming of the Third church. A possible historical analogy from early Christian history would be that there would have been 'crisis in mission' for the early Church after AD 70. Depending on whether one took the point of view of Jerusalem or of Antioch, the 'crisis' would be seen as 'a setback for the Christian mission' or 'a sign of ferment and vitality … an opportunity to free Christian communities to find and experience new life in faithful mission'.[9] From the latter perspective the post-colonial crisis in mission can also be seen as part of the dying stages of Western ethnocentrism, with the Western church still largely unaware of the shift in Christianity's centre of gravity to the non-Western world. Thus it becomes possible to set forth, in an entirely new light, the impact of the southward shift of the Church upon the theology of mission in the twentieth century, and to see that in some significant ways it is the contribution from the Two-Thirds World that has made possible important breakthroughs in mission.

The Two-Thirds World in Twentieth-century Ecumenical Theology – the Symbolic Role of M. M. Thomas

In a recent University of Tübingen doctoral thesis, subsequently published, the crisis in the theology of mission in the WCC was traced through the thought of one man – the Indian lay theologian, Dr M. M. Thomas – whose theology is seen as 'highly representative of the WCC's changed concept of mission', especially since the fourth General Assembly in Uppsala, 1968.[10] On the basis that there is an essential link between one's view of Scripture and one's theology of mission, the author came to the conclusion that M. M. Thomas's theology of mission was incompatible with the Biblical theology of mission. According to Dr Sumithra, by making 'humanisation the goal of mission', Thomas 'has consciously' departed from 'the Church's understanding of her mission' as transmitted through the centuries.

Without making an exhaustive study of his theology, it seems to me that when M. M. Thomas's thought and career are placed in the context of the emergence of the Two-Thirds World church, it becomes possible to arrive at distinctly different conclusions. Rather than a predetermined 'biblical theology of mission', it is M. M. Thomas's responses to the new realities and challenges which have faced mission itself that give us a clue as to whether or not his contribution is continuous with earlier phases of missionary endeavour.

There is little doubt that his stature at the international and ecumenical level notwithstanding, M. M. Thomas cannot properly be understood, as Dr Sumithra shows, apart from his involvement as a Christian in India's political, social and religious struggles to find a path from the colonial and communal shackles of the past into a new integrated modern and more open and just society. In this, M. M. Thomas has also embodied the struggles of all the dominated, oppressed and marginalised peoples of the nations who were just emerging from colonial rule and affirming their human dignity and cultural identities.[11] It was his ability to relate the struggles of his native India, and those of the rest of the Two-Thirds World, with forces and developments in international politics and economics, and to articulate an intellectual and theological vision unifying them all, that explains in part, at least, his leadership role within the ecumenical movement. It is to this dimension of M. M. Thomas that I wish to draw attention, in order to show how, in some very important respects, he exemplifies the holistic vision on Christian mission which the Two-Thirds World church was beginning to contribute at a time when Western Christian thought on mission was labouring under destructive dichotomies and polarisations.

The body of literature to which I relate my discussion is a collection of letters, a record of theological correspondence with some leading Western missionary statesmen and missiologists, and published under the title, *Some Theological Dialogues*.[12] These are more revealing of the man than his formal writings; I have chosen to comment on four of the eight dialogues.

In 1960 the Dutch missionary scholar, Hendrik Kraemer, well known for his *The Christian Message in a Non-Christian World* at the 1938 International Missionary Conference at Tambaram, India, wrote *World Cultures and World Religions: The Coming Dialogue*.[13] In a review of the book in the *International Review of Missions*,[14] M. M. Thomas expressed appreciation for the book, but also expressed some doubts:

> One puts the book down asking several questions. Can one man, even if it is Kraemer, do justice to the 'inwardness' of the renascence of so many of the cultures of the East? Is the same theological tool adequate for understanding and interpreting inner dialogues that are taking place within the soul of diverse cultures and religions? And in any event, has Dr. Kraemer the right theological tool? This reviewer is not competent to answer those questions. But he has serious doubts about them all.[15]

M. M. Thomas was raising a question that would be persistently asked in Africa, Asia and Latin America about the suitability and adequacy of the categories of Christian theology fashioned within Western Christendom to deal with the new realities in the new lands of the Christians. The West, in its immediate past, had not faced such questions; how could it pronounce on them for the rest of the world? For Thomas,

> the inadequacy of the theology from which Dr. Kraemer derives his criterion of cultural discrimination and judgement is precisely its one-sided emphasis on the religious ultimates which leaves what may be called the human ultimates without Christian significance. Dr. Kraemer's theology can discriminate easily between God and idol in the cultural renascence, but it provides no criterion to distinguish between the human and inhuman in it. Of course it is possible to argue that true spiritual worship is ultimately the only basis of true humanism, but that argument does not do justice to the fact that a devotion to the truly human in a real sense implies and expresses a partial but true response to God, and is at least the door at which the knocking of God-in-Christ is heard.[16]

Here, it seems to me, M. M. Thomas was expressing a very important idea and one which has a respectable precedent in early patristic theology in Justin Martyr and Clement of Alexandria, and also an apostolic example in Paul on Mars Hill in Athens; it is the idea that Christian insight itself must discern in every pre-Christian and non-Christian tradition what is continuous with Christian affirmation and what is not. This task of critical discernment is crucial in mission precisely because there is always more than one strand within every non-Christian tradition. Dr Thomas considered Dr Kraemer's theology weak in this region and he expressed himself in words which indicate the importance he attached to the idea: 'It is my faith that there can be no renewal of the theology of mission in the mid-twentieth century without a proper theology of values'.[17] Rather curiously, when Dr Kraemer replied to the review, he did not answer Dr Thomas's critique. However, he wrote later:

> Your real viewpoint is that the theological framework I adopt does not provide a principle of discrimination at the cultural and human levels ... For you in your situation, my framework is not usable, were it alone for the reason that I am too exclusively concentrated on the matter of truth and criterion. The fact that, to my own feeling, I have always combined and feel able to combine my framework with your (and my) concern, does not prove that it is the best possible framework for *you* in *your* situation.[18]

It would seem that Kraemer really missed the point of Thomas's critique and, despite his claim in the letter following the review that he understands Thomas, he did not. If Kraemer did understand, it does not appear in his responses.

M. M. Thomas also entered into theological dialogue with Canon Max Warren, the General Secretary of the Anglican Church Missionary Society. In 1955 Canon Warren's book, *Caesar – the Beloved Enemy*,[19] was published. In it Canon Warren had attempted to develop a Christian interpretation of British imperialism in Asia and Africa in the modern period in terms of Divine Providence, and he sent a copy of the book to M. M. Thomas.

Dr Thomas's reply to Canon Warren shows how Thomas's experience of imperialism 'from the underside' enabled him to perceive more clearly and more holistically the issues involved in a theology of mission that takes imperialism seriously. His major criticism of Canon Warren's book was the latter's distinction between theology and demonology, whereby the theology of imperialism was equated with the acts of God, whilst the demonic aspects of imperialism were consigned to a 'demonology of imperialism'. For Thomas this approach revealed a misconception of the subject and conferred a false 'messianism' upon imperialism: 'What you have called Demonology of Imperialism is integral to its theology and cannot be separated'. Thomas explained why:

> It seems to me that the result of this narrow definition of Theology leads you to build your Theology of Imperialism, not from the redeeming forgiving act of God in Christ, but from a theologically questionable doctrine of Providence based almost entirely on the reading of history and the 'works' of Imperialism. This, I feel, has led you to emphasise the mission and vocation of Imperialism as the foundation for your Theology; so much so that I have the general feeling that you have not taken serious account of the demonic perversion that has occurred in Imperialism when the very sense of mission and vocation has been exaggerated. It is not the lack of a sense of mission and vocation, but its elevation as the basis of a Messianism that has made Imperialism so demonic. Any Theology of Imperialism should, to my way of thinking be an attempt not to justify Imperialism by its sense of vocation or mission, but to show how God in Christ has mercifully judged and redeemed Imperialism from the demons that afflicted it.[20]

Thomas found equally unacceptable Warren's Western bias that took no serious account of the victims of imperialism, and of the response to imperialism in nationalism.

As Thomas pointed out, nationalism itself did not constitute 'the divine act of judgement and redemption upon Imperialism', for that would amount to making 'the same mistake, and of forgetting the demonic character of Nationalism'. Rather, an adequate theology of imperialism should relate the divine act of judgement and redemption to both imperialism and nationalism. Lacking in this total view and holistic focus, Warren's treatment, for Thomas, was seriously flawed: 'This mistake has resulted from your defining the word Theology as separate from Demonology. Theology proper should be the story of God's acts of overcoming the Demons.'[21] When Warren replied to Thomas, he accepted the latter's criticisms and also acknowledged that Thomas's thinking was in advance of his own:

> You are so right in saying that my [treatment] was one-sided. You have made me see very clearly that in following up the subject I must now work on (a) Demonology of Imperialism and (b) the theology of Nationalism and then (c) to see how in a real measure Nationalism 'redeems' Imperialism in the sense of transforming it (not overlooking your point about the demonic in nationalism). I am ever so excited by this and grateful to you for being so faithful in writing at such length to me about it.[22]

It becomes quite obvious from this dialogue that as the post-missionary and post-colonial era gathered momentum, it was M. M. Thomas's thinking on the 'theology of imperialism', and not Max Warren's, as previously formulated, that held the promise of a balanced and positive sense of identity for the missionary movement as a Christian enterprise from the West. For, in Thomas's theology of imperialism, Western missions, insofar as they were Christian, were redeemed from the false and self-justifying messianic complex of imperialism and so rescued from going down with the collapse of the empires. Clearly the sharper vision was the one from 'the underside', from the periphery, not from the centre of empire.

M. M. Thomas's theological dialogue with the author of the important book, *Christianity in World History*,[23] the Dutchman, Arend van Leeuwen, reveals an aspect of Thomas's thought which is misunderstood and obscured by the kind of criticism of his theology made by Beyerhaus and Sumithra. Thomas wrote a review of van Leeuwen's book in the *Ecumenical Review* of October 1964. The dialogue that ensued included an actual meeting at Union Theological Seminary, New York in 1966.

In his review, Thomas made essentially the same criticism he had made of Kraemer's *World Cultures and World Religions: The Coming Dialogue*, namely, the inability of Western theological scholarship to do full justice 'to the struggles within the traditional religions and cultures of the East to break the cosmic monism' of their past. Perhaps this was not surprising since van Leeuwen's approach owed a great deal to Kraemer, who wrote the foreword to the book. To describe this 'cosmic monism', van Leeuwen had invented the term 'ontocracy' to denote an overall religious pattern which he applied not only to the ancient religions of India, but also to those of the ancient Near East, with the exception of the 'theocratic' and prophetic religion of ancient Israel. For van Leeuwen, there was a direct line of development which linked the Israelite tradition through Western Christianity to modern technology and modern Western secular culture as the fruits of Christianity. Accordingly, the secularisation process ought to be welcomed as part of the mission of Western Christianity to liberate the ontocratic East from its cosmic monism. But for Thomas, it was this absolutisation of the civilisations of East and West, as 'ontocratic' and 'theocratic' respectively, which caused Western scholarship to misread the inward struggles of the cultures of the East:

> I am not saying that any radical break with the ontocratic pattern has taken place in traditional Indian culture nor that the Christian doctrines of Creation and Incarnation can easily be understood in or adapted by it. But I am convinced that if the break with ontocracy is taking place in Indian culture through the impact of the West, it is not altogether discontinuous with the genuine struggles within the traditional Hindu religion and culture itself in that direction. At least, there are points in Hindu culture which are more or less ontocratic. I think the encounter of Christian mission with Eastern life and thought will be more fruitful if there is a good deal more discrimination and sensitiveness to the 'more or less' on the part of the theologians of Western culture and mission.[24]

But Thomas's even more incisive comment was on van Leeuwen's inability, precisely because of the 'same absolutisation of a general picture', adequately to recognise that there was 'the persistence of the presence of old ontocratic paganism in the collective unconsciousness of the West' with a 'capacity to take new forms and even swallow up the Christian elements of Western cultural dynamics'.

Van Leeuwen had argued that it was 'impossible' for the West to return to the cosmic monism of paganism; Thomas was not so sure:

> Indeed, the ideologies of self-redemption of the world, the movements towards complete subjectivisation of self and history, the tendencies towards a technocracy of impersonal modern mass society, and towards a secularism which is indifferent to the dimension of spirit, either in the height or in the depth, are sufficient warnings that it is not impossible for the West to lose the sense of the transcendent or eschatological dimension of culture and to revert to a new paganism. Here too, instead of a blanket description of the West, more discrimination is needed in evaluating the more and the less in the Western culture also.[25]

In his reply, van Leeuwen conceded Thomas's first point, allowing that it was 'a question of the way Indians will reinterpret the past' though he himself had 'serious doubts concerning the adequacy of this interpretation'.[26] However, on the major thesis of his book, namely that the secularisation process itself was the working out of the theocratic and prophetic principle inherent in the Biblical view of reality in its continuing impact upon the world through Western culture, van Leeuwen was adamant that

> religion and religions are not absolute entities, but ... are involved in mankind's history on its way between creation and recreation, and it is the very historicity of religions which is being revealed in the secularisation processes of our century. Since man in Biblical view is a creature and a historical being, I do not see any essential reason for belief that any religion might dispose of eternal truth unaffected by historical change.[27]

On this thesis of a full-blown secularisation, Thomas differed quite firmly from van Leeuwen, as he was to write later:

> I endorse van Leeuwen's statement that agreement between us is much larger than disagreement, especially on the priority of the prophetic tradition and spirituality [i.e. the biblical] over the mystic [i.e. the ancient Indian tradition] in the Christian witness in the modern world. But I do differ from him on the question how far we should work for secularisation versus the

renewal of traditional religion, and what value mystic religion has within the prophetic framework ... I believe the Church should be deeply concerned with the renascence of traditional religions as they move into the theological circle of Messianism, and that the mystic tradition has a continuing role of humanising Messianism where it goes astray from the Messianism of the Suffering Servant to that of the conquering King.[28]

And yet, in Beyerhaus's book mentioned above, he connected in a blanket statement 'Arend van Leeuwen, Harvey Cox and M. M. Thomas ... with an influential theological trend which interprets and justifies the secularisation process as being a legitimate fruit of the Gospel'.[29]

It is true that M. M. Thomas seems to be continually seeking an open and 'secular' framework for his theology of mission. But to understand this, one must look to his Indian context. Obviously Thomas agreed with the Indian social reformer, Ambedkar, on what constituted the three sources of power in Indian society, namely: property, social status and religion. For Ambedkar, this meant that social transformation required a simultaneous struggle against the propertied class, the upper caste and Brahminic Hinduism, or, put differently, against economic exploitation, social oppression and religious fatalism. Since Thomas's own commitment is towards 'a transformation of modernity in Jesus Christ',[30] he considered it crucial that Christian thinking should come to grips with 'spiritual penetration' as he called it – with the world of scientific technology, the revolts of the poor and oppressed peoples and secular ideologies as well as other religious faiths. But this was because he believed that 'compulsions of spiritual vision are behind the momentum of these worlds of science, technology and revolts, and men and women pursue them in the name of their moral and spiritual integrity'.[31] However, because 'these spiritual visions are partial and not holistic, and when affirmed as absolute, they tend to misdirect people', Christian mission to the modern world has to help to integrate them into the wholeness of the Christian vision – the wholeness that is in Jesus Christ. It is this vision which Thomas called humanisation, a vision in which proclamation and confession of Jesus Christ as ultimate reality is implicit.

The truth of this evaluation of Thomas's thought is conveyed by Lesslie Newbigin's concluding and illuminating comment in his dialogue with M. M. Thomas on the latter's book, *Salvation and Humanisation*:

> Perhaps our differences arise because we are stressing the opposite sides of ... mutually necessary propositions. You are stressing the necessity for the Church to be fully opened up to these secular movements. I am stressing the fact that if there is to be a Church at all, there must be an active effort to bring people into full commitment to Jesus through baptism and incorporation into the sacramental congregation-liturgical life of the Church. I feel the force of your contention and I hope I am as open to it as an ageing ecclesiastic can be. I hope and believe that you share my concern that evangelism – in the sense of the open and explicit proclamation of Jesus as Saviour and the invitation to men to be committed to him in the fellowship of the Church – is in danger of being left to people who do not at all understand your concern for openness. This seems to me to be one of the really dangerous things in our situation.[32]

It is something of this same understanding of M. M. Thomas that caused Donald McGavran too, in his dialogue with M. M. Thomas, to wonder 'just how wide the gulf is', theologically, between Thomas and himself.[33]

If we are to follow Newbigin and McGavran in their appreciation of Thomas, we may ask the question whether the so-called 'betrayal' of the evangelistic motivation in mission, which is often traced to Uppsala in 1968, might not be yet another aspect of the Western crisis in mission arising more out of the secularisation of theology within Western culture itself (as we have seen in van Leeuwen), rather than related in any significant measure to M. M. Thomas's vision of Christian mission as humanisation.

M. M. Thomas thus emerges as a major figure in the ecumenical missionary theology of the twentieth century, and one who may have helped to move Christian thinking in a holistic direction more than his critics allow. Therefore, Thomas's long and distinguished career within the ecumenical movement and the wcc, including his Moderatorship of the Central Committee between the Fourth and Fifth General Assemblies (1968–75), may even be symbolic. His role as well as his missionary vision may come to symbolise the theological leadership which Christians from the Two-Thirds World were beginning to give in vast areas of Christianity in the world, a 'theological leadership' which Lesslie Newbigin actually acknowledged in a letter to him in November 1971.[34]

The Two-Thirds World in Twentieth-century Missionary Theology – the Evangelicals

Perhaps in no area has the theological initiative of the Two-Thirds World been more marked than in the development in the last twenty to thirty years of the missionary theology of institutional evangelicalism. An outline history of this development traced through agreed evangelical statements on evangelism and social responsibility is given by René Padilla, in his article, 'Evangelism and Social responsibility from Wheaton '66 to Wheaton '83'.[35] If it is true that, as Padilla notes in his article, 'today, most evangelicals would hardly fit the stereotype of a person who is solely committed to "saving souls" and who closes his or her eyes to bodily needs', this has come about largely because of the role that Two-Thirds World theologians have played in moving evangelical theology of mission from a polarisation of evangelism and socio-political involvement to a recognition that 'both are parts of our Christian duty'. This recognition came at the International Congress on World Evangelisation held in July 1974 at Lausanne, Switzerland. More tentative steps had been taken earlier, as at the Wheaton (April 1966) Congress on the church's world-wide mission, the Berlin World Congress on Evangelism (October 1966), and various regional congresses on evangelism, sponsored by the Billy Graham Evangelistic Association: South-East Asia (Singapore, November 1968), United States (Minneapolis, September 1969), Latin America (Bogota, November 1969) and Europe (Amsterdam, August 1971). At each of these meetings it was increasingly evident that it was through Christians from the Two-Thirds World that the social implications of the Gospel were being brought to prominence. René Padilla, commenting on these regional congresses, wrote: 'At all of them, with surprising regularity, there were speakers who brought up the question of Christian social involvement as an issue intimately related to evangelism'.[36] Meanwhile, in the United States, which had become the single most important source of missionary personnel and funding, a major event marking an awakening of social conscience among evangelicals came with the *Chicago Declaration of Evangelical Social Concern*, in November 1973. This Declaration was 'essentially an affirmation of God's total claim on the lives of his people, a confession of failure in demonstrating God's justice in society, and a call for evangelicals to demonstrate repentance in a Christian discipleship that confronts the social and political injustice of our nation'.[37] Clearly evangelical missionary theology was transcending its traditional dichotomy between evangelism and social respons-ibility.

What happened at Lausanne in 1974, therefore, was the breaking, upon the international stage, of this gathering storm. Though the Congress had been 'expected to concentrate on the *how* of world evangelisation', the impact of the Two-Thirds World overturned that. The decisive contribution came from Latin America in two major papers. René Padilla's paper on 'Evangelism and the World' exposed the 'worldliness' of an evangelism that exported 'the American way of life' to the rest of the world as equivalent to the Gospel, and which, by failing to address the fundamental issues of repentance and discipleship in relation to social justice, poverty and oppression, reduced the Gospel to 'cheap grace'.[38] Samuel Escobar (of Peru), in a paper on 'Evangelism and man's search for freedom, justice and fulfillment', drew attention not only to the evangelical heritage of social involvement as a necessary accompaniment of verbal pro-clamation, but warned of the danger of an evangelical betrayal of the Gospel, if the Gospel was perceived as irrelevant to the social struggles and the condition of oppressed peoples.[39] *The Lausanne Covenant*, in affirming that 'the message of salvation implies also a message of judgement upon every form of alienation, oppression and discrimi-nation ...'.[40] ensured that future developments would be in the direction of the agenda of the Two-Thirds World.

In stating that evangelism and socio-political involvement are both 'part of our Christian duty',[41] *The Lausanne Covenant* itself also made evangelism 'primary ... in the church's mission'[42] without clarifying the nature of the primacy of evangelism. Two important specialist meetings, the Consultation on the Relationship between Evangelism and Social Responsibility (Grand Rapids, June 1982) and more significantly, on the Church in Response to Human Need

(Wheaton, June 1983), were to take the affirmations of Lausanne 1974 further yet. Not only did evangelism and social responsibility now become 'integrally related in our proclamation of and obedience to the Gospel' and therefore 'in reality a marriage',[43] but it was 'the whole of human life – individual as well as societal, physical as well as spiritual' – which came to be viewed as subject to the transforming power of God through the Gospel.[44] In the most far-reaching statement on the Church's mission issued by Evangelicals, the consultation document, 'Transformation – the Church in Response to Human Need', declared:

> We ... joyfully proclaim that the Kingdom [of God] has broken into human history in the resurrection of Christ. It grows like a mustard seed, both judging and transforming the present age.
>
> Even if God's activity is focused on the church, it is not confined to the church. God's particular focus on the church – as on Israel in the Old Testament – has as its purpose the blessing of the nations (Gen. 12:1–3; 15:17; Is. 42:6). Thus the church is called to exist for the sake of its Lord and for the sake of humankind (Matt. 22:32–40) ... the church is called to infuse the world with hope, for both this age and the next.[45]

The Two-Thirds World and the Emergence of a New Consensus in Missionary Theology

The Lausanne Covenant has, however, also stated that 'the Gospel does not presuppose the superiority of any culture to another ...' and that 'missions have all too frequently exported with the Gospel an alien culture ...'.[46] Thus in the evangelical theology of mission too, a Western value-setting for the apprehension as well as the expression of the Christian faith has now effectively ended. As a result of the historical development of the evangelical missionary theology after Lausanne, not only has the significance of the Two-Thirds World contribution been confirmed but also a situation has now arisen in which the polarised categories, 'ecumenical' and 'evangelical', have become increasingly perceived as misleading precisely because of the Two-Thirds World impact. The emergence of Evangelical mission theologians from the Two-Thirds World with clearly ecumenical sympathies has ensured that there is now an 'overlap' of traditions'.[47] This is 'an overlap between the evangelical and ecumenical traditions, in which 'many in the ecumenical tradition have been struggling to recapture proclamation, invitation evangelism and the call to conversion and many in the evangelical tradition have also been struggling to recapture biblical and prophetic mandate for justice … a movement for integral evangelism'.[48] What is significant is that this 'movement' emerged at the Stuttgart Consultation on Evangelism in March 1987, organised by the WCC Commission for World Mission and Evangelism. Evangelicals played a dominant role at Stuttgart which was one of the influential preparatory meetings for the San Antonio Missionary Conference.

It is equally important to realise that this 'movement' 'has not been a convergence of these two traditions'. Rather, it has occurred as Christians in the Two-Thirds World, freed from the polarisations between evangelical and ecumenical in the West, as well as the uneasy Western conscience about the 'spiritualisation' or 'secularisation' of the Gospel, have read the Bible and sought to communicate the Gospel from perspectives that take their cultural and social contexts seriously.

The Two-Thirds World and the Gospel as Good News to the Poor

Reading the Bible in the Two-Thirds World context of poverty, powerlessness and religious pluralism is probably the single most important characteristic of this new theology of mission. It is by thus appropriating the Scriptures and the Gospel in context, that this new theology of mission has been able to acquire fresh insights into the Gospel and into the nature of the Christian mission itself, such as the discovery that the Gospel is good news to the poor.

It is important to understand how the discovery of the Gospel as good news to the poor – by which is meant the materially poor, socially oppressed and underprivileged – has become a fundamental challenge for mission and theology from the Two-Thirds World. In the case of Africa, the Cameroonian theologian, Engelbert Mveng, has even spoken of 'anthropological poverty', a category which, for him, denotes more than poverty on the material level, and takes account of the exploitation and sufferings which African people have experienced and which make them the most humiliated people in history, in their social and cultural identity as well as in their humanity.[49]

That the Gospel is good news to the poor is not arrived at solely by an academic study of the Scriptures. On its own, that could lead into an intellectualist abstraction that misses the point. As Vinay Samuel and Chris Sugden show in *Evangelism and the Poor – A Third World Guide*:[50] 'We have not interpreted the biblical view of the poor until we interpret its meaning in our own context. To find the meaning in biblical context alone does not answer the question of the meaning of the Bible for us.'[51] In other words, the fact that the question of the poor in relation to mission and theology is being raised by churches of the poor in the Two-Thirds World, rather than from the affluent churches of the West, is part of the meaning of the Gospel as good news to the poor. Thus, to cite an instance from North America, where the Two-Thirds World reality can also be identified, Black Americans also survived the experience of slavery by hanging on to the Jesus whom they found in the Bible and in worship. As James Cone notes, in his *God of the Oppressed*:

> After being told six days of the week that they were nothings by the rulers of white society, on the Sabbath, the first day of the week, black people went to church in order to experience another definition of their humanity. These six days of wheeling and dealing with white people always raised anxious questions of whether life was worth living. But when blacks went to church, and experienced the presence of Jesus' spirit among them, they realised that he bestowed a meaning upon their lives that could not be taken away by white folks.[52]

Another Black American theologian has written:

> In their independent church traditions, the slaves reinterpreted the meaning of the Gospel, knowing in their hearts that obedience to God does not imply the denigration of their own self-worth. The encounter with Jesus Christ in the lives of black people who struggle for freedom has been the experience of affirmation. This hope of liberation and this survival experience has been the primary source of black Christology.

Jesus Christ in his explicit identification with the oppressed had identified himself with the black experience in North America.[53]

It is in the context of actual poor churches and communities, as is the case of the well-known 'grassroots ecclesial communities' (Communidades eclesiales de base) in Latin America, and of countless similar groups found all over the Two-Thirds World, that one understands that the Gospel is indeed 'Good news to the poor'.[54] They can read the Bible and experience, in the midst of their poverty and powerlessness, the reality of the power of the Kingdom of God through faith in the Jesus who, in order to save the world, became poor.[55]

'Blessed' then 'are the poor'[56] and 'those who know they are spiritually poor',[57] that is, who share the outlook of the poor, not because they are poor, but because 'the Kingdom of God is theirs'; theirs is the divine preferential option for the poor, because the Gospel as 'good news to the poor' is the good news of God's kingdom and God's justice.[58]

It follows therefore that the Gospel's content is defined by what it means to the poor, namely, justice, just relationships, with God, among humans and with the environment; the fact that the rich too can be saved denotes the power of God to do what is impossible to humans.[59] However, 'the road to the Kingdom, at least for the rich, is signposted by the search for justice in whose service the rich must offer their possessions as a sign of … solidarity with the less privileged'.[60]

If Christianity, then, is the 'religion of the poor of the earth', who are at the centre of God's concern, among whom the saviour came as a poor man among the poor, then, as Canadian scholar Jon Bonk has shown, 'the affluence-based mission of the Western church' may prove to be a much less 'vitally Christian spiritual force' in the future.[61] One must hope that the Western church, with large sections of it in moral and spiritual decline, will experience a profound conversion to the essential wholeness of the Gospel and to the wholeness of mission which goes beyond evangelism and becomes involved in the struggle for justice to the poor both locally and around the world. As René Padilla has pointed out, 'when Jesus told the rich young man to sell everything and give to the poor, he was thinking more about the spiritual need of the young man than the material need of the poor'.[62] This is another way of saying that the 'evangelisation [or re-evangelisation] of the West is inseparable from the rediscovery of the Gospel as "good news to the poor"'.[63]

In conclusion, I should like to recall an event in recent ecumenical history which may well indicate that if Friar Tuck is removed from the 'outlaw' gang in Sherwood Forest, the Robin Hood story inevitably collapses. When, in 1970, the Central Committee of the WCC (during the Moderatorship of M. M. Thomas) decided to make financial grants to African liberation movements for non-violent purposes, the critics of the decision saw it as evidence that the WCC was abandoning 'spiritual' matters in favour of 'an over-concern with the secular'. Consequently, with the approach of the Fifth General Assembly in Nairobi, Kenya (December 1975), delegates from some Western churches, in the words of Adrian Hastings, 'churches without any past commitment to pacifism ... went, some of them, with teeth clenched to challenge some supposed third world take-over of the World Council and in particular, to fight the leadership on the grants issue'.[64] It is hard to disagree with Hastings's view that

> The Nairobi assembly was not prepared in any way to go back on the 'Programme to combat Racism'. The grants had, indeed, become more of a symbol than anything else: a symbol that Christianity was not what Malan and Verwoerd and Vorster and Smith had claimed it to be – a bastion in the fortress of white supremacy. And yet, in a remarkable way, this whole issue was all the same reduced in import and subsumed in a deeper vision in which the artificial contrasts ... between 'horizontal' and 'vertical' approaches ... between 'liberal' and 'evangelical' almost faded away. Here the African contribution was not insignificant, and just because African Protestantism of almost any denominational brand is so devoutly 'evangelical' and yet so emphatically committed to the righting of racial injustice.

It is entirely fitting then that the issue should have been resolved 'in a context of prayer'. And Adrian Hastings continues:

> Here too the deciding contribution may well have been the African rather than the more self-conscious 'spirituality first' message of some Western delegates. The African churches, in

their immense material poverty, are so manifestly prayerful – their services so long, so well attended, so absorbing.[65]

In 1990, when momentous changes began in South Africa, for so long the land with an ideological Christianity harnessed in the service of injustice and oppression, it was possible to forget that on 16 June 1985, on the ninth anniversary of the shootings in Soweto in 1976, the South African Council of Churches issued a 'call to prayer for an end to unjust rule'. In the theological rationale they set out for this extraordinary call to prayer, the Council of Churches wrote:

> We have continually prayed for the authorities, that they may govern wisely and justly. Now in solidarity with those who suffer most, in this hour of crisis we pray that God in His grace may remove from His people the tyrannical structures of oppression and the present rulers in our country who persistently refuse to heed our cry for justice as reflected in the Word of God as proclaimed through His Church both within this land and beyond. In constant and solemn awareness of the responsibility we take upon ourselves in this regard, we pray that God's rule may be established in this land. We pledge ourselves to work for that day, knowing that this rule is good news to the poor, because the captives will be released, the blind healed, the oppressed set at liberty and the acceptable year of the Lord proclaimed. (*Luke* 4:18–19)[66]

And so they prayed. In his sermon on the occasion, Allan Boesak, then President of the World Alliance of Reformed Churches (WARC) and Vice-President of the South African Council of Churches, said: 'I believe that God will hear us as we pray for the removal of those who persist in disobeying God's will, I believe that God *has* seen us, I believe that God *will* hear us, I believe that God *will* use us'.[67] Politicians who presume to hold power in the world may claim events as vindicating their policies. And yet, from the standpoint of the Gospel, there is no doubt where the deeper insight lies. There is probably no more palpable demonstration that the Christianity of Jesus is indeed the religion of the poor of the earth.

Notes and References

1. Andrew F. Walls, 'Towards understanding Africa's place in Christian history', in J. S. Pobee (ed.), *Religion in a Pluralistic Society*, Leiden: E. J. Brill, 1976, pp. 180–9, and I happen to know that he made the observation several years before the publication!
2. Walbert Buhlmann, *The Coming of the Third Church – An Analysis of the Present and Future of the Church*, Slough: St. Paul Publication, 1976; first published in German as *Es kommt die dritte Kirche – Eine Analyse der kirchlichen Gegenwart und Zukunft*, 1974.
3. Ibid., pp. 6f.
4. David B. Barrett (ed.), *World Christian Encyclopaedia – A Comparative Study of Churches and Religions in the Modern World AD 1900–2000*, Nairobi: Oxford University Press, 1982.
5. Walbert Buhlmann, *The Coming of the Third Church*, p. 23.
6. Johannes Verkuyl, *Contemporary Missiology* (English translation by Dale Cooper), Grand Rapids: Eerdmans, 1978, p. 277.
7. Walter Freytag, *Reden und Aufsätze*, Bd I, p. 111, quoted in Sunand Sumithra, *Revolution as Revelation – A Study of M. M. Thomas' Theology*, Tübingen: International Christian Network, and New Delhi: Theological Research and Communications Institute, 1984, p. 5.
8. Peter Beyerhaus, *Missions: Which Way? Humanisation or Redemption*, Grand Rapids: Zondervan, 1971.
9. G. H. Anderson and Thomas Stransky (eds), *Mission Trends I – Crucial Issues in Mission Today*, New York: Paulist Press and Grand Rapids: Eerdmans, 1974, p. 1.
10. See Sunand Sumithra, *Revolution as Revelation – A Study of M. M. Thomas' Theology*, Tübingen: International Christian Network and New Delhi: Theological Research and Communications Institute, 1984.
11. See M. M. Thomas, *Religion and the Revolt of the Oppressed*, Delhi: SPCK, 1981.
12. M. M. Thomas, *Some Theological Dialogues*, Madras: Christian Literature Society, 1977.
13. Hendrik Kraemer, *World Cultures and World Religions: The Coming Dialogue*, London: Lutterworth Press, 1960.
14. See *International Review of Missions*, April 1961.
15. M. M. Thomas, *Some Theological Dialogues*, p. 24.
16. Ibid., pp. 26–7.
17. Ibid., p. 27.
18. Ibid., p. 29.
19. Max Warren, *Caesar – The Beloved Enemy*, London: SCM Press, 1955.
20. M. M. Thomas, *Some Theological Dialogues*, p. 36.
21. Ibid., p. 37.
22. Ibid., p. 38.
23. Arend van Leeuwen, *Christianity in World History*, London: Edinburgh House Press, 1964.
24. M. M. Thomas, *Some Theological Dialogues*, pp. 78–9.
25. Ibid., p. 80.
26. Ibid., p. 88.
27. Ibid., p. 91.
28. Ibid., p. 93.
29. Beyerhaus, *Missions: Which Way?*, p. 21.
30. M. M. Thomas, *Religion and the Revolt of the Oppressed*, p. 2.
31. Ibid., p. 56.
32. M. M. Thomas, *Some Theological Dialogues*, p. 128.

33. Ibid., p. 148.
34. Ibid., p. 128.
35. René Padilla, 'Evangelism and social responsibility from Wheaton '66 to Wheaton '83', in Padilla and Sugden (eds), *How Evangelicals Endorsed Social Responsibility (Texts on Evangelical Social Ethics 1974–1983 (ii) A Commentary)*, Nottingham: Grove Books Ltd, 1985.
36. Ibid., p. 7.
37. Ibid., p. 9.
38. René Padilla, 'Evangelism and the world', in J. D. Douglas (ed.), *Let the Earth Hear His Voice – International Congress on World Evangelisation, Lausanne, Switzerland* (Official reference volume: Papers and Responses), Minneapolis: World Wide Publications, 1975, pp. 116–46.
39. Samuel Escobar, 'Evangelism and man's search for freedom, justice and fulfillment', in Douglas, *Let the Earth Hear His Voice*, pp. 303–26.
40. *The Lausanne Covenant – An Exposition and Commentary by John Stott* (Lausanne Occasional Papers no. 3), Wheaton: Lausanne Committee for World Evangelization, 1975, para. 5.
41. Loc. cit.
42. Ibid., para. 6.
43. See René Padilla, 'Evangelism and Social Responsibility', p. 16.
44. Loc. cit.
45. Paras. 49, 50 and 51. Text in Vinay Samuel and Chris Sugden (eds), *The Church in Response to Human Need*, Grand Rapids: Eerdmans and Oxford: Regnum Books, 1987, pp. 254–65.
46. *The Lausanne Covenant*, para. 10.
47. Like the Latin American Theological Fraternity, Partnership in Mission-Asia and the African Theological Fraternity, and the networks that link them with kindred spirits in the 'One-Third Word' (i.e. the West).
48. Vinay Samuel and Albrecht Hauser (eds), *Proclaiming Christ in Christ's Way – Studies in Integral Evangelism* (Essays presented to Walter Arnold on the occasion of his 60th birthday), Oxford: Regnum Books, 1989, pp. 13–14.
49. See Engelbert Mveng, 'African Liberation Theology', in Leonardo Boff and Virgilio Elizondo (eds), *Third World Theologies – Convergences and Differences*, Edinburgh: T. and T. Clark, 1988, pp. 15–27.
50. Vinay Samuel and Chris Sugden, *Evangelism and the Poor – A Third World Guide*, Oxford: Regnum Books, 1982.
51. Ibid., p. 22.
52. James Cone, *God of the Oppressed*, New York: Orbis Books, 1975, pp. 12–13.
53. George Cummings, 'Who do you say that I am? A North American minority answer to the Christological question', in Vinay Samuel and Chris Sugden (eds), *Sharing Jesus in the Two-Thirds World*, Grand Rapids: Eerdmans, 1984, pp. 220–1.
54. *Luke* 4:18.
55. *2 Corinthians* 8:9.
56. *Luke* 6:20.
57. *Matthew* 5:3.
58. *Matthew* 6:33.
59. *Matthew* 19:26 and parallels.
60. Julio de Santa Ana, *Good News to the Poor – the Challenge of the Poor in the History of the Church*, Geneva: World Council of Churches, 1977, p. 96.
61. Jonathan Bonk, 'Mission and Mammon. Six theses', *International Bulletin of Missionary Research*, vol. 13, no. 4, October 1989, pp. 174–81.

62. René Padilla, 'Mission in the 1990's', *International Bulletin of Missionary Research*, vol. 13, no. 4, October 1989, pp. 149–52.
63. Ibid., p. 150.
64. Adrian Hastings, *A History of African Christianity 1950–1975*, Cambridge: Cambridge University Press, 1979, p. 233.
65. Ibid., p. 234.
66. Text in *Journal of Theology for Southern Africa*, vol. 52, September 1985, pp. 56–61.
67. Ibid., p. 55.

9

Towards a New Understanding of
Christian History in the Post-missionary Era

As in previous chapters, I shall begin by recalling what I consider are earlier pointers to the theme which I should like to discuss. In 1971, an American Jesuit scholar, John Schumacher, who was working in theological education teaching history in the Philippines, published an article under the title: 'The Third World and the Twentieth Century Church' in the international journal *Concilium*.[1] The editors of the well-known series, *Mission Trends*, found the article significant enough to include it in their first volume.[2] What makes Father Schumacher's article important is how he relates the emergent Third World Church to the study of Christian history in view of the changed situation of world Christianity. Written against the background of events within the Roman Catholic Church following the Second Vatican Council, Father Schumacher's article sought to establish fundamentally one point: 'The entrance into the full life of the Church of the peoples of the Third World, acutely conscious of their aspirations to national development and self-realisation, has had a manifold effect on the whole Church's self-understanding.'[3] Father Schumacher identified four areas in particular in which the principal elements in the new self-understanding are due primarily to the Third World or Two-Thirds World, as we would say. The *first* was the realisation that there was an essential cultural plurality in unity which belongs within the universal church; no longer would it be taken for granted that the manifestations of the Christian presence would merely replicate patterns and forms in the West. *Secondly*, there was a new attitude to the values of non-Christian religions, and consequently a new perception of the church's relation to them. In

Father Schumacher's view, it is the impact of the Third World which has compelled the twentieth-century church to look at non-Christian religions, not merely to understand them, but also to 'find in them true religious values which perhaps have been obscured in the Western Christian presentation or formulation of God's Word to man'. The *third* area of influence from the Third World upon the universal church has been to bring about a broader understanding of the role of the church as witness to the Word of God among men, the effect of this being to cause the church to adopt a humbler, servant posture among the peoples it encounters, rather than the stance of crusader or inquisitor. The *fourth* area of the Third World's impact upon the church's self-understanding was 'a fuller concept of the mission of the Church as embracing not only the ministry of the Word and sacraments but active involvement in economic and all human development' and the struggle for justice in the world.[4]

Apart from these four elements which he considered 'specific contributions of the Third World', other elements too in contemporary church's self-understanding, such as 'the new understanding of religious freedom and the altered concept of ecumenical relations among the Christian churches', though they had their 'principal origin in a European or North American milieu', were 'the fruit of Third World experience'. As Father Schumacher put it: 'The lived experience of Protestants and Catholics working in the Third World has made its own contribution here too'.[5] Consequently, for Father Schumacher, the Christian life of the churches of the Third World constituted an important theological factor, a *locus theologicus* for Christian scholarship and so belonged not on the margin but in the mainstream of Christian history.

Yet, according to Father Schumacher, Christian scholarship, and ecclesiastical historiography in particular, was continuing to ignore the weight and significance of the Third World churches, treating them 'more as manifestations of the Christian life of the church which evangelised them than as new incarnations of the church in cultures having their own contribution to make to the fullness of the people of God'.[6] What was required to correct this imbalance was for ecclesiastical historiography not only to become 'conscious of the new centre of gravity of the people of God' but also to show how the history of the people of God in the nations of the Third World forms 'an integral part of the continuation of the history of salvation into which the younger churches have been inserted in God's due time, as the Gospel came from Jerusalem through Greece and Rome to Europe, and to the Third World through Europe'. Within this understanding of ecclesiastical historiography, for Father Schumacher, 'it is surely far more important to know the progress of Christian life during a single century among one entire people of the Third World than to investigate the *minutiae* of the history of any number of medieval European monasteries, long since extinct', unless the Church historian is to be 'merely an ecclesiastical antiquarian'.[7]

In the same period, a similar questioning of the trend of Christian scholarship was expressed in an article by the Kenyan Anglican theologian, John Mbiti, at the time the Director of the World Council of Churches Ecumenical Institute, Bossey, in Switzerland. The article 'Theological impotence and the universality of the Church' was published in *Lutheran World* and subsequently reissued in the *Mission Trends* series.[8] John Mbiti is seldom found making critical remarks about the Western church and Western theology but the following is a rare instance:

> It is utterly scandalous for so many Christian scholars in [the] old Christendom to know so much about heretical movements in the second and third centuries, when so few of them know anything about Christian movements in areas of the younger churches. We feel affronted and wonder whether it is more meaningful theologically to have academic fellowship with heretics long dead than with the living brethren of the Church today in the so-called Third World.[9]

What Mbiti was calling attention to was the danger, as he perceived it, of the church becoming 'kerygmatically universal', while it remained 'theologically provincial'. In other words, for Mbiti, as 'the axis of Christendom appeared to shift from the Northern to the Southern regions of the world' so that 'the centres of the Church's universality were no longer in Geneva, Rome, Athens, Paris, London, New York, but Kinshasa, Buenos Aires, Addis Ababa and Manila', there did not seem to be a corresponding shift towards 'mutuality and reciprocity in the theological task facing the universal church'. The problem was in a one-sidedness in theological learning in the church:

Theologians from the new (or younger) churches have made their pilgrimages to the theological learning of the older churches. We had no alternative. We have eaten theology with you; we have drunk theology with you; we have dreamed theology with you. But it has all been one-sided; it has all been, in a sense, your theology. ... We know you theologically. The question is do you know us theologically? Would you like to know us theologically?[10]

As a result of this absence of mutuality and reciprocity in theological learning in the church, Mbiti saw that there was 'a real and yet a false dichotomy at the heart of the Church's very experience of universality. This dichotomy is real because it is there; it is false because it ought not to be there'. One indicator of the lopsidedness in the church's experience of universality and therefore a false universality, was the fact that the theology that was brought from the pilgrimage to the theological learning in the older churches seemed unable to cope with the new concerns in the new churches. To illustrate his point, Mbiti told a story:

> He learned German, French, Greek, Latin, Hebrew, in addition to English, church history, systematics, homiletics, exegesis and pastoralia, as one part of the requirements for his degree. The other part, the dissertation, he wrote on some obscure theologian of the Middle Ages. Finally he got what he wanted: a Doctorate in Theology. It took him nine and a half years altogether, from the time he left his home until he passed his orals and set off to return. He was anxious to reach home as soon as possible, so he flew, and he was glad to pay for his excess baggage which, after all, consisted only of the Bible in various languages he had learned, plus Bultmann, Barth, Bonhoeffer, Brunner, Buber, Cone, Küng, Moltmann, Niebuhr, Tillich, *Christianity Today, Time Magazine* ...
>
> At home relatives, neighbours, old friends ... all gather to welcome him back ... Dancing, jubilation, eating, feasting – all these go on as if there were nothing else to do, because the man for whom everyone had waited has finally returned.
>
> Suddenly there is a shriek. Someone has fallen to the ground. It is his older sister ... he rushes to her. People make room for

him and watch him. 'Let's take her to the hospital,' he calls urgently. They are stunned. He becomes quiet. They all look at him bending over her. Why doesn't someone respond to his advice? Finally a schoolboy says, 'Sir, the nearest hospital is 50 miles away, and there are few buses that go there.' Someone else says, 'She is possessed. Hospitals will not cure her!' The Chief says to him, 'You have been studying theology overseas for 10 years. Now help your sister. She is troubled by the spirit of her great aunt.' He looks around. Slowly he goes to get Bultmann, looks at the index, finds what he wants, reads again about spirit possession in the New Testament. Of course he gets the answer: Bultmann has demythologised it. He insists that his sister is not possessed. The people shout, 'Help your sister, she is possessed!' He shouts back, 'But Bultmann has demythologised demon possession.' ...

Fantasy? No, for these are the realities of our time.[11]

Mbiti added that the story is entirely fictional and not based on the experience of a real person. In order to overcome the false universality which produced this 'theological impotence' according to Mbiti, the church in the North and the church in the South should 'embrace each other's concerns and stretch to each other's horizons'. This was all the more important as the axis of Christianity tilted southwards 'towards areas, situations, cultures, concerns, traditions, religions and problems which are largely different from those which have precipitated or necessitated the theological output of the Church in the West over the last 500 years at least'.[12]

We shall not follow John Mbiti into the details of his discussion of some of these concerns of the church in the South, which the church in the North may need to 'embrace', such as the theme of survival in all its dimensions – national, communal and personal – which he singled out as a major preoccupation for Christians in Africa. The story he told makes the point adequately. What is important is to understand the grounds upon which Mbiti was making these observations: it was essential to recognise the theological significance of the concerns of the church in the South, not merely for the sake of the South; rather 'only in that way can the universality of the Church be meaningful both evangelistically and theologically'.[13]

To speak of the southward shift of Christianity is not to be taken to mean that it is the South alone which now matters theologically. Rather, what must be stressed is that an important effect of the southward shift of the church's axis has been to give to Christianity what John Mbiti called new 'centres of universality'. The meaning of this new reality for understanding the nature of Christian history, and therefore of Christian missionary theology in our post-missionary era, will be examined in the remainder of this chapter.

Undoubtedly these articles by John Schumacher and John Mbiti were raising important questions about theology and Christian identity as the church was now becoming truly universal for the first time in its history. Christianity was indeed entering upon a new intellectual phase, with a new and unique sense of this universality. In his survey of 'The Christian tradition in Today's World', in the volume, *Religion in Today's World*,[14] Andrew Walls traced the process of this effectual universal diffusion of Christianity to a considerably earlier period seeing 'a culmination and acceleration' since 1945, hence since the start of the decolonisation era. The convergence of the two processes has been decisive since it has meant that the new and unique sense of Christianity's universality was also in effect the 'decolonisation' of Christianity. For obvious reasons it has been in the recently decolonised parts of the world, the new centres of Christianity's universality, that this new Christian intellectual climate has been felt most intensely.

These developments in Christianity have come to maturity since the 1970s and 1980s when one began to speak of 'Third World theology' or 'Theologies of the Third World' as a distinct element within the broad field of Christian scholarship, distinguishable from the Western or European tradition.

Theologies of the South – a New Way of Doing Theology

The constraints of this book prohibit a detailed analysis of the theologies of the South. What is important is to understand the general direction and broad trends, and to appreciate those characteristics that the emergent theologies from the new centres of Christianity's universality have in common.

It would perhaps be an exaggeration to say that the emergence of the theological activity of the South has involved a complete break with the tradition of the West. Latin American Liberation theology, for instance, owed a lot to the political theology associated with the work of German Reformed theologian, Jürgen Moltmann, as well as to some areas of French Roman Catholic thought in the twentieth century, especially that represented by Father Yves Congar. But these theologians were themselves open to the Third World. Nevertheless, in some important respects, theological activity as a specifically Christian activity has undergone some radical transformations in the new centres, particularly in relation to mission.

It is important to understand how, in the minds of its promoters, this new theological activity became closely linked with meetings, conferences and associations, even when they had already embarked upon a career of theological writing. It is usual for instance, to take Gustavo Guttierrez's *A Theology of Liberation*[15] as the literary inauguration of Latin American Liberation theology. Latin American Liberation theology, as a theology from the South or 'from the periphery', belongs, however, within the movement that was effectually launched only with the formation of the Ecumenical Association of Third World Theologians in August 1976, when twenty-two theologians from Latin America, Asia, Africa, the Caribbean and Black America met at Dar-es-Salaam in Tanzania. According to Sergio Torres Gonzales (from Chile), the first Executive Secretary:

> The first major achievement of Dar-es-Salaam was to create a new space for self-expression ... the Third World theologians were separated and without any forum of common communication. The Dar-es-Salaam dialogue allowed them to meet and to establish together a space or permanent forum where their humiliated and suffering voice could be heard, with the hope that God would hear this people ...[16]

This could equally be said of the conference in March 1982 in Bangkok, Thailand on the theme of Christology, which launched the International Fellowship of Evangelical Mission Theologians from the Two-Thirds World comprising the Latin American Theological Fraternity, Partnership In Mission-Asia and the African Theological Fraternity. The editors of the Conference Proceedings defined the conference's own self-understanding:

The Conference was more than a forum to present papers. It was a creative workshop to facilitate and promote reflection in community. It was a meeting and a fellowship of persons, testing and affirming insights gained from diverse cultural and theological backgrounds to deepen their understandings of Christ. ... the product of the Conference was thus more than a collection of papers. It was the creation, experience and development of community.[17]

This leads us to perhaps the single most important observation on the transformation of theological activity in the new centres. Whilst individual promoters have continued their literary output under their own names, the theological activity itself is seen as a shared activity in that it emerges out of a shared experience. The 'testing and affirming of insights' takes place in the context of a shared 'space', in 'the experience and development of community'. But here the notion of community is understood as embracing more than the circle of scholars. The explicit claim is that this is the 'theology of the people'. In the words of Engelbert Mveng of Cameroon (Executive Secretary of the Ecumenical Association of African Theologians), on African theology (and this would apply especially to South African Black theology):

It expresses the faith and hope of our oppressed peoples. It illustrates the experience of the living Christian communities in Africa. It is therefore not an academic theology even if some of its promoters move in university circles.

And on the question of the linguistic medium of this theological activity, Mveng continues:

When the objection is made that this theology is not written in native languages, we reply that it is *lived* in native languages, in the villages and in the neighbourhoods, before being translated into foreign languages by its own rightful heirs, the African theologians.[18]

Perhaps even more than in African theology, it is in Latin American Liberation theology that theological activity as the experience of community and as 'theology of the people' has been most forcefully exploited. In the words of Brazilian theologian Leonardo Boff:

> Liberation theology has defined another place in which theology is 'done': not so much the university or institute and more the community and in service to the community ... Those who do this theology are not so much individual theologians as the communities who bring their problems, solutions, actions and thinking to be taken up and worked on by theologians.[19]

It is probably the case that Boff's own literary career cannot be adequately understood apart from his close association with the 'grassroots ecclesial communities' of which he has become 'national adviser'. The whole rationale of the Minjung theology from South Korea is captured in the name: Minjung – people, ordinary people as the subjects of history and theology.

It is this conception of theology as fundamentally the experience of community in the sense we have outlined which underlies what the conference in Dar-es-Salaam felt to be the 'most novel aspect' of the emergent theologies from the South, and which led the participants to speak of an epistemological break with traditional academic theology as they knew it in the West. On this point they expressed themselves quite clearly in their final statement:

> We reject as irrelevant an academic type of theology that is divorced from action. We are prepared for a radical break in epistemology which makes commitment the first act of theology and engages in critical reflection on the praxis of the reality of the Third World.[20]

This is perhaps not the place to enter into an extensive discussion on the nature of this 'first act' of commitment to 'the praxis of the reality of the Third World', but in its various manifestations in theologies of the South it has come to mean the commitment to liberation, that is to liberation in all its dimensions, spiritual as well as socio-political, individual as well as collective and cosmic. Here 'liberation' becomes synonymous with 'theology', or rather theological activity. It is the idea, in the words of the Indian theologian, Samuel Rayan, that in theology, 'truth is not something that can be known and spoken independently of its realisation in life'.[21] In the Third World reality of poverty, powerlessness and religious pluralism, such a commitment ties theological activity inextricably into the service of liberation.

It is the very commitment to this 'first act of theology' – or as

Samuel Rayan puts it, the commitment to 'liberational praxis to effect real change in human relations in the direction of greater equality and justice'[22] – that led also to the realisation that such theological activity needed a spirituality, that 'a theology seeking to be of service to the people must necessarily be a theology that starts with a meeting with God, a meeting that takes place within a situation of challenge, a situation that awakens Christians to a contemplative commitment'.[23] Some, like Engelbert Mveng, have spoken of this spirituality of liberation as the spirituality of the Beatitudes of the Gospels, 'not as the eschatological result of liberation, but rather its theological foundation'.[24] In other words, it is from the standpoint of the liberation of the Kingdom of God that theological activity can confront the 'other kingdom' which 'breeds poverty, destitution, injustice, tears, hard-heartedness, iniquity, discord and war, intolerance and persecution'. For Mveng, this quality of the spirituality of liberation makes the theology of liberation itself of universal relevance:

> It is the spirituality of the Beatitudes which allows us to put our finger on the universal character of liberation theology. Every sinner is a slave to be freed through Jesus Christ … if Liberation theology was invented by the Third World, it is in reality the theology of all sincere Christians and therefore of the Universal Church.[25]

We shall not follow Mveng into a discussion of the universality of the theological activity in the South in the way he states it. What I wish to stress, rather, is the way in which the conception of theology as born of community and spiritual experience has helped to restore to the theologies of the South, at least in their intellectual frame of reference and methodology, the unity of theology and spirituality. This, no doubt, has been helped by the massive presence of religion on these continents and by the fact that in several areas too the Christian churches have been experiencing growth and religious awakening. As a consequence a so-called 'secular theology', or the transformation of theology into a social ethic, has so far been avoided. Even Latin America Liberation theologians who at the start were much less interested in the question of religion in its own terms because of their inclination towards Marxian categories of social analysis, soon came to recognise that their reality also includes a 'popular religiosity' which is a religious phenomenon to be taken seriously. Some years after *A Theology of Liberation,* Gustavo Guttierez was to write a different kind of book, *We Drink From Our Own Wells.*[26] Accordingly, the theologies of the South seem to have been able to affirm with much greater confidence that not only is theology born of spirituality, but also, in its Christian specificity, is born of faith in Jesus Christ and the following of Jesus in the perspective of liberation. Thus Sri Lankan Jesuit theologian Aloysius Pieris has written, 'Spirituality is not the practical conclusion of theology but the radical involvement with the poor and the oppressed, and is what creates theology. We know Jesus the *truth* by following Jesus the *way.*'[27] Samuel Rayan of India also makes this point but in different terms, stressing more clearly its rooting in community: 'Theology is spiritual activity, a function of our faith in Christ, interior to our faith-union with God. Worship opens us up to the call of the Spirit who pervades history and enables the poor.'[28] Bishop Tsibangu of Zaire has insisted that the African theologian needs to be 'a person of deep faith, and a solidly metaphysical life'.[29]

Because of the strong element of 'the experience of community' in the theologies of the South, these theologies have a distinct inclination to being 'ecclesial' theologies, which is not to say that they are confessional or denominational. Rather, this simply expresses the way in which the theologies of the South are rooted in the churches, and are produced from within the churches, to the extent that they proceed on the basis of seeking to understand and articulate the longings and aspirations of the communities they represent. This same inclination has tended to make the theologies of the South ecumenical. The tendency has been towards being Christian and true to context – Asian or Latin American or African, rather than being simply Roman Catholic, or Lutheran or Reformed. Theologians of the South are hardly found discussing or defending, for example, the Catholic or the Protestant view of a particular doctrine for its own sake. When Allan Boesak wished to affirm his identification with the Reformed tradition in the history of Christianity, it was to say he was 'Black and Reformed'.[30]

This characteristic of the theologies of the South points to one of the profoundest criticisms of Western theology made by the theologians of the South, that Western theology was for so long presented in all its particulars as *the theology* of the church when in fact it was geographically localised and culturally limited, European and Western, and not universal. The southward shift of the Church, with the growth and vitality of the Christian communities of the South has changed all that. Some theologians of the South speak of this phenomenon as 'the displacement of theology from the centre to the periphery' and would like to ascribe a particular form of universality to the new theological methodology from the South, on the basis that it is a *new way* of doing theology, the way of liberation. This, to my mind, is simply a plea to be taken seriously, the affirmation of the space that is needed for authentic expression.

Christian History – its New Shape

I too should like to argue that the church's learning experience in the South has a universal relevance. However, I understand that relevance differently and I intend to arrive at my conclusion by a different route, by discussing what this southward shift of the church means for our understanding of the nature of Christian history.

In the first place, rather than speak of a 'displacement from centre to periphery', I wish to say with John Mbiti that what the southward shift of the church has done is to cause to emerge 'new centres of Christianity's universality'. Wherever the faith has been transmitted and assimilated are equally 'centres of Christianity's universality'. This is not to deny that there have been (and the modern Western world is not the first of these) instances of Christian recession. What is important is that a shift in the centre of gravity of Christianity is precisely that: a shift in the centre of gravity of *Christianity*. It is a pointer to the nature of the faith and much less to the significance of the human agencies of its transmission. Any absolutisation of the pattern of Christianity's transmission should consequently be avoided and the nature of Christian history itself be re-examined. We are constantly in danger of re-inventing the Deuteronomic law of the single sanctuary[31] and of requiring, in the old language of the Western church, that *ubi ecclesia ibi Christus* (where the church is, there is Christ), whereas the deeper Biblical insight is that *ubi Christus ibi ecclesia* (where Christ is, there is the church).

Since it is on the basis of the experience of faith in the living Christ in the Christian communities of the South that we speak of the present shift, it also signifies that there is no *one* centre from which Christianity radiates, and that it was never intended to be so. From this viewpoint, it would appear that the Lord's words: 'You will be witnesses for me in Jerusalem, in all Judaea and Samaria and the ends of the earth'[32] were not intended to be read as indicating a linear geographical progression of Christian history, meaning 'from Jerusalem, through Greece and Rome to Europe ... to the Third World through Europe'[33] for we cannot absolutise that pattern. Rather the Lord's words are to be taken as stressing the universality of the good news conveyed in terms in which the disciples would have understood the world. The early chapters of the book of *Acts* indicate that the Jerusalem church was often overtaken by events, and the whole book can be read as the process whereby the early Christian leaders, predominantly Jewish, were brought to understand the mind of Christ which they had initially failed to grasp, as they inquired: 'Lord, will you at this time give the Kingdom back to Israel?'.[34] Within the lifespan of that early apostolic leadership, Jerusalem became 'periphery'. And yet the one apostle through whose ministry this especially came about, could anticipate that in the mercy of God, Jewry would become again a centre of faith in Jesus the Messiah.[35] So Jerusalem, where it all began, would need to believe again.

As with Jerusalem, so now, following the Western missionary penetration into the non-Western world, the Western world, in the words of Karl Rahner 'a milieu that has become unchristian',[36] also needs to be re-evangelised. Indeed, we may say that it is precisely because the Western missionary enterprise has brought about the crumbling of the final vestiges of the notion of a territorial Christianity, namely, Western Christendom, that we can now appreciate something of the nature of Christian history that seeks to approximate the mind of Christ. To that extent, the Western missionary endeavour has accomplished a feat comparable to St Paul's, even though it may not always have used, if we are to believe Roland Allen, St Paul's methods.[37]

If it was the Great Commission to make the good news available to the whole world which launched Christian history, then it is legitimate to expect that all Christian history should be read in the light of the original impulse. In other words, it is the terms of the

Great Commission that ought to furnish us with the means of understanding and testing the direction and the major forces operating
within any segment of Christian history. In a study of Christian
history we should look for what the Great Commission teaches us to
expect.

In a recent discussion of the subject Andrew Walls has written:
'The words of the Great Commission [Matt. 28:19–20] require that
the various nations are to be made disciples of Christ'. He draws
attention to the fact that it is 'the *nations*, not some people within the
nations, who are to be discipled'; and then he continues:

> In other words, national distinctions, the things that mark out
> each nation, the shared consciousness and shared traditions,
> and shared mental processes and patterns of relationship, are
> within the scope of discipleship. Christ can become visible
> within the very things which constitute nationality.[38]

In his St Colm's Lecture for 1989, Walls related the subject to conversion:

> Conversion is not about adopting someone else's pattern of life
> and thought, however ancient and however excellent, that is
> not conversion but proselytisation .... Conversion involves the
> turning towards Christ of everything that is there already, so
> that Christ comes into places, thoughts, relationships and
> world views in which He has never lived before.[39]

Applied to Christian history, the terms of the Great Commission
calling for the 'discipling' and the 'conversion' of the nations, would
lead to the realisation that no Christian history anywhere ever ceases
to be a missionary history – a history of conversion, a history of the
constant seeking and application of the mind of Christ to the issues
and questions within a particular context, culture or nation – unless
conversion has ceased to matter, unless that seeking and application
of the mind of Christ has ceased to be made in that context, culture or
nation. In a recent published article I have sought to show that as an
alternative to the current dominant anthropology-based missiology
which tends to reduce everything to the categories of 'the West and
the rest', the whole of Christian history might be better read as
mission history, and so made to yield, from within it, clues to the

queries and the puzzles that one may encounter elsewhere in the study of the Christian story. Missiology becomes not just learning to communicate the Gospel to other peoples and cultures, but also an exercise in self-understanding within Christian scholarship.[40] It can only be a failure in this respect which explains Father John Schumacher's complaint twenty years ago that ecclesiastical historiography, particularly that in the West, was ignoring the weight and significance of the Third World, whereas he considered that 'the principal elements of the whole Church's self-understanding' were the contribution of the Third World.

If all Christian history is to be understood as missionary history – the application of the mind of Christ to, and in, context, conversion in context – the emergence of the 'new centres of Christianity's universality' makes our time perhaps the most exciting of all. For whilst today no individual or individual church can speak the Word of God by itself alone, today also the universal church resembles what it will look like at the end (according to the vision of *Revelation* 7) more than it has ever done before. The promise of Pentecost has become fulfilled more abundantly than on the first day; and cross-cultural mission now comes truly into its own, for the whole church has more opportunity to hear and share the good news as all of us 'hear in our own languages [contexts, cultures and nations] about the great things that God has done'.[41]

The universal relevance of the church's missionary histories in the Christian communities of the South comes, then, to consist in this – in the extent to which those histories have in fact been the histories of 'the great things that God has done'. This view is also the answer to those Western Christian scholars who have doubted whether the cross-cultural missionary learning that has been gained within so-called 'pre-modern cultures' (that is of the South) can assist in mission to the 'modern Western world'.[42] Has the modern Western world, in Christian recession, but with its increasing interest in the practice of the occult, so outgrown religious and spiritual hunger that it is impervious to the experiences of Christian transcendence recorded in the religious worlds of the South? What, then, is the significance of such cross-cultural missionary learning if it is shown to be truly of the Gospel? Even though whatever may be accounted universal is nonetheless experienced within a particular context, as

Max Stackhouse writing on the theme, 'One Faith, Many Cultures', has observed:

> a decisive criterion for a Christian understanding of contextu-
> ality is whether or not it leads to inter-contextual understanding
> of both the 'texts' of Christian faith and the interdependence of
> the contexts of the Church. Only intercontextual views of
> contextuality could be reflective of the trans-contextual power
> of God present in each context.

Stackhouse later continues: ·

> If that was not so, we would be called, above all, to understand
> the perils of any contextuality which does not reach toward
> intercontextual and trans-contextual possibilities.[43]

Stackhouse's observations lead naturally to the recognition that what the plurality of centres of Christianity's universality provides is not a linear unidirectional pattern of Christian history, but a pattern of overlapping circles of Christian life in context, with no absolute centres or peripheries. Every centre is a potential periphery and vice versa. Christian history in the post-missionary era, therefore, brings Christians everywhere potentially into the experience of shared space for self-expression, the experience of community. I use the term potentially, because whilst such 'ecumenical sharing of resources' is a crucial pointer to the nature of Christian history itself, it requires a willingness to come into it, it requires openness on all sides. To recall and paraphrase John Mbiti's words: we have eaten theology with you ... will you eat theology with us?

At the 1978 Lambeth Conference, there were eighty bishops from Africa; in 1988 there were 175. With the present trend of growth in the Anglican Church in various parts of the continent, it is expected that in 1998 there could well be over 300 African bishops. As the 1988 conference ended, an African bishop is reported to have com-mented: 'Anyone who wants a resolution passed in 1998 will have to come to terms with the African bishops'.[44] Will that happen? Will Western bishops be prepared to come to terms with African bishops? The answer to that question is neither simple nor straight-forward.

The above discussion has been about history, not prophecy. Yet prophecy itself is rooted in a judicious historical discernment concerning the things and the ways of God. For a puzzle which lies so evidently in the Christian future, it is appropriate to look to Christian history for some guidance. To consult the Scriptures may confer some special privileges upon our findings and urge them more intently upon our attention.

Towards the end of his long and profound *Letter to the Romans*, in Chapter 15, the seasoned apostle Paul suddenly turned to a subject that was obviously preoccupying him: his impending visit to Jerusalem to deliver gifts of money from the Gentile churches to the poor churches in Judaea. This was obviously important to the apostle, for he described it as being 'in the service of God's people there'.[45] Paul was evidently pleased that the churches in Macedonia and Achaia had freely decided to give the offering, even though he was thoroughly convinced that the Gentiles had an obligation to help the Jews and that for a simple reason: 'Since the Jews shared their spiritual blessings with the Gentiles, the Gentiles ought to use their material blessings to help the Jews'.[46]

If it was all so simple and straightforward, then what explains Paul's urgent request for prayer in vv. 30–2?

> I urge you, brothers, by our Lord Jesus Christ and by the love that the Spirit gives: join me in praying to God for me. Pray that I may be kept safe from the unbelievers in Judaea and that my service in Jerusalem may be acceptable to God's people there. And so I will come to you full of joy, if it is God's will, and enjoy a refreshing visit to you.

Was Paul anxious lest the Jewish Christians, even in their evident need, should in spiritual pride reject the gifts of their ill-rated Gentile brethren? If this were to happen, not only would it mean failure of an attempt to get resources from one group of Christians to another, but more importantly it would be a major setback for the Gospel. The whole operation had to do with God and Christ and the Good News in an infinitely more profound way, as he had previously written to the Corinthians.[47] A deeper insight into the apostle's mind on the present question is given us in *Ephesians* 2 and 3, for the passing of material gifts from the Gentiles to the Jews was the opportunity to demonstrate openly – before principalities and powers pulling in the opposite directions – the validity of the missionary proclamation of the Good News, and the meaning of Christ as the clue to the design of God in history. This was to create, out of hostility, alienation and mutual suspicion, a new people, one people, the people of God with no walls separating them and keeping them enemies.[48] 'The secret is that by means of the Gospel the Gentiles have a part with the Jews in God's blessings; they are members of the same body and share in the promise that God made through Christ Jesus.'[49] It ought, then, to be through ecclesiastical historiography probing all Christian history as missionary history, as the history of the great things that God has done and is doing – contextual, intercontextual and trans-contextual – that the stubborn barriers that divide people behind the 'fetish' symbols of 'modern' and 'pre-modern', 'civilised' and 'uncivilised' are transcended and made to yield instead, the evidence of what God has been about since the foundation of the world.

The shape of Christian history in the age of the many new centres of Christianity's universality offers, therefore, the opportunity for all the different missionary histories to 'key into' the 'mainframe' of the one story of the enormous crowd that no one could number, from every race, tribe, nation and language. In their diverse tongues they stood in front of the throne of the Lamb and they all called out in one loud voice: 'Salvation comes from our God who sits on the throne, and from the Lamb'.[50]

Notes and References

1. *Concilium*, September 1971.
2. See John Schumacher, 'The Third World and the Twentieth Century Church', in Gerald H. Anderson and Thomas F. Stransky (eds), *Mission Trends No. 1: Crucial Issues in Mission Today*, New York: Paulist Press and Grand Rapids: Eerdmans, 1974, pp. 205–14.
3. Ibid., p. 207.
4. Ibid., pp. 207–11.
5. Loc. cit.
6. Ibid., p. 212.
7. Loc. cit.
8. John Mbiti, 'Theological impotence and the universality of the Church', *Lutheran World*, vol. 21, no. 3, 1974; see Gerald Anderson and Thomas Stransky (eds), *Mission Trends No. 3: Third World Theologies*, New York: Paulist Press and Grand Rapids: Eerdmans, 1976, pp. 6–18.
9. Ibid., p. 17.
10. Ibid., pp. 16–17.

11. Ibid., pp. 6–8.
12. Ibid., p. 10.
13. Ibid., p. 9.
14. Andrew F. Walls, 'The Christian tradition in Today's World', in F. B. Whaling (ed.), *Religion in Today's World*, Edinburgh: T. and T. Clark, 1987, pp. 76–109.
15. Gustavo Guttierrez, *A Theology of Liberation – History, Politics and Salvation*, New York: Orbis Books, 1973; first published in Spanish in 1971.
16. See S. Torres Gonzalez, 'Dar-es-Salaam 1976', in Leonardo Boff and Vergilio Elizondo (eds), *Third World Theologies – Convergences and Differences*, Edinburgh: T. and T. Clark, 1988.
17. Vinay Samuel and Chris Sugden (eds), *Sharing Jesus in the Two-Thirds World*, Grand Rapids: Eerdmans, 1984, p. viii. (First published in 1983 in Bangalore, India, by Partnership in Mission (PIM)-Asia.)
18. Engelbert Mveng, 'African Liberation Theology', in Boff and Elizondo, *Third World Theologies*, p. 18.
19. Leonardo Boff, 'What are Third World Theologies?', in Boff and Elizondo, *Third World Theologies*, p. 13.
20. Sergio Torres and Virginia Fabella (eds), *The Emergent Gospel – Theology from the Developing World*, London: G. Chapman, 1978, p. 269.
21. Boff and Elizondo, *Third World Theologies*, p. 131.
22. Ibid., p. 129.
23. Ibid., p. 119.
24. Ibid., p. 19.
25. Loc. cit.
26. Gustavo Guttierrez, *We Drink From Our Own Wells: The Spiritual Journey of a People* (translated by Matthew J. O'Connell), London: SCM Press, 1984.
27. Aloysius Pieris, *Towards an Asian Theology of Liberation*, New York: Orbis and Edinburgh: T. and T. Clark, 1988, p. 82.
28. Boff and Elizondo, *Third World Theologies*, p. 130.
29. T. Tshibangu, 'The task of African theologians', in Kofi Appiah-Kubi and Sergio Torres (eds), *African Theology en Route*, New York: Orbis Books, 1979, p. 74.
30. See Allan Boesak, *Black and Reformed – Apartheid, Liberation and the Calvinist Tradition*, Johannesburg: Skotaville Publishers, 1984.
31. *Deuteronomy* 12.
32. *Acts* 1:8.
33. See John Schumacher, 'The Third World and the Twentieth Century Church', p. 213.
34. *Acts* 1:6.
35. *Romans* 9–11.
36. Karl Rahner, *The Shape of the Church to Come*, London: SPCK, 1974, p. 32.
37. See Roland Allen, *Missionary Methods – St. Paul's or Ours?* Grand Rapids: Eerdmans, 1962; first published in 1912 by World Dominion Press.
38. I am indebted to Andrew Walls for the understanding of the terms of the Great Commission in this section of my discussion. Andrew F. Walls, 'The translation principle in Christian history', in Philip C. Stine (ed.), *Bible Translation and the Spread of the Church – The Last 200 Years* (Studies in Christian Mission 2), Leiden: E. J. Brill, 1990, pp. 24–39; quotation on p. 25.
39. Andrew F. Walls, *The Significance of Christianity in Africa*, Edinburgh: Church of Scotland/St Colm's Education Centre and College, 1989, p. 20.
40. See Kwame Bediako, 'World Evangelization, Institutional Evangelicalism and the future of Christian World Mission', in Vinay Samuel and Albrecht Hauser (eds), *Proclaiming Christ in Christ's Way – Studies in Integral Evangelism* (Essays

presented to Walter Arnold on the occasion of his 60th birthday), Oxford: Regnum Books, 1989, pp. 52–68.

41. *Acts* 2:11.
42. See Lesslie Newbigin, 'Can the West be converted?', *International Bulletin of Missionary Research*, vol. 11, no. 1, January 1987, pp. 2–7.
43. Max Stackhouse, 'Contextualisation, Contextuality and Contextualism', in Ruy O. Costa (ed.), *One Faith, Many Cultures*, New York: Orbis Books, 1988, pp. 6–7 and 12–13.
44. Vinay Samuel and Chris Sugden, *Lambeth: A View from the Two-Thirds World*, London: SPCK, 1989, p. 4.
45. *Romans* 15:25.
46. *Romans* 15:27.
47. See 2 *Corinthians* 9.
48. *Ephesians* 2.
49. *Ephesians* 3:6.
50. *Revelation* 7:9–10.

10

The Gospel and the Transformation of the Non-Western World

☯

> Take my face and give me yours!
> Take my face, my unhappy face.
> Give me your face,
> With which you return
> When you have died,
> When you vanished from sight.
> You lie down and return –
> Let me resemble you, because you have joy,
> You return ever more alive,
> After you vanished from sight.
> Did you not promise me once
> That we too should return
> And be happy again after death?[1]

Thus runs a prayer text of primal religion from South Africa. This section on Christianity as a non-Western religion began in Chapter 6 with a discussion of the primal imagination and the opportunity it offers for new formulations of the apprehension of the transcendent in Christian experience. This prayer returns to this theme, serving as a fitting point of entry into a concluding discussion on the transforming impact of the Gospel upon the life-patterns, the value-systems and the ideas which have hitherto shaped human outlook and destiny in the non-Western world.

The non-Western world is a large and diverse world, but unified to a significant extent by the impact of the Western world, both through the economic, political and cultural expansion of the West and through the Western missionary transmission of the Gospel

reaching back over four centuries. As has been shown, only a superficial reading of the missionary history of the Christian religion can
lead to the conclusion that the Western missionary enterprise has
done little more than transmit a 'Western religion'. An 'infinitely
culturally translatable' reality, the Christian faith has, in the process
of its assimilation in the non-Western world, overturned any Western cultural possessiveness of it. As this fact has become more
apparent in the post-missionary setting of the non-Western
churches, and as Christianity's centre of gravity has shifted to the
non-Western world, so also has it been possible to recognise the
Christian religion as a non-Western religion. To assess the prospects
of the Christian religion it is therefore essential to study that part of
the non-Western world that has become Christian, at least to the
extent that it gives evidence of having significantly welcomed the
Christian religion and seems poised to seek ways of making it incarnate in large areas of its life.

The Significance of Africa in the Non-Western Christian Experience

Africa, perhaps, provides the most interesting context for such a
study. Latin America, which like twentieth-century Africa is largely
Christian, has been a Christian continent for much longer. Its
present Christian ferment is as much a re-working of Christian sub-
stratum (for Roman Catholics) as it is the result of some radical evangelism (for Protestants, mainly Pentecostals). Asia so far does not
demonstrate a similar uniform, massive Christian allegiance, except
in a few regions, as in the Philippines and South Korea. Oceania is
perhaps the closest to the African situation.

The comparison of Africa with Oceania is also interesting because
Christian penetration has come into contact there with primal religious traditions in something approaching their primordial forms.
This is also true for certain regions of India that have experienced
mass movements to Christianity in the twentieth century. If, as Sri
Lankan theologian, Aloysius Pieris, has suggested, the major Asian
religions of 'Hinduism, Buddhism and to some extent Taoism' must
be understood as 'metacosmic soteriologies' which rest on a 'domes-
ticated' primal substratum which he calls 'cosmic religion',[2] then one

cannot exclude the prospect that as Asian Christian theologians relate the Christian faith ever more deeply to Asian cultures, Asia also might yield evidence to confirm the historical connections between Christianity and primal religion.

By virtue of its scale, the African story is particularly interesting and almost a test case of the whole process. In the second decade of the twentieth century it was possible for a Western Christian scholar and missionary to write a book about the primal religions of Africa and call it *The Religion of the Lower Races*.[3] In the century's closing decades, when Africa appears to have tipped the balance and transformed Christianity, according to its best-known statistician, 'permanently into a primarily non-Western religion',[4] there is the opportunity to think of Christianity itself in new ways.

The Transformation Through the Gospel in Non-Western Terms

The significant transforming impact of the Gospel upon the non-Western world arises from non-Western responses to the Gospel in its own terms and not in terms of Western expectations. What needs to become explicit in the process of such an impact is the experience of Christ within the religious, social and cultural settings of African, Asian and Latin American Christians; they respond to their own, not to other people's experience of Christ.

'Take my face and give me yours.' In its primal religious setting, the prayer is addressed to the moon, and so exemplifies the widespread African phenomenon of sky symbolism in which the celestial bodies become symbolic, focal points for the experience of transcendent realities, very often of the Supreme God. The waxing and waning of the moon here symbolises immortality, thus the prayer is a plea for participation in immortality, a plea for transcendence. That much of the religious imagery as well as the expressed sentiments in such a prayer can pass with ease into Christian experience and spirituality, is perhaps the proof that in Africa, as Adrian Hastings wrote in 1976,

> it is in the experience of vernacular prayer, both public and private, both formal and informal, and in the spirituality which

grows up from such experience, that the roots for an authentic African Christianity will most surely be found.[5]

It is important to note not only that African Christianity is overwhelmingly vernacular, but also that it is through the vernacular that the living forces of the primal imagination are perpetuated and carried forward into Christian usage. Even prayers derived from Western sources, in translation, take on resonances rooted in primal spirituality. When John Mbiti wrote in 1968 that in passing from primal religion into Christianity, 'the man of Africa will not have very far to go before he begins to walk on familiar ground',[6] what he had in mind was the 'wholeness of African life', which in its religiousness found an echo and an answer in the 'wholeness' of the Gospel of Christ. Because of the significance of the vernacular across the whole spectrum of African Christian experience (not least in the rise of independent churches) where it encountered the translated Scriptures, it is possible to restate John Mbiti's conclusion from different premises. The African evidence may perhaps confirm the dictum by Aloysius Pieris that 'language is the "experience" of reality, religion is its expression', which makes language, each language, a distinct way of apprehending and experiencing truth.[7] Thus, in Africa, it is not in African adoption of Western social and cultural mores, not even when these are specifically associated with Christian transmission, but in African languages and in their significance in the whole process of the local assimilation of Christianity, that one must look for the true proportions of the Gospel's impact in African life. In 1982 Andrew Walls wrote:

> The notion that religions are not mutually exclusive entities which succeed one another in the process of conversion, but that the whole social life of a community must be taken together was perhaps more readily learned in Africa than elsewhere.[8]

There is a specific application that relates to the significance of language. The early and profoundly vernacular character of African Christianity has meant that not only has the primal imagination found a place, permanently, in the Christian mind, but also, through the persistence of the primal world-view carried by indigenous languages, Christ has, to quote Paul Jenkins, 'as it were, shouldered his way' into that world and altered the way people view it and seek spiritual help.[9] The requests that would have been addressed to spiritual powers and their human agents in a primal religious setting have come to be addressed to Christ too; the Christian minister in Africa is often called to the performance of duties ranging from prayer for fertility, the dedication of a baby at an 'outdooring', for success in an examination, the blessing of a newly built or occupied house, to the blessing of a newly purchased motor car to ensure safety for user and vehicle alike.

This leads to the recognition of perhaps the most important impact that the Gospel has had on African life, as seen in the African response to Christ. Far from obliterating the African primal view of things, in its essentially unified and 'spiritual' nature and replacing it with a two-tier modern Western view comprising sacred and secular dimensions, the Christian faith has in fact reinforced the African view. Even though African Christian communities were generally the earliest to be exposed to Western education through the missionary enterprise, African Christians have, on the whole, avoided any significant secularisation of their outlook. New knowledge in science and technology has been embraced, but it has not displaced the basic view that the whole universe in which human existence takes place is fundamentally spiritual. The African experience here points to the African insistence, as Aylward Shorter has rightly noted, that technology has to be 'without materialism. God is an inner necessity for humankind.'[10]

What the Gospel has done, therefore, is to affirm a spirituality that was there already, even if it has also pruned off some of its features and sharpened its focus, this time, upon Christ. It is hardly surprising that the Christologies that have emerged in African theology so far are predominantly 'pneumatic', presenting a Christ who is a living power in the realm of spirit. African Christological titles like 'Eldest Brother' (H. Sawyerr), 'Ancestor', 'Great Ancestor' (J. S. Pobee, C. Nyamiti, K. Bediako), are neither 'from below', nor strictly 'from above'; rather they are indicative of the way the primal imagination grasps the reality of Christ in terms in which all life is essentially conceived – as spiritual.[11] The 'intuitive' theology of the Prophet Harris is paradigmatic of an African experience that is likely to emerge as academic theologians probe into the actual lived experience of African Christians under the impact of the Gospel.

Perhaps the Gospel's affirmation of the essential spirituality of the African primal world-view explains why African theology has so far been predominantly a theology of inculturation. True, it seems to have been much less preoccupied, consciously that is, with the quest for an 'African spirituality' and much more with 'African theology'. And yet, the actual content of African theology may indicate that it is the affirmation of the primal spirituality which has provided its foundation. Since the 1960s it has been greatly concerned with the theological reinterpretation and rehabilitation of the pre-Christian primal tradition and can be said to have been quarrying amid the spiritual treasures of the African past. If the result of this theological investigation has been to show, in the words of Desmond Tutu, that 'the African religious experience and heritage were not illusory ...' and that 'many of Africa's religious insights had a real affinity with that of the Bible',[12] then African theology can also be said to be part of the vindication of the primal spirituality of the past. African theology as the theology of inculturation has thus involved a twofold process: on the one hand 'the evangelisation of African culture in such a way as to enable it to be integrated into the eternal Christian heritage and to continue to make this heritage more "Catholic"', and on the other hand, 'the Africanisation of Christianity to the point where it becomes a constituent of the spiritual and cultural inheritance of Africa'.[13] In that sense, African theology has been about the redemption of African culture. Earlier Western missionary theology had taken a negative view of African culture, underestimating it and even dismissing it as of scant significance. But it was the Gospel itself which, by declaring that God has never left Himself without witness in the life of humankind,[14] gave the impetus to African Christian scholars to embark on the study of the heritage of African peoples. After nearly two decades of investigations into the primal religions and spiritualities of numerous African societies, often with authors studying their own particular peoples, Africa's theologians came to a virtual consensus on a matter of prime concern: recognising 'the radical quality of God's self revelation in Jesus Christ' – they were nonetheless convinced that 'this knowledge of God was not totally discontinuous with African peoples' previous traditional knowledge of Him'.[15]

More informed Western interpretation of African tradition was to arrive at similar conclusions. However, it has been important for Africa's self-respect that African theologians should reach these positions through their own scholarship, since the redemption of African culture has, at a deeper level, been about the redemption of African humanity. It was vital that the melancholy history of Africa's contact with the Western world should be transcended through the discovery of Africa's role within redemptive history, so liberating Africa to work out her own unique contributions to the fullness of the apprehension of Christ in anticipation of the *eschaton*.

It is true that this positive appropriation of Christianity as belonging within the spiritual and cultural inheritance of Africa has not been unanimously welcomed. There are African intellectuals who, reacting to the historical entanglement of the Christian missionary endeavour with Western colonial dominance, have retained a suspicion of the Christian religion in Africa. On the other hand, there are secular-minded Westerners who are distrustful of any claim that a religious conviction can form the basis for developing a viable social and intellectual tradition for new and young nations seeking paths to modernisation. African Christians are not bound to accept either of these criticisms at face value.

To the one, it can be pointed out that the alleged close alliance between the missionary endeavour and colonial dominance is an overdrawn picture which conceals a historical *naïveté*. In many parts of the continent, Christian missionaries had established independent centres of influence far in advance of any European administrations, colonial or commercial. Yet more significant is the fact that in actual evangelisation and church planting, many of the pioneer missionaries were Africans. This is the case whether one considers the significant African missionary force which emerged out of the tiny settlement of Sierra Leone to serve the Anglican Church Missionary Society in West Africa, and even beyond, or the evidence uncovered by Louise Pirouet, regarding the work of Ganda evangelists often operating as 'foreign missionaries' in areas other than their home base.[16] And all this was before the continent-wide emergence of African independent prophets with the distinctive African initiatives that they have exemplified. 'There is something symbolic', as Andrew Walls has pointed out, 'in the fact that the first church in tropical Africa in modern times was not a missionary creation at all'. The 1100 so-called 'Nova Scotians', Christians of African birth or descent who arrived in Sierra Leone in 1792, brought their own preachers and leaders, and their churches had been functioning for twenty years when the first missionary arrived'.[17]

Equally, there is something intrinsically right about Lamin Sanneh's claim that the history of African Christianity must seriously recognise African Christian antecedents in antiquity, including Biblical history. On this view, the flight of Joseph, Mary and the infant Jesus to Egypt has to be reckoned to be 'the first tradition connecting the African continent with the Christian story'.[18] At least one prominent African theologian has written that 'Christianity in Africa can rightly be described as an indigenous, traditional and African religion'.[19] Thus, although in more recent history as Godwin Tasie and Richard Gray have pointed out, 'The alliance between Christian missionaries and European colonialism was intimate, it was never complete, the equation of missionaries and Christianity was never absolute. There was always a gap between [Western] missionaries and African Christianity.'[20]

To the other criticism, it can be objected that Western secular categories need not be any more successful in interpreting African realities than some aspects of the Western missionary estimations of African culture and tradition were in the past. Indeed, it can be argued that the Western secular outlook on life and history may itself be the product of what Lamin Sanneh has called a 'cultural self-flattery',[21] which conceals an undue limitation of the range of human experience by jettisoning the dimensions of transcendence and spirituality. The secular outlook wedded to technology can give an illusion that humanity has effectively tamed and even dismissed the spiritual realities and cosmic forces which are presumed to operate within a primal frame of reference. In the words of Aloysius Pieris:

> Technology is as ambivalent as the cosmic forces it claims to domesticate. Its unwise use, far from making cosmic forces really submissive to humanity, has only provoked them to retaliate and enslave humans with pollution, consumerism, materialism and a host of evils that a technocratic society has produced in the First World [the West]. Besides, it has deprived the human mind of myth and ritual, two things by which humanity enacts its deep yearnings and keeps itself sane in mind

and body. Can technology liberate the person? Certainly not in the form in which 'Christian' nations have offered it to us. It takes away cosmic religion from the masses and replaces it with neurosis. It takes away religious poverty only to give us mammon instead.[22]

And yet the full African Christian response (and indeed I would include, *mutatis mutandis*, also the Asian and Latin American), will be not merely that 'the Africanness which has its roots in the soil of our continent ... is basically a religious phenomenon',[23] but rather, that in Christ, African Christians have found a principle of understanding and interpretation which is superior to any thing that a secular world-view is able to offer.

Christianity and the African Future

'No one can miss the vitality of the [Christian] religion in much of the [African] continent', Lamin Sanneh wrote in 1983.[24] The question now is to explore what possible promises this African religion holds for moulding and transforming African life in the future. This discussion will relate particularly to African political thought, and to the institution of polygamy.

One could write the history of post-independent African as the history of political instability. Ali Mazrui has described the spate of military overthrows of elected civilian administrations as the warrior tradition of Africa taking its revenge on its new educated class, that is, educated on Western models.[25] I should like to suggest that African religion too can give a clue to African politics, and that African Christianity may have an important role to play in the moulding of new political models and ideals.

Issues affecting church and state tend to be seen as relating essentially to the church and the political institutions that have come into place following decolonisation. Such an approach ignores the fact that in many parts of Africa, the church had a previous history of relating to the pre-colonial traditional state. Furthermore, in contemporary independent Africa, the coming of central government has not totally eclipsed the traditional state, and there are many Africans who are thoroughly 'modern' in the sense of being at home with the new centralised political organisation who also maintain a significant degree of loyalty to traditional rule associated with kinship and its attendant obligations. In fact, it would be no exaggeration to say that in places where traditional rule and its rituals and symbols still exert some influence on people's lives, the church, because of its own closeness to grassroots, possesses a deeper and richer experience in relating to traditional rulers than to central government. Whilst traditional rulers have been known to willingly dissociate themselves from some actions and duties of their office that Christian conscience finds offensive, in order to retain their link with the church, Christian leaders seem, on the whole, to have had less impact on the policies of the presidents and heads of state of the new republics. In John Pobee's study of the relationship between the socialist government of Kwame Nkrumah and the churches in Ghana between 1949 and 1966, it is the churches which come out worse, for their ineptitude and 'lack of theology' in their numerous clashes with the late Osagyefo.[26]

That adopted title of Nkrumah is itself a pointer to the political mission that may belong to the church in the future. When Nkrumah took the honorific title which eventually became something of a personal name, Osagyefo (Redeemer, Saviour, or else Messiah), he was adopting a title reserved for traditional sacral rulers. He must have known what he was doing, for Nkrumah was not royal, nor was he concerned to promote the interests of traditional rulers. In the religious cosmology that undergirds the traditional social organisation, the traditional ruler was regarded as the channel through whom cosmic forces operate for the well-being of the community while his power was derived from his position as 'one who sits on the stool (throne) of the ancestors'. The power of the ruler among the living members of the community, being sacral power, is therefore, strictly speaking, the power of the ancestors. Even the royal title, Nana, properly applies to the ancestors.

It is a fact that throughout history, Biblical faith has been a desacralising force in the world. That Christianity has had a similar impact in Africa is evident from the history of the relationship of traditional rulers to the churches. Indeed, in several areas this can be written as a process of desacralisation. If, in the field of politics, a sufficient level of desacralisation was achieved in people's attitudes, it may well explain, at least in part, the fact that in the new independent republics, there was no overt return to the 'ontocratic' pattern of the traditional state.[27] It has not, however, been impossible for re-sacralisation to occur. Harold Turner – who wrote on this subject several years ago and gave part of the credit for the desacralisation process to the independent churches in their role as modernisers – recognised that Nkrumah and other heads of state of his generation (Azikiwe, Banda, Kenyatta, Houphouët-Boigny, Lumumba) who were founders of independence, were 'given a messianic and some-times almost divine status'. Turner, however, dismissed the trend as 'more superficial than substantial' which did not belie the radical secularisation and modernisation that have occurred.[28]

It is my view that the terms in which Turner discussed the subject obscured a fundamental issue that the desacralisation with which he credited the independent churches failed to resolve, and which perhaps explains why it was quite often these independent churches which were most effusive in the ascription of 'messianic status' to Osagyefo. Turner was more interested in tracing a development 'from an ontocratic to a modern society'. That, in actual fact, is an institutional problem. The deeper problem is the sacralisation of power; the political history of African countries since independence shows that the sacralisation of power is not the prerogative of the 'founders of independence', nor, for that matter, of the old 'ontocratic' order.

What African societies seem to stand in need of is a new conception of power that will eliminate from politics its present sacral overtones. But desacralisation need not mean secularisation, while the 'spiritual' character of the African view of life should remain. The real problem here is that though the traditional sacral state had its own mechanism for restraining autocratic rule through the institution of royal coun-sellors, nevertheless, by locating the source of power in the realm of ancestors, it effectively placed power within the range of human capriciousness. It is this conception of power that modern presidents and heads of state have inherited. What is needed is an understanding of power that secures its source beyond the reach of human manipu-lation, at least conceptually, and so transforms the exercise of power in human community from rule into service. African Christianity may have no greater political mission in African societies than to assist in this transformation of outlook, a subject to which I will return later.

The other issue in African social life to which African Christianity should make a contribution from the standpoint of its full participation in the history of redemption is that of polygamy. It is not inconceivable that a really serious African wrestling with the problem from the standpoint indicated above may well be led to deeper insights into the subject for the simple reason that the West has from time to time had misgivings about marriage. That this is so can be seen in the fact that not only has the Western church produced the Christian ascetic ideal and, for a period at least, promoted it as the highest form of the spiritual life, but there is also the modern problem of homosexuality within the Western church and how to deal with it. Africa, on the other hand, has been overwhelmingly committed to marriage, heterosexual marriage. What will the understanding of Christian marriage be in a continent which appears to believe so deeply that to be unmarried is to remain in a state of permanent adolescence?

The discussion of polygamy has so often started from an assumption that it is *the* African form of marriage, so that the essential universal challenge of the Gospel concerning marriage has sometimes been obscured. Writing in 1962, the Ghanaian philosopher William Abraham claimed that African marriage was 'polygamous in definition' and so found himself having to defend it as 'not immoral'. And yet, when he weighed the merits of polygamy against those of monogamy, he could conclude that within the self-same Africa,

> It must nevertheless be admitted that the preference, certainly the longing of women, is for monogamy. Monogamy implies the acquisition of new sensibilities, a readiness to attain an integrated discipline, an offering of the self in service and sacrifice, a closed communion. One might even say it is a delightful prejudice. It is always an ideal.[29]

In other words, there is more than one strand within the African tradition. The failure to recognise that 'there is nothing inherently African about the institution of plural marriages' and hence the tendency in some circles in Africa to treat monogamy as merely a Western institution being forced upon Africans, leads to a misunderstanding both of monogamy itself and of 'the West's painful inconsistency on the subject'.[30] Western society's coupling of legal monogamy with ease of divorce and remarriage, as well as the various other forms of cohabitation, in effect amounts to the practice and legitimisation of plural marriage. What significance should be given in discussing polygamy, to the insight that 'the other African tradition' relates to the views and sensibilities of women? Is this not equally important, if not more so? Is it of any significance, for instance, that the 'modern proponents' of polygamy are 'mostly men'?[31]

African Christian reflection on the subject, availing itself of its 'feminine' insights – which means men and women listening and reflecting together – may come up with some interesting conclusions.

Within the constraints of this chapter, I can only give some indicators of possible directions of such reflection. If African Christianity were to take seriously its own background in the primal unity of humanity as man/woman, I have little doubt that it will grasp that insight that in the well-known apostolic commentary[32] on the primary text of *Genesis* 2:24, 'the hidden truth', 'the mystery' of the Genesis text relates to the marriage relationship itself, that there is such a thing as the mystery of marriage, a positive mystery which affirms marriage and does not give it a spiritually secondary status.

If the way the apostle passes the Genesis text first through the prism of Christ and the church before letting its light refract upon the man–woman relationship is the norm of interpretation, then Paul implies that the Genesis statement contains a mystery that has existed from the very origins of the institution of marriage, but which is made known only with the coming of Christ. The meaning of the mystery is revealed in the understanding of the *spiritual* relationship between Christ and the church. This also means that the unity of man and woman in *Genesis* 2, dramatised by the formation of woman from man (and continually reaffirmed also in the birth of man from woman),[33] is to be seen as a kind of parable which is ultimately made plain in the spiritual union between Christ and the church as His Bride. Accordingly, the man–woman relationship in marriage is meant to serve as a reflection of the all-embracing and eternal spiritual union between Christ and the church. Although the Christ–church relationship appears to follow the man–woman union, in actual fact the former anticipates the latter and is its paradigm. All true marriage therefore is intended to approximate this model of spiritual union as much as possible.

If this is the theology of marriage, then marriage itself becomes a fruit of the Kingdom of God which comes with the coming of Christ, and is a context for discipleship. But polygamy is incapable of fostering the kind of discipleship in exclusive and sacrificial loving which *Ephesians* 5:21–33 requires, and so cannot abide. As Lamin Sanneh writes: 'We need to avoid the danger of describing it in such a way that it is made to embody all the ideals of the African past. There was much abuse in the system and its benefits were not always the unmitigated boon claimed.'[34] Therefore, not through prompting and prodding from the West, but by assuming its firm and self-assured place within the history of redemption, African Christianity must courageously recognise polygamy as *not* a peculiarly African form of marriage, but as a *theologically* false way, a merely *human* contrivance and one which is ultimately incapable of fostering the righteousness of the Gospel of the Kingdom of God. And yet the fact of its incidence within *redeemed* African humanity means that it has been taken into the divine call to conversion and is to be brought into the same relation to the mind of Christ as everything else in African society. It forms part of the fabric of the nations to be discipled.[35] Christ must become visible in African marriage as in every other facet which constitutes Africanness – a costly, demanding and intensely theological process.

It is reasonable to anticipate that African Christianity will make significant contributions towards the transformation of African societies, particularly in relation to the two areas of African thought and practice discussed above. This may be expected because Christianity in the non-Western world has introduced, as has been noted earlier, genuinely novel ways of thinking of the Christian religion as being relevant to a vast range of issues and problems in daily life. Curiously, this cannot be understood in isolation from the nature of the faith's transmission. Thanks to the modern missionary movement, Christianity in the non-Western world is both a scriptural and a vernacular religion lived through hearing the Word of God 'in our own language'. It has, therefore, provided the conditions in which the ordinary people's experience of faith can become more significant and important for theological articulation than has happened in the development of the theological tradition of the West.[36] This, in turn, can have far-reaching implications for understanding the nature of theology. Essentially, theological activity in non-Western

Christianity is also being seen increasingly as involving the participation of people who are not academic and professional theologians. In the words of Samual Rayan (of India),

> It is likely that the greater the part played by the poor in insighting and articulating the meaning of the faith for today, the lesser will be the use of sophisticated scientific mediations and erudite language. Should not theology be expressed more and more in art forms – in dance and drama, in pictures and lines, in carving and sculptures? It should become embodied above all in new and beautiful relationships, in deeds of love, and finally in the new social order itself, in the beauty and shape of the just and free and equal fellowship of God's children and Christ's friends.[37]

Surely here Samuel Rayan speaks for us all, and so perhaps provides the clearest testimony that Christianity, in becoming a non-Western religion, has become in actual experience the most universal of all religions.

Notes and References

1. Quoted in Aylward Shorter, *Prayer in the Religious Traditions of Africa*, Nairobi: Oxford University Press, 1975, p. 116.
2. Aloysius Pieris, *An Asian Theology of Liberation*, Edinburgh: T. and T. Clark and New York: Orbis, 1988.
3. E. W. Smith, *The Religion of the Lower Races*, New York: Macmillan, 1923.
4. David B. Barret, 'AD 2000: 350 million Christians in Africa', *International Review of Mission*, vol. 59, no. 233, January 1970, pp. 39–54.
5. Adrian Hastings, *African Christianity – An Essay in Interpretation*, London: Geoffrey Chapman, 1976, p. 49.
6. John Mbiti, 'Christianity and East African culture and religion', *Dini na Mila*, vol. 3, no. 1, May 1968, p. 4.
7. Aloysius Pieris, *An Asian Theology of Liberation*, p. 70.
8. Andrew F. Walls, 'A bag of needments for the road: Geoffrey Parrinder and the study of religion in Britain', *Religion*, vol. 10, pt 2, Autumn 1980, p. 145.
9. Paul Jenkins, 'The roots of African Church history: some polemical thoughts', *International Bulletin of Missionary Research*, vol. 10, no. 2, April 1986, p. 68.
10. Aylward Shorter, *African Christian Spirituality*, London: Geoffrey Chapman, 1978, p. 114.
11. Harry Sawyerr, *Creative Evangelism – Towards a New Christian Encounter with Africa*, London: Lutterworth Press, 1968; J. S. Pobee, *Toward an African Theology*, Nashville, Tenn.: Abingdon Press, 1979; C. Nyamiti, *Christ as our Ancestor – Christology from an African Perspective*, Gweru: Mambo Press, 1984; K. Bediako, 'Biblical Christologies in the context of African Traditional Religions', in Vinay Samuel and Chris Sugden (eds), *Sharing Jesus in the Two-Thirds World*,

Bangalore: Partnership in Mission-Asia, 1983, and reissued by Grand Rapids: Eerdmans, 1984; subsequently see *Jesus in African Culture – A Ghanaian Perspective,* Accra: Asempa Publishers, 1990.

12. Desmond Tutu, 'Whither African Theology?', in Fasholé-Luke et al. (eds), *Christianity in Independent Africa,* London: Rex Collings, 1978, p. 366.

13. E. Mveng, 'African Liberation Theology', in Leonado Boff and Vergilio Elizondo (eds), *Theologies of the Third World – Convergences and Differences,* Edinburgh: T. and T. Clark, 1988, p. 18.

14. *Acts* 14:17.

15. See K. Dickson and P. Ellingworth (eds), *Biblical Revelation and African Beliefs,* London: Lutterworth Press, 1969, p. 16.

16. Louise Pirouet, *Black Evangelists: The Spread of Christianity in Uganda, 1891–1914,* London: Rex Collings, 1978.

17. Andrew F. Walls, *The Significance of Christianity in Africa,* Edinburgh: Church of Scotland/St Colm's Education Centre and College, 1989.

18. Lamin Sanneh, *West African Christianity – The Religious Impact,* London: C. Hurst, 1983, p. 1.

19. John Mbiti, *African Religions and Philosophy,* London: Heinemann, 1969, p. 229.

20. Godwin Tasie and Richard Gray, in Fasholé-Luke et al. (eds), *Christianity in Independent Africa,* pp. 3 and 4.

21. Lamin Sanneh, in a review of Salman Rushdie's *The Satanic Verses* in *The Christian Century,* 21–28 June 1989, pp. 622–6.

22. Aloysius Pieris, *An Asian Theology of Liberation,* p. 79.

23. See Aylward Shorter, *African Christian Spirituality,* p. 45.

24. Lamin Sanneh, *West African Christianity,* p. 250.

25. Ali Mazrui, *Political Values and the Educated Class in Africa,* London: Heinemann, 1978.

26. See J. S. Pobee, *Kwame Nkrumah and the Church in Ghana 1949–1966,* Accra: Asempa Publishers, 1988.

27. For the word, denoting the effectual union of throne and altar, see Arend van Leeuwen, *Christianity in World History: The Meeting of the Faiths of East and West* (English translation by H. H. Hoskins), London: Edinburgh House Press, 1964.

28. H. W. Turner, 'The place of independent religious movements in the modernisation of Africa', *Journal of Religion in Africa,* vol. 2, no. 1, 1969, pp. 43–63, see pp. 50f.; reprinted in Turner, *Religious Innovation in Africa (Collected Essays on New Religious Movements),* Boston, Mass.: G. K. Hall and Co., 1979.

29. William E. Abraham, *The Mind of Africa,* London: Weidenfeld and Nicholson, 1962, pp. 82 and 189–90.

30. Lamin Sanneh, *West African Christianity,* pp. 248–9.

31. Ibid., p. 249.

32. *Ephesians* 5:31–33.

33. *1 Corinthians* 11:12.

34. Lamin Sanneh, *West African Christianity,* p. 248.

35. *Matthew* 28:19.

36. See my 'The Roots of African theology', *International Bulletin of Missionary Research,* vol. 13, no. 2, April 1989, pp. 58–65; and subsequently 'Cry Jesus! Christian theology and presence in modern Africa', *Vox Evangelica,* vol. XXIII, April 1993, pp. 7–25.

37. Samuel Rayan, 'Third World theology: where do we go from here?', in Leonardo Boff and Vergilio Elizondo, *Theologies of the Third World,* p. 138.

PART 3

*Into the Twenty-first Century –
Africa as a Christian Continent*

The Prospects and Challenges

11

The Making of Christian Africa
The Surprise Story of the Modern Missionary Movement

African Christianity and Africa's Primal Background –
Unexpected Association?

A former Duff Lecturer discussed the fortunes and prospects of Christianity in Africa in the following terms:

> However anxious a missionary may be to appreciate and retain indigenous social and moral values, in the case of religion, he has to be ruthless ... he must admit and even emphasise that the religion he teaches is opposed to the existing one and the one has to cede to the other.[1]

These words, by the German missionary scholar Dietrich Westermann, came to be regarded, at least in subsequent African reactions, as somewhat representative of the traditional Western missionary view of Africa. For Westermann, the transmission of Christianity in Africa necessarily entailed the complete elimination of the pre-Christian primal religions of Africa, since, in his opinion, 'giving the new means taking away the old'.[2] It was another Western interpreter of the missionary expansion of the Christian religion, Bishop Kenneth Cragg, who later made the most trenchant response to Westermann, in the simple question: 'If the old is taken away, to whom is the new given?'[3]

Of course, since both Westermann and Cragg wrote, over fifty and twenty years ago respectively, we have had the benefit of other studies of Christianity in Africa, not least by African Christian writers.

From what we know of this African Christian scholarship, and especially of the genesis and development of what has been known as 'African theology', we are now able to conclude quite firmly that we cannot understand the fortunes of Christianity in Africa if we ignore the impact of the continent's primal religious background. As has been demonstrated by Lamin Sanneh in connection with West Africa, the places reflecting the most marked accession to the Christian religion are also the areas of the highest concentration of the old traditional religions.[4] Perhaps even more remarkable has been the evidence of the large number of new religious movements – admittedly many but not all are Christian – that have emerged from the meeting of the Christian religion and African primal religious traditions. Islam's meeting with Africa has not produced any comparable evidence.

The primal religions of the continent have thus been a significant factor in the immense Christian presence in Africa. While this cannot be taken to mean that there has not been any 'paradigm-shift' in African religious consciousness, it does confirm that the African apprehension of the Christian faith has substantial roots in the continent's primal traditions at the specific level of religious experience. At the least we can say that if it did not have the primal religions as its sub-stratum, the story of Christianity in Africa at the close of the present century would be very different.

In a sense, though, there is probably only one word that can truly describe the present status of Christianity in Black Africa. That word is *surprise*. The surprise lies not just in the much-publicised demographic breakthrough that now makes Africa one of the heartlands of the Christian religion; the surprise lies at a deeper level, quite simply in the fact that Africa has become so massively Christian at all.

The View at Edinburgh 1910 – 'Can the Animist be Converted?'

If we wish to gauge the state of Christian missionary thinking at the beginning of our century, we need to look no further than the World Missionary Conference of 1910 held in Edinburgh. At that conference, which was called to consider the 'missionary problems in relation to the non-Christian world' and particularly to seek ways in which the Christian Gospel could make a greater impact upon the world's non-Christian religions, it was the primal religions of Africa, roundly called 'Animism', which, without doubt, caused the most concern.

Admittedly Africa did not constitute the whole of the evidence for Animism at the Conference. Nevertheless, 60 per cent of the missionaries' responses, which provided the basic material for the report of Commission IV, related to the African field. The general feeling was that there was 'practically no religious content in Animism', by which was meant 'no formulated religious observances or doctrines', nor was there 'any preparation for Christianity'.[5]

It was not so much that Christian mission had registered more significant successes amid the other non-Christian religions that were identified, namely: Chinese religions, religions of Japan, Islam and Hinduism. Rather, of all the non-Christian religions, Animism was probably the most difficult for the Western Christian missionary mind to penetrate. Not only was Animism devoid of literature and lacking in scholars to expound its meanings, but Animism, a designation taken from E. B. Tylor's *Primitive Culture*,[6] was also held to be 'the religious beliefs of more or less backward and degraded peoples all over the world', as W. H. T. Gairdner wrote in his account of the conference.[7] The problem was not just with Animism; the real stumbling-block was the Animist.

Perhaps a more recent missionary question will illuminate this point. Bishop Lesslie Newbigin, following his missionary exertions in India, has now posed the question: 'Can the West be converted?'[8] In the process, he has inaugurated a movement of earnest minds intent on seeking the answer to his question, one which may well be of the utmost importance for the Christian mission in our time. At the start of the missionary movement from the West, the troublesome question was, however: 'Can the Animist be converted? For, the Animist was held to be the same as 'the savage and the uncivilised'. Now, as then, the whole world-wide church may profitably participate in seeking the answer to the modern question: 'Can the West be converted?' When, at the start of the Western missionary movement the question was raised: 'Can the Animist be converted?', it was a European debate about other peoples.

Africans as Type of 'the Savage and Barbarous Heathens'

It is worth recalling that the modern missionary movement was inheritor not only of the notion of a territorial Christianity which saw Europe, and such extensions of its ways of life as existed, as the embodiment of the Christian religion; it was heir also to the idea of a 'great chain of being', which ranked 'White', 'Red', 'Yellow' and 'Negro' races in that descending order in a grand schema of humanity. The theory of the 'great chain of being' found application also in the treatment of humanity's religions, so that in the third edition of the *Encyclopedia Britannica* of 1797, one read under 'Religion':

> When the different systems of religion that have prevailed in the world are comparatively viewed with respect to their influence on the welfare of society, we find reason to prefer the polytheism of the Greeks and Romans to the ruder, wilder religious ideas and ceremonies that have prevailed among savages; Mahometanism, perhaps, in some respects to the polytheism of the Greeks and Romans; Judaism however to Mahometanism; and Christianity to all of them.[9]

It is true that there were persons of a more radical temper, like William Carey who held no belief in the religious superiority of Europeans or 'of those who bear the Christian name'.[10] This, however, in no way weakened the common conviction that the 'civilised' culture and institutions of Europe owed their enlightened status to Christianity, held to be the most civilised of all religions. In the fourfold division of the world's religions into 'Christian, Jewish, Mahometan, Pagan', which Carey used, 'Pagan' constituted a category apart, for lacking monotheism, which was taken to be a major test of religion. Peoples of Africa and Asia equally qualified to be called Pagan. Indians and Chinese, however, were accounted 'civilised' Pagans for possessing literature and for being literate. Africans, on the other hand, believed to be 'without literature, arts, sciences, government, Laws, and also cannibalistic and barbarous', were reckoned to be 'savage and barbarous pagans', 'as destitute of civilisation as they are of true religion', wrote Carey, quoting from his sources. Such ideas were part of the stock of general knowledge, and they persisted into the intellectual climate of the nineteenth century, when they became fused with evolutionary and racially-based theories of human achievement, history and progress.

In an intellectual climate that confused race and culture, as Philip
Curtin has shown,[11] it is not hard to understand how educated persons would entertain serious doubts about the possibility of 'savage
and barbarous' peoples ever becoming Christians. It is to the credit
of the modern missionary movement that its history could be seen as
the history of the acceptance and the rejection of these notions. For
towards the end of the slave trade era, in the late eighteenth century,
when European humanitarianism coincided with the awakening of
missionary concern, both humanitarians and their opponents were
agreed on the image of Africans: Africans were not only 'savage' and
'barbarous', they were also in 'the very depths of ignorant superstition'. The difference was that while their racist opponents claimed to
identify a natural and inherent inferiority in the 'savages', the
humanitarians located the fault 'not in their nature but in their condition'.[12] Therefore, as the missionary movement swung into action at
the start of the nineteenth century, it was also to demonstrate to its
detractors at home that, as one Secretary of the Wesleyan Missionary
Society, John Beecham, wrote, to stir up interest in a projected mission
to Ashanti in West Africa, the Gospel itself was 'the great civiliser of
barbarous men'.[13]

The 'Savage Heathen' as a Missionary Problem

Such confident assertions regarding the efficacy of the Gospel could,
however, give the erroneous impression that all missionary circles
easily overcame their doubts over the ignorant, superstitious and
barbarous savage.

It is well known that the Church of Scotland was relatively late in
engaging in foreign missionary outreach, that is, in relation to the
actual involvement of Scottish people in missionary activity. But this
cannot be taken to mean that the mind of the Kirk was closed as such
to mission. After all, the Scots Confession affirms quite prominently
that 'this glad tidings of the Kingdom shall be preached through the
whole world, then the end shall come ...'. Rather, the modern mission
history of the Church of Scotland helps us understand, in a peculiar
way, that process of agonising over what to do about 'barbarous
peoples' which became so much a part of the missionary movement
as a whole. In 1796, in response to overtures made to it to lend its

support to the newly formed missionary societies, the General Assembly instead passed a resolution that 'to spread abroad the knowledge of the Gospel among barbarous and heathen nations seems to be highly preposterous in so far as it anticipates, nay, it reverses the order of nature'.[14] The Assembly was not being obtuse; it did not know what to do. The intellectual climate in Europe so defined 'the barbarous and the heathen' that, if the terms of the Scots Confession were to be implemented, then 'means' ought to be found and used to do so. And four years before, in the Calvinistic circles of his provincial colleagues in the English Midlands, the self-taught cobbler-turned-preacher, William Carey, had actually written and circulated an eighty-seven-page booklet under the title: *An Enquiry into the Obligations of Christians to Use Means for the Conversion of the Heathens.*[15] The same process of agonising questioning regarding what to do about 'barbarous and heathen' peoples was also taking place elsewhere.

The formation of missionary societies and eventually of Foreign Mission Committees and Boards by churches was itself one such 'means' devised for seeking the conversion of the heathens, though it could only be a first stage. To return to Scotland, the long process in the Church of Scotland, which led from Dr John Inglis's famous sermon in Edinburgh in 1818, arguing the case for an official Scottish missionary project, to the final adoption of a definite scheme by the General Assembly in 1825, cannot be fully understood apart from the eighteenth-century and nineteenth-century European perception of non-European peoples. The new missionary scheme that was to be established had to be on educational lines, 'since little could be expected from mere preaching to an uneducated and barbarous people', according to the Committee's convenor, Dr Inglis.[16] Perhaps it is not surprising then, that Scotland, where what to do about 'the barbarous heathens' became such a missionary problem, was to be so closely associated with educational missions. When Alexander Duff sailed for India in October 1829, to implement the Committee's mandate, he took with him a library of 800 books dealing with a large variety of subjects. Unfortunately, in the shipwreck on the Atlantic coast of Southern Africa the following February, all the books were lost, except two, a copy of Bagster's Bible and a Scottish Psalter. But Duff was not discouraged; he would try again.

In view of the fact that the urge to make a humanitarian response to the slave trade was such a significant factor in the rise of the missionary movement, one might wonder why Africa did not feature in a well-laid missionary scheme like the one which took Alexander Duff to India. Duff himself, of course, had a concern for Africa. He visited Southern Africa on his way from India in 1863 to study the opportunities for an extension of the African missions of the Free Church; and in his later years, as Convenor of the Free Church Foreign Missions Committee, the Free Church's missionary work in Southern African made some significant advances, including the launch of the Livingstonia Mission.

Perhaps an explanation to this problem may be found by examining another Indian missionary story. When the brilliant young Cambridge graduate, Henry Martyn, inspired by Jonathan Edward's *Life of David Brainerd*[17] and some of William Carey's writings, came to the conclusion that God was calling him to missionary work abroad, the thought was greeted with dismay by his teachers who 'thought it a most improper step for him to leave the University to preach to ignorant heathen, which any person might do'.[18] As early as 1802 Martyn applied to the Church Missionary Society, their first English candidate. Conceivably he could have been accepted for Sierra Leone, for the CMS was established with interest in both Africa and the East, as its original name, the 'Society for Mission in Africa and the East', makes clear. For complex reasons this did not happen: the family's fortune collapsed suddenly and financial burdens were imposed upon the young man. He accepted an appointment as chaplain in the East India Company, though he would have been 'infinitely better pleased', we are told by his biographer, 'to have gone out as a missionary, as poor as the Lord and his apostles'.[19] Perhaps the CMS too did not know what to do with the brilliant young university graduate who desired to go to preach the Gospel to the 'ignorant heathen'. Martyn, in fact, technically, was not a 'missionary': he was a chaplain.

An insight into the thinking of the CMS on the nature of missionary work and the qualifications required for it is given in a portion of a memorandum on missionary recruitment, prepared shortly before the Society's foundation by Rev. John Venn, rector of Clapham, soon to be elected its President:

It is obvious that the Church of England can allow no persons to officiate in any respect as ministers who have not been episcopally ordained. Episcopal ordination, bearing respect to the present improved state of society in this island, is justly conferred upon those only, whose education and learning qualify them for the rank English clergy hold in society. It is evident however, that a missionary, dwelling among savages rude and illiterate, does not require the same kind of talents, manners or learning as are necessary in an officiating minister in England.[20]

The CMS saw itself in a dilemma. Concerned to be consistent with normal Anglican order, it should insist on sending ordained men as missionaries. However, since a missionary 'dwelling among savages rude and illiterate' did not need what was required for the Christian ministry at home, Venn would have liked to see a lower order of unordained persons sent as missionaries. He was concerned lest a person unsuited for the home ministry should use ordination into missionary service as a backdoor into that more respectable form of the Christian ministry! For our purposes of course, the statement is valuable for the light it sheds on the Henry Martyn story: obviously Martyn was overqualified for missionary work among 'savages rude and illiterate'. It is perhaps instructive that to Sierra Leone, the earliest of the CMS fields of activity dating from 1804, no ordained English missionary was sent before 1824.[21]

Africa – the Success Story of the 'Savage and Barbarous Heathen'

Ironically, the work of the CMS in Africa was to provide the effective answer to those who doubted the conversion of the 'savage and barbarous heathens'. Its missionary work produced 'probably the most widely-known African Christian of the 19th century',[22] Samuel Ajayi Crowther. First met as a young boy of around thirteen when he was rescued from a Portuguese slave ship, he later became the first African bishop in the Anglican Communion. Following early school education in Freetown, Sierra Leone, Crowther was brought to England in 1843 for ordination, as there was no bishop nearer than

London. His achievement in the ordination examination, which was conducted by the Regius Professor of Greek in Cambridge, caused, we are informed by his biographer, no little stir in learned circles used to discussing the 'mental capacity of the Negro' and concluding that it was 'always deficient as regards logical faculty'.[23] Crowther later came to England in 1851 to urge the cause of the city of Abeokuta in the conflicts of the time which opposed the trading interests of various Yoruba communities in Western Nigeria. In his St Colm's Lecture of 1989, on the theme: 'The significance of Christianity in Africa', Andrew Walls commented on Bishop Crowther's significance:

> When the Rev. Samuel Crowther, later to be bishop [in 1864], came to London, and people heard this grave and gracious black clergyman address public meetings in excellent English, when he visited the Palace and answered Prince Albert's intelligent questions about African trade, missionary work appeared to have reached its final justification. Its aim henceforth must be to produce more of the same. An African clergyman and an English clergyman should be identical in everything but colour.[24]

Indeed, not just Bishop Crowther and his abilities, but the entire Christian establishment of Sierra Leone which he represented, literate and academically respectable, amounted to 'strong evidence of the progressive possibilities of the African mind and character'.[25] So wrote the Bishop's biographer, reflecting awareness of nineteenth-century European opinion which doubted such possibilities. In the 1870s, Fourah Bay College in Freetown, established as a Christian institution in 1827, and eventually affiliated to the University of Durham, was offering degree courses in Arts and Theology, which was more than most early European missionaries to Africa had acquired.

Bishop Crowther's missionary endeavours in the Mission to the Niger territories from Sierra Leone were many sided: in language study and the early development of a literary culture in some of West Africa's important languages, in Bible translation, in his recognition of the importance of tone in a tonal language and in his increasing insight into the issues and approaches in inter-religious encounter in the African context. All this showed the wisdom and correctness of Henry Venn's confident expectation of 'an African Church led by Africans', a reality which Crowther seemed to embody in himself.[26] In the contemporaneous and comparable, though also different, story of the Basel Mission in the Gold Coast, as shown in earlier chapters, missionary Christianity had, by the 1860s and 1870s, produced a number of educated Christians with a clear self-consciousness as Africans and Christians, and who were keenly alive to their intellectual and missionary responsibilities to their societies. Some missionaries were justly exulting in the fruit of their work. Here a missionary Joseph Mader announces to Basel in his annual report of 1870: 'We must expect a new generation on the Gold Coast after 10 years: a nation called to freedom and independence, able to give political expression to this and gaining its aim in due course.'[27] Obviously the missionary effort had proved that Africans did 'possess the mental capacities to participate on equal terms in "civilisation", that is, the European discourse of life ... that given the same opportunities, Africans could do just as well as Europeans.'[28]

Into the Twentieth Century – Imperial Experience and Uncertain Missionary Fortunes in Africa

The imperial age was, however, soon to overtake the missionary expectation, and to cast its shadow on missionary attitudes to Africans. In the late nineteenth century, European thought about Africa altered significantly from the humanitarianism of the early 1800s onwards. What is more startling is the feeling which one gets, that as the twentieth century began, the missionary movement seemed to behave as though there had not been almost a century of missionary involvement in some parts of Africa. Perhaps, unconsciously, the missionary movement was entering a critical phase. Certainly by any reading of the accounts, the World Missionary Conference of 1910 seemed to proceed on the assumption that there had been no Samuel Ajayi Crowther. We have already noted that to understand Africa and Africa's religious traditions, the Conference turned to the theories of a writer who had never lived in Africa, while its own missionary correspondents in the field could, without any self-doubt, write that their experiences in the midst of Animism had not 'altered in any form or substance, their impression as to what constitutes the most important vital elements in the Christian Gospel'.[29] It was not entirely ruled out that 'the Christian faith itself may learn from even Animism', but in the view of Temple Gairdner 'surely this was the humblest of all possible teachers ... the least sublime of the five great creeds'.[30]

By the next international missionary conference in Jerusalem in 1928, the missionary concern was with 'non-Christian systems', and the 'humblest ... the least sublime of all the creeds' had given way to 'secular civilisation' on the list of issues which deserved special treatment. African questions would again be marginalised at the missionary conference in 1938, in Tambaram, India. It all seemed as if the missionary movement had learnt nothing from Africa, and that in the twentieth century the missionary task was to be, in the words of the title of an otherwise most sensitive book by J. H. Oldham and Miss B. D. Gibson,[31] 'the remaking of man in Africa'.

And yet, in the twentieth century it has been the missionary movement which has had to think again about its work. So far as Africa is concerned, the real watershed in the missionary consciousness was the 'Africa' international conference of September 1926 in Le Zoute, Belgium, chaired by Scotsman, Dr Donald Fraser, Secretary of the United Free Church of Scotland Foreign Mission Committee and former missionary in Nyasaland, now Malawi. Unlike Edinburgh 1910 which had had no African participant, Le Zoute 1926, though attended by Western missionaries in the majority, also included African churchmen representing their churches and mission communities.

More important still, the account of the conference, published as the *Christian Mission in Africa*,[32] under the editorship of Edwin Smith, gives every indication that the missionary movement was now reflecting on and learning from its African experience. On the question of the existence of any preparation for Christianity in the African religious past, Le Zoute struck a quite different note from Edinburgh, affirming that it was now recognised that 'Africans have been prepared by previous experience for the reception of the Gospel and that their experience contains elements of high religious value'.[33] In an important paper written specially for the conference and published in the special Africa number of the *International Review of*

Missions of that year, Dietrich Westermann give probably the first extensive positive treatment of what he called 'the Value of the African's Past', saying, among other things:

> Can a system of life by which a race has lived through many centuries be entirely worthless? Must it not contain elements of divine education and guidance that should not be destroyed but be brought to full evolution? May it not be a preparatory stage for fuller life?[34]

Of course, when in 1935 Dr Westermann gave his Duff Lectures, he sounded a much less sanguine note on the African's *religious* past. Yet it was Westermann who, at Le Zoute, raised for the mission boards and committees – and so for the missionary movement as a whole – probably the most searching question of all, which had ultimately to do with the European image of Africa. It was Westermann who, by raising the issue of the calibre of some of the missionary personnel being sent to Africa and their capacity for sustained impact, caused the Conference to declare that:

> Surely the day has gone when the best men could be picked out for India and China and the rest sent to Africa, as if any man or woman were good enough for Africa. The time for amateurs has passed – if it ever existed. Nothing is too good for Africa.[35]

The conference even passed resolutions on the subject, recommending to mission boards, committees and agencies that they 'provide full opportunity and time to African missionaries, by means of recognised courses at home or on the field, to study native languages, customs and religion, that they may make an effective approach to the African mind.'[36]

African Christianity as an African Story

Valuable and important as these declarations at Le Zoute were, they are not as central to the story of African Christianity in the twentieth century as they may sound. By the early decades of the century, the missionary movement had unleashed forces that would lead to a major Christian breakthrough on the continent, and yet one which Western missionaries on the whole did not see because they did not expect it. Furthermore, the foundations for the breakthrough had been laid, in fact, by some of these 'amateurs', men of 'humble background and modest attainments' who, as Walls has shown in a most illuminating study on the subject, 'would not have been considered for ordination at home' and yet who

> in order to reach the mission field, or in order to be more effective there, set themselves to intellectual effort and acquire learning and skills far beyond anything which would have been required of them in their ordinary run of life.[37]

Such a one was Robert Moffat (of Bechuanaland) who had been an Englishman's gardener in Cheshire, before he became 'one of God's gardeners' as Edwin Smith called him in his biography.[38] When Moffat experienced a spiritual awakening as a result of his association with Methodists, and subsequently felt the initial stirrings of a missionary vocation, his first thought was: 'I have never been to college; no missionary society will accept me.' Another was Johannes Christaller (of the Gold Coast), son of a tailor and a baker's daughter, who, on returning to his native Germany would not be awarded an honorary doctorate by the Theological Faculty of Tübingen because he had no university degree. Yet this is the missionary about whose work Noel Smith wrote:

> Christaller's work achieved three things: it raised the Twi language to a literary level and provided the basis of all later work in the language; it gave the first real insight into Akan religious, social and moral ideas; and it welded the expression of Akan Christian worship to the native tongue.[39]

Scotland did better for Moffat: Edinburgh University awarded him a Doctor of Divinity.

There is therefore a further sense in which the emergence of Christian Africa in the twentieth century was to be a surprise story of the modern missionary movement. By its deep and early vernacular achievement, that is relative to Europe's own missionary past, the modern missionary movement had actually ensured that Africans had the means to make their own responses to the Christian message, in terms of their own needs and categories of meaning. As early as the late nineteenth and early twentieth century, as a result of a variety of factors including frustration with European missionary paternalism and control, Africans had set about establishing what came to be called African independent churches (or African instituted churches, in some of the more recent literature). Many of the earlier investigations of this phenomenon tended to focus on their sociological and political causes; rarely were religious and properly Christian factors taken seriously into account. Only later did it become more widely acknowledged that the Christian Gospel in Africa had in fact 'had a liberating effect, setting man free, free from fear, fear of witches and the power of darkness, but above all conferring a freedom from an inner dependence on European tokens of grace or favour, to aim for higher things and a finer sensitivity'.[40] These are the words of one of the most able and most sensitive of the European interpreters of African Christianity, Swedish Bishop Bengt Sundkler, in his book *Zulu Zion and Some Swazi Zionists*. Part of the process which I am referring to as the eventual realisation of the surprise story of Christian Africa is reflected in the difference between his first pioneer study on the independent churches, *Bantu Prophets in South Africa*[41] and the later *Zulu Zion*. Having concluded in the earlier book that these 'syncretistic sects', as he called them, were 'the bridge over which Africans are brought back to heathenism', he later acknowledged a mistake in this interpretation. In 1976 he wrote: 'From the point of view of those involved, Zion was not turned to the past, but to the future, and was their future'. Anyone interested in following up this subject should study the two books *together*.

The careers of William Wade Harris, John Swatson, Sampson Oppong, Joseph Babalola, Garrick Braide in West Africa; of Joseph Kimbangu in Congo/Zaire; of Isaiah Shembe in Southern Africa and several other dynamic prophetic figures across the continent – none of whom was commissioned by a missionary society, yet whose ministries contributed significantly to the growth of the mission churches – all occurring in the same general period when the Le Zoute conference was lamenting missionary failures, is sufficient indication that the making of Christian Africa in the twentieth century has been 'to a surprising extent the result of African initiatives'.[42] It is interesting that at Le Zoute Harris was in fact mentioned as 'Africa's most successful evangelist', and there were those who wished that the prophet were present to talk 'about preaching to Africans'.[43]

Andrew Walls again noted in his St Colm lecture:

> There is something symbolic in the fact that the first church in
> tropical Africa in modern times was not a missionary creation
> at all. It arrived ready-made, a body of people of African birth
> or descent who had come to faith in Christ as plantation slaves
> or as soldiers in the British army during the American War of
> Independence, or as farmers or squatters in Nova Scotia after it.[44]

The first church in Sierra Leone arrived there in 1792, the year of
William Carey's *Enquiry into the Obligations of Christians to Use
Means for the Conversion of the Heathens*. Carey, for one, looked
forward to the emergence of theologians, 'great Christian thinkers,
nay, able divines' from among the 'heathens'. The general expectation was, however, that it was the non-Christian monotheists, then
the 'civilised pagans', in that order, who would lead the way. As far
as 'barbarous and uncivilised heathens' were concerned, it was presumed they had more ground to cover; it was never conceived that
heathen Africans would be among those who would make the most
significant response to the Gospel message. The recognition that the
forms of the religious life associated with 'barbarous and uncivilised
heathens' has in fact been the basic background of the majority of
Christians everywhere, including the Christians of Europe, throughout Christian history, lay in the future. Even mid-twentieth-century
books like the late Bishop Stephen Neill's *The Christian Society*,[45]
which attempts to set forth 'the Christian people as a society of men
and women existing in time and space, acting and reacting continually with its environment',[46] could have a chapter under the heading
'The Faith and the Great Religions', followed by one on 'The Gospel
and Primitive Peoples'. This realisation has indeed been recent.

Mission as the De-stigmatisation of all Human Cultures

In his epoch-making book, *Translating the Message – The Missionary Impact on Culture*, Lamin Sanneh has shown how the clue to
Christian mission consists in understanding that 'Christianity from
its origins ... resolved to relativise its Judaic roots ... and to
destigmatise Gentile culture ...'.[47] Had the modern missionary movement from the West been more alive to the dynamic potential of this

dual force of Christianity in its historical development, modern missionaries would have realised that their achievement was more significant than anything in Christianity's previous history of expansion, with the possible exception of the apostolic precedent itself. However, being deeply affected by their own cultural ethnocentrism, and expecting non-Western incarnations of the faith to become extensions of their own European Christianities, that result was not evident to them. It is only in recent years that it has become more widely recognised that

> of the two processes at work in Christianity, [namely] historical transmission and indigenous assimilation, ... the more significant ... without hesitation ... is the process of assimilation, for it is within that that the historical process itself becomes meaningful.[48]

The reception of the Christian message among the ill-rated Africans was consequently to be more far-reaching than the missionary movement had anticipated: it was to be a surprise story. One such surprise relates to the realisation that, contrary to the commonly-held view, the fortunes of modern Christian mission in Africa were relatively free from dependence on European political and imperial interests. As Godwin Tasie and Richard Gray state in their introductory survey to the symposium, *Christianity in Independent Africa*:

> although the alliance between Christian missionaries and European colonialism was intimate, it was never complete. The message and impact of the missions could in varying degrees be distinguished from the apparatus of alien rule.[49]

This, coupled with 'the fact that European missionaries were not the sole representatives of Christianity in Africa', ensured that the survival of the faith was much less tied to the vicissitudes of empire than was presumed. In this context, African 'political independence proved a relatively insignificant factor'.[50] Well before the dismantling of the European empires, in the so-called African independent churches, and also in the mission churches, through access to the Scriptures in African mother-tongues, African Christians were discarding such Western value-setting for the faith as there may have been, and were developing indigenous responses to the Christian

Gospel, claiming validity for them from the Scriptures. Not what Western missionaries did (or did not do), but what Africans did, and have done with the Gospel, is what has proved the more enduring element in the making of Christian Africa in the twentieth century.

In concluding his study, *West African Christianity – The Religious Impact*,[51] Lamin Sanneh felt able to suggest that African Christianity may well have entered upon a universal vocation in the onward march of the people of God in history, a destiny comparable to that of Gentile Christianity in the early Christian centuries. The indicators are that Sanneh's assessment was well founded.

In the early 1970s Andrew Walls published an article on the subject of the shift in the centre of gravity of Christianity. Its title was 'Towards understanding Africa's place in Christian history'.[52] That article was written several years before its publication at which time, by any reckoning, this watershed in the history of Christianity was yet to register in the regular textbooks. Since then the study of the problems and issues arising from the impact of the Christian faith in the various contexts of its transmission and reception in the world has grown apace. The validity of Bishop Newbigin's question referred to near the beginning of this chapter may be taken to indicate that the event has substantially registered. We are in a new world, a new *Christian* world, different, that is, from the world as perceived at Edinburgh in 1910. It is no longer possible to speak of 'fully missionised lands' as against 'not yet fully missionised lands' as was done then; yet it was because, for several decades to 1910, many saw the world in those terms and decided to do something about it that we have the new Christian world we now see, as we approach the threshold of the twenty-first century.

In a wide-ranging article published in 1991 in the *International Bulletin of Missionary Research*, Andrew Walls suggested that this 'global transformation of Christianity requires nothing less than the complete rethinking of the Church history syllabus'.[53] Let us hope that we do not have to wait till the end of the twenty-first century for the response to this new call from Edinburgh!

Notes and References

1. Dietrich Westermann, *Africa and Christianity* (The Duff Lectures, 1935), London: Oxford University Press, 1937, p. 94.
2. Ibid., p. 2.
3. K. Cragg, *Christianity in World Perspective*, London: Lutterworth Press, 1968, p. 57.
4. Lamin Sanneh, *West African Christianity – The Religious Impact*, London: C. Hurst, 1983, pp. 227–41.
5. See *World Missionary Conference 1910: Report of Commission IV – The Missionary Message in Relation to Non-Christian Religions*, Edinburgh and London: Oliphant, Anderson and Ferrier, 1901, p. 24.
6. E. B. Tylor, *Primitive Culture – Researches into the Development of Mythology, Philosophy, Religion, Art and Custom* (2 vols) (3rd edn revised), London: John Murray, 1891. (First published in 1871.)
7. W. H. T. Gairdner, *Edinburgh 1910 – An Account and Interpretation of the World Missionary Conference*, London: Oliphant, Anderson and Ferrier, 1910, p. 139.
8. Lesslie Newbigin, 'Can the West be converted?', *International Bulletin of Missionary Research*, vol. 11, no. 1, January 1987, pp. 2–7.
9. See article 'Religion', in *Encyclopedia Britannica* (3rd edn), vol. 16, Edinburgh, 1797, p. 77.
10. William Carey, *An Enquiry into the Obligations of Christians to Use Means for the Conversion of the Heathens* (reprinted from the edition of 1792), London: Hodder and Stoughton, 1891, p. 65.
11. Philip Curtin, *The Image of Africa – British Ideas and Actions, 1780–1850*, Madison: University of Wisconsin Press, 1964.
12. T. F. Buxton, *The African Slave Trade and its Remedy*, London: Frank Cass, 1840, p. 457.
13. John Beecham, *Ashantee and the Gold Coast, Being a Sketch of the History, Social State and Superstition of the Inhabitants of These Countries With a Notice of the State and Prospects of Christianity Among Them* (with introduction and notes by G. E. Metcalfe), London: Dawson's of Pall Mall, 1968, p. 339. (First published in 1841.)
14. See Alec R. Vidler, *The Church in an Age of Revolution: 1789 to the Present Day* (Pelican History of the Church, vol. 5), Harmondsworth: Penguin Books, 1977, p. 248.
15. William Carey, *An Enquiry into the Obligations of Christians*.
16. R. W. Weir, *Foreign Missions of the Church of Scotland*, p. 33, cited in William Paton, *Alexander Duff – Pioneer of Missionary Education*, London: Edinburgh House Press, 1923, p. 47.
17. See Jonathan Edwards, *Memoires of Rev. David Brainerd – Missionary to the Indians of North America*, New York and London: Fink and Wagnalls, 1885.
18. Constance Padwick, *Henry Martyn: Confessor of the Faith*, London, 1922, p. 56, cited in Clinton Bennett, 'The legacy of Henry Martyn', *International Bulletin of Missionary Research*, vol. 16, no. 1, January 1992, p. 11.
19. Padwick in Clinton Bennett, 'The legacy of Henry Martyn', p. 10.
20. M. Hennell, *John Venn and the Clapham Sect*, London: Lutterworth Press, 1958.
21. See Andrew F. Walls, 'The missionary vocation and the ministry – the first generation', in Mark Glasswell and Edward Fasholé-Luke (eds), *New Testament Christianity for Africa and the World*, London: SPCK, 1974, pp. 141–56.
22. Andrew F. Walls, 'The legacy of Samuel Adjai Crowther', *International Bulletin of Missionary Research*, vol. 16, no. 1, January 1992, pp. 15–22.

23. Jesse Page, *The Black Bishop, Samuel Ajayi Crowther*, London: Hodder and Stoughton, 1908, p. 71.
24. Andrew F. Walls, *The Significance of Christianity in Africa* (The St Colm Lecture, 1989), Edinburgh: The Church of Scotland, St Colm's Education Centre and College, 1989, p. 13. The story is also told of an English naval officer who met the bishop in the Niger Territory and was said to have been so impressed with him and his conduct 'with his simple, unaffected manner and his perfect pronunciation of English, that in speaking to him you could scarcely realise that you are speaking to a black man'. (Jesse Page, *The Black Bishop*, p. 250.)
25. Ibid., p. 38.
26. See Andrew F. Walls, 'The legacy of Samuel Ajayi Crowther', pp. 15–22.
27. Quoted in Hans Debrunner, *A History of Christianity in Ghana*, Accra: Waterville Publishing House, p. 163.
28. Andrew F. Walls, *The Significance of Christianity in Africa*, p. 13.
29. See *World Missionary Conference 1910*, p. 35.
30. Gairdner, *Edinburgh 1910*, p. 141.
31. J. H. Oldham and B. D. Gibson, *The Re-making of Man in Africa*, London: Edinburgh House Press, 1931.
32. E. W. Smith, *The Christian Message in Africa – A Study Based on the Work of the International Conference at Le Zoute, Belgium, September 14–21, 1926*, London: Edinburgh House Press, 1926.
33. Ibid., p. 46.
34. D. Westermann, 'The value of the African's past', *International Review of Missions*, vol. 15, 1926, pp. 427–8.
35. E. W. Smith, *The Christian Message in Africa*, p. 46.
36. Loc. cit.
37. Andrew F. Walls, 'The missionary vocation and the ministry', p. 153.
38. E. W. Smith, *Robert Moffat – One of God's Gardeners*, London: Edinburgh House Press, 1925.
39. Noel Smith, *History of the Presbyterian Church of Ghana 1835–1960*, Accra: Ghana Universities Press, 1965, p. 55.
40. Bengt Sundkler, *Zulu Zion and Some Swazi Zionists*, London: Oxford University Press, 1976, pp. 318–19.
41. Bengt Sundkler, *Bantu Prophets in South Africa*, London: Oxford University Press, 1948.
42. Andrew F. Walls, *The Significance of Christianity in Africa*, p. 5.
43. E. W. Smith, *The Christian Mission in Africa*, p. 42.
44. Andrew F. Walls, *The Significance of Christianity in Africa*, p. 5.
45. Stephen Neill, *The Christian Society*, London: Collins, 1952.
46. Ibid., p. 7.
47. Lamin Sanneh, *Translating the Message – The Missionary Impact on Culture*, New York: Orbis Books, 1989, p. 1.
48. Lamin Sanneh, 'The horizontal and the vertical in mission: An African perspective', *International Bulletin of Missionay Research*, vol. 7, no. 4, October 1983, p. 166.
49. G. Tasie and Richard Gray, 'Introduction' in Edward Fasholé-Luke et al. (eds), *Christianity in Independent Africa*, London: Rex Collings, 1978, p. 3.
50. Ibid., p. 4.
51. Lamin Sanneh, *West African Christianity – The Religious Impact*, pp. 250–1.
52. Andrew F. Walls, 'Towards understanding Africa's place in Christian history', in J. S. Pobee (ed.), *Religion in a Pluralistic Society*, Leiden: E. J. Brill, 1976, pp. 180–9.
53. Andrew F. Walls, 'Structural problems in Mission Studies', *International Bulletin of Missionary Research*, vol. 15, no. 4, October 1991, p. 146.

12

Christian Religion and the African World-view

Will Ancestors Survive?

The African World-view and its Potential for Christian Experience and Theology

Beginning from the basic apprehension of the universe as a unified cosmic, essentially spiritual, system, we have been able to show elsewhere in this book that the primal imagination could help us avoid destructive dichotomies in epistemology and so offer guidance towards an organic view of the knowledge of truth – increasingly felt to be desirable in Christian theology. In this chapter one aspect of the African primal world-view, the place and significance of ancestors, will be used as a focus for a further discussion of some of the theological issues which emerge in the encounter of the Christian faith with primal religious traditions.

My own interest in the subject goes back several years to my reading of Geoffrey Parrinder's *West African Religion*.[1] Geoffrey Parrinder was probably the first Western interpreter of African primal religions to recognise that 'in many West African languages, convenient categories exist for the consideration of the religion' concerned.[2] In that recognition and in his use of the discovery, Parrinder was establishing a most important principle that was applicable not only to the story of Africa's 'old' religions, but even more to the continent's 'new' faiths: the principle of interpreting a religion through the language in which the faith is experienced and expressed. The relevance of the principle, especially to the interpretation of African Christianity, in view of its Western missionary inheritance, was, to me, beyond doubt.

Equally significant for me was a statement in Edwin Smith's 'Foreword' to Parrinder's book in which Smith anticipated a sequel to Parrinder's work. Smith's comment raises so many interesting issues that he should be quoted at some length:

> I hope that some day Dr. Parrinder, or someone equally competent, will follow up this study of the pagan religion with a study of the actual religion of those Africans who in various degrees of reality have accepted Christianity. It is not to be expected that they have made, or can make, a complete break with the past, however much they profess to do so. What in Christianity most attracted these polytheists and how precisely did they react to it? Do preachers and teachers deliberately set themselves to relate the new religion to the old? The Church has adopted African names for translating 'God'; but how far is the popular theology coloured by the old beliefs? Aggrey we know, always thought of God as Father–Mother, or rather Mother–Father; and I doubt not this sense of the motherhood of God lingered on from his early training in a pagan family. Christianity may thus be enriched from pagan sources. On the other hand, it may be debased when the lower elements of paganism are perpetuated. West African polytheism will follow European polytheism into oblivion. One could wish that some at least of its best features were sublimated: on the credal side by recognition in daily life of ubiquitous spiritual forces working in the universe; on the practical side by the transference to the new religion on a higher level of something of the symbolism, the colour, the artistry, the gaiety that marked the old ...[3]

Even though Edwin Smith's evolutionary orientation kept intruding, threatening to distort what he wished to convey, his observations nonetheless point us in the direction of some very important developments to follow. It even seemed as if 'pagan' Africa, through Dr Aggrey, could make some contribution to feminist theology of modern times!

What is of particular interest is Edwin Smith's intuition that 'the actual religion' of African Christians would retain the spiritual experience of multiplicity, incorporating 'recognition in daily life of ubiquitous spiritual forces working in the universe'. The only problem I have with Edwin Smith's observation is the impression he seems to give that such an experience of spiritual plurality in the 'actual religion of those who could not be expected to have made or to make, a complete break with the past', would be less than full Christian experience. The thesis of this chapter is that the place and significance of ancestors in the African primal world-view actually offers opportunities for 'filling out' some dimensions of spiritual experience and historical consciousness which are inherent in the Christian religion.

Dynamic and 'Sifting' in African Religious History

Conceivably, it might be objected that by isolating ancestors for particular treatment in this way would be to 'atomise' the primal world-view which presents itself, after all, as 'a unified cosmic system'; to remove one element would be to break up and so destroy the harmony of the whole. This is an important objection. Yet it would stand only if one were to ignore what has actually happened in the process of religious change in Africa. Historical studies of African primal religions have shown that these religions, far from being 'passive traditional cosmologies', have, in fact, been dynamic institutions, able to adapt and respond to new situations and human needs in society. Indeed, African primal religions have been shown to have 'founders and proselytisers and converts and prophets ...' and it even becomes possible to explore a 'salvation-history' within them.[4]

This quality of an inner dynamic in the religious histories of Africa's primal religions also explains the following statement by K. A. Busia, regarding the Ashanti of Ghana and their religion:

> The gods are treated with respect if they deliver the goods, and with contempt if they fail; it is the Supreme Being (that is GOD) and the ancestors that are always treated with reverence and awe, a fact which an onlooker who has seen Ashanti chiefs and elders making offerings or pouring libations to the ancestors can hardly fail to observe. The Ashanti, like other Akans, esteem the Supreme Being and the ancestors far above gods and amulets. Attitudes to the latter depend upon their success, and vary from healthy respect to sneering contempt.[5]

This statement of Busia's is important. While Parrinder's fourfold classification of categories within West African religions, namely Supreme God, divinities or gods, ancestors and charms or amulets, was a helpful and workable one, within the religions themselves African believers have generally been quite clear in their minds as to who is God and who are *not* gods, as any speaker of an African language well knows. Parrinder recognised this when he noted that this classification 'represents a distinction in the African mind, as shown by the separate terms' used.[6] It was through his study of the language of the Akans that Johannes Christaller came to the conclusion that a people who were presumed polytheists were 'to a great extent rather monotheists, as they apply the term for *God* only to one supreme being'.[7] In Patrick Ryan's important article on the distinction of 'God' from 'gods' in West African religions[8] – of Yorubas and Akans – Ryan concluded that 'the Yorubas and Akans are better equipped linguistically than are Semites, Greeks, Romans and their inheritors to express the absolute uniqueness of God', and that they had this capacity 'before Muslims and Christians arrived in the West Africa forest zone'.[9] *Olorun* is God (Yoruba), so is *Onyame* (Akan); *orisa* and *abosom* are *not* gods. Furthermore, *orisa* and *abosom* are disposable; but not *Olorun* or *Onyame*, not God ... nor, as it turns out ... ancestors.

Christian Conversion in Africa: New Perspectives and Questions

This leads us to look afresh at African Christian conversion. The seeming ease with which the God of the African religious past has found access through African Christian Scriptures into African Christian consciousness becomes a significant factor. In contra-distinction to the earlier missionary history of Europe, in Africa there was not the likelihood of the true God doing battle with a false God. The God of the Africans has turned out, after all, to be the God of Israel whom the Christians worship. This may appear to labour a point which might be considered self-evident. For are not the Scriptures quite explicit on the matter? 'Is God the God of the Jews only? Is he not also the God of the Gentiles? Of course he is the God of the Gentiles also, for God is one.'[10]

Yet the testimony of the Scriptures did not convince some early missionaries from Europe that God was in Africa before them. The clue to the problem lies in the fact that the truth of the apostolic declaration is not of the nature of a dogmatic assertion, a theological *datum*; rather it is of the nature of a truth of recognition, given and received in the process of the transmission of the Gospel. It is by reading the New Testament books as documents of cross-cultural and inter-religious missionary encounter, which they are as Bishop Kenneth Cragg has shown, that we realise this quality of the Scriptural affirmations.[11] In other words, the very process of the cross-cultural transmission of the Gospel can also be revelatory.

In the African field, then, the evidence makes one wish to ask new questions, not only about the nature of African primal religions themselves and their undergirding world-view but also fresh questions regarding the character of Christian conversion within the African world-view. John Mbiti has commented that 'the man of Africa' in meeting with the Christian Gospel, 'will not have very far to go before he begins to walk on familiar ground'.[12] Is it the case that in African Christian conversion, it is as much a question of what the convert sheds from the primal spiritual universe, as of what is taken on board in order to repair the torn fabric of the primal harmony? Dutch theologian Anton Wessels has commented on this African evidence, observing:

> In addition to the two great world religions, Christianity and Islam, Africa also knows of African religion, rather religions. Although African religion(s) [sic] also have their own adherents, it remains important to observe that this peculiar African religiousness has attached itself to Christianity and Islam, so that it may even be asked which has had the greater influence on which.[13]

Wessels then recalls the view of Lamin Sanneh that in the African forms of both Christianity and Islam, it is African primal religions which have, in · large measure, influenced the 'shape of both religions'.[14] It becomes possible therefore to apply Lucy Quimby's methodological principles for the treatment of African religious traditions to the particular phenomenon of African Christian conversion, in that the evidence compels the scholar to 'shift his focus from [the] religion as an abstract ideal to [the] religion as a particular African society defines and practises it ... to look at religion as a composite of a variety of forms of religious behaviour and beliefs, as believed and acted out by a variety of individuals within the society being studied'.[15] From this perspective, one can appreciate even more fully the observation by Andrew Walls made in an article published in 1980:

> The recognition that religions are not unitary mutually exclusive entities which replace each other in the process of religious change, but that a person's or a community's religious experience has to be taken in itself and within its own social setting, was perhaps more readily learnt in Africa than elsewhere.[16]

The African primal world can now be looked at in a completely new light: from the standpoint of a dynamic African religious history. If it is West Africa which, in the words of the well-known Yoruba scholar on African primal religions, Bolaji Idowu, 'may be said to be the home of divinities',[17] what happens to the West African divinities may be taken as significant for the disposability of gods (or divinities) across Africa. Idowu's own interpretation of Yoruba religion is a useful indicator of this phenomenon. He acknowledges that in Yoruba religion 'divinities so predominate the scene that it is difficult for the casual observer to notice that under them there is one vital cultic basis'.[18] In his interpretation of this practice, he in fact continues the process of 'sifting' which has always been present in African religious tradition. For Idowu, the Yoruba divinities are in reality manifestations of the Supreme God, 'His ministers, acting as intermediaries between Him and the world of men'.[19] They have no absolute existence, and are disposable. 'A people's idea of God can undergo modification by way of enrichment and correction',[20] and 'to those who have outgrown them [the divinities] all reality is concentrated in the Deity'.[21] The significance of Christianity for Yoruba religion is that it has 'helped to emphasise the belief of the Yoruba in the Supreme God'.[22] Most other African writers on the subject, whose backgrounds are generally less encumbered with divinities, but who, like Idowu, are Christian writers with a predominantly theological interest, have come to similar conclusions, all arguing for an essentially theistic and unitary character of African pre-Christian religion.[23]

When divinities leave the scene, they do not, however, take ancestors with them. Furthermore, African theology has, so far, not seriously suggested that ancestors may be quite as disposable as are divinities. One African theologian has even remarked that 'to take the ancestors from an African is robbing him of his personality'.[24] The notable exception, of course, has been the theological viewpoint championed by Byang Kato.[25] Kato, however, drew his conclusions on the basis of his belief that the entirety of the African heritage in religion and the Christian faith constituted two quite distinct and discontinuous entities, with little or no common ground between them. As I have sought to show elsewhere,[26] Kato, in that sense, laboured under a misconception.

The fact is, unlike divinities – generally non-human spirits, and often associated with natural forces – ancestors are the human, if somewhat 'apotheosised' spirits of a person's or community's elders and so are not quite so easily susceptible to demonisation in the Christian consciousness. In one early African treatment of the subject, a Roman Catholic churchman, Mgr S. N. Ezeanya (of Nigeria), wrote:

> Belief in Angels replaces belief in minor divinities without much difficulty. Ancestral cult prepares the ground for the doctrine of the Communion of Saints. The strong attachment to ancestors makes it easy to promote both devotion to the saints and prayers for the departed.[27]

Clearly the responses to 'minor divinities' and to 'ancestors' are different, and Mgr Ezeanya's approach on ancestors indicated the general direction which later discussion was to take. Simply put, ancestors represent a more enduring reality in the African world-view than do divinities, other non-human spirits, amulets and charms. In the very graphic way in which Christian Baëta of Ghana stated it, Africans 'live with their dead'.[28] It becomes essential, therefore, that there should be a Christian theology of ancestors.

A Fresh Look at Ancestors in African Tradition

The discussion of the place of ancestors in the African world-view in relation to Christian discipleship has tended to be stumped over the question as to whether Africans 'worship' their ancestors or 'venerate' them.[29] When the problem is approached from this angle, then ancestors are cast in the role of rivals of Christ.

There is, it is true, an obvious Christological dimension to any consideration of the place of ancestors in the spiritual universe of Christian consciousness. When Jesus Christ appears in the world of distributed power, which I consider the universe of the African primal world to be,[30] some important changes are bound to occur. He comes into a world where he has not been named previously. As John Mbiti has put it: 'The Gospel enabled [African] people to utter the name of Jesus Christ ... that final and completing element that crowns their traditional religiosity and brings its flickering light to full brilliance.'[31] For Mbiti, 'without him [Jesus Christ] the meaning of our [African] religiosity is incomplete'.[32] Mbiti's clear affirmation of the ultimate and irreplaceable significance of Jesus Christ for African religious tradition is one with which I fully concur. I myself have argued elsewhere that 'once Jesus Christ comes, the ancestors are cut off as means of blessing and we lay our power-lines differently'. Unlike the 'old' African primal universe in which spiritual power is broadly refracted, so that human religious response and activity must be directed to a variety of centres of influence, ranging between God, divinities and ancestors, from the standpoint of the Gospel, God's saving activity towards us is focused on Christ, mediated through the Holy Spirit.[33] That argument is, however, Christological, and like other recent explorations into an Ancestor-Christology in African theology,[34] it is meant to show that Christ, by virtue of his Incarnation, death, resurrection and ascension into the realm of spirit-power, can rightly be designated, in African terms, as Ancestor, indeed Supreme Ancestor.

Christology is not, however, the burden of this chapter. It is ancestors in themselves, as our 'natural' ancestors, so to speak, and not as possible rivals of Christ, who interest us. One of the values of an Ancestor-Christology is precisely that it helps to clarify the place and significance of 'natural' ancestors. By making room among the 'living-dead' for the Lord, the judge of both the living and the dead, it becomes more evident how they relate to Him, and He to them. Because ancestors, even in their realm of spirit existence, remain in African understanding essentially human just like ourselves, they

cannot therefore ultimately be rivals of Christ in Christian consciousness. Just as there exists a clear distinction between God and
divinities, so also there exists a qualitative distinction between Christ
as Ancestor and natural ancestors.

One suspects that one reason for the debate over whether
Africans 'worship' their ancestors or 'venerate' them is a failure to
realise that African ancestors, strictly speaking, do not become after
death what they were not before death. In his very penetrating
analysis of 'Ancestor worship in Africa' (as he called it),[35]
anthropologist Meyer Fortes has served us well in this connection.
Observing that African ancestor cults have 'a remarkably uniform
structural framework',[36] Fortes stresses that not only are they 'not
co-terminous with the worship of the dead',[37] but also that they do
not have the metaphysical implications of the Western notions of the
immortality of the soul. The Western notions in this regard assume 'a
kind of law of the conservation of entities in a total universe made up
of two complementary regimes, a regime of nature and a regime of
deity. By this reckoning, souls are indestructible essences that
animate bodies and succeed them in the timeless realm of God,
pending resurrection in a corporeal form'.[38] The African concepts of
personality on the other hand, not based on such sharp dichotomies
between the realm of the secular and the sacred – the 'regime of
nature' and the 'regime of deity' in Fortes's terminology – 'refer to
activities, relationships and experiences that are deemed to fall
wholly within the regime of nature'.[39] Then, relating his discussion to
funeral rites, Fortes wrote, with deep insight:

> So mortuary ceremonies, though couched in language and rites
> that appear to personify the dead, are in fact not directed
> towards consigning them to, and equipping them for spiritual
> existence in a supernatural realm, but towards discorporating
> them from the social structure. At the personal level this
> resolves the dislocation and assuages the grief of bereavement.
> But death and mortuary rites, though they must precede, do
> not confer ancestorhood. Specific rites are needed for that. The
> dead has first to be 'brought back home again', re-established
> in the family and lineage, by obsequial rites, and will even then
> not receive proper ritual service until he manifests himself in
> the life of his descendants and is enshrined.[40]

For by being 'brought back home again' and re-established, an ancestor's 're-instatement ... establishes his *continued relevance* for his society, not as a ghost, but as a regulative focus for the social relations and activities that persist as the deposit, so to speak, of his life and career.[41] It follows therefore that:

> An ancestral 'spirit' is not thought of as a kind of nebulous being or personified mystical presence but primarily as a *name* attached to a relic, the stool, standing for ritual validation of lineage ancestry and for mystical intervention in human affairs.[42]

In this last observation Fortes was basing his conclusion primarily on Ashanti ideas and practices, but I have found striking confirmation of Fortes's main thesis in the contemporary thought and practice of the Akuapem Traditional State in south-eastern Ghana. I take particular interest in the subject, since it falls within the range of matters concerning applied theology which occupy the Akrofi-Christaller Memorial Centre in the Akuapem royal capital, Akropong. Of all Akan ritual acts dealing with ancestors, there is none which gives as deep an insight into how ancestors are perceived as the act of libation, the pouring down of liquid substance to the accompaniment of an appropriate form of words. The following evidence is important because it is provided by the current traditional King (Omanhene) of Akuapem, Nana Addo Dankwa III.[43]

On the controversial question of 'ancestral worship' Nana Addo Dankwa expresses his view quite forcefully:

> The Akans regard the ancestors still as heads and parts of the families or communities to which they belonged while they were living human beings ... . Since Akans are not supposed to worship anybody within the living community, it follows that the ancestors, being part and parcel of the living community, also cannot be worshipped.[44]

But if neither ancestors themselves nor their relics (in the case of royal ancestors, their stools or thrones), are worshipped as divinities, it is in the act of libation that their true significance is understood. The act of libation is commonly held to be a purely religious act, virtually the traditional equivalent of Christian prayer. Nana Addo

Dankwa disagrees: 'Libation, originally, was never intended to be a completely religious act. Libation ... consists of three separate acts, the first two being purely cultural acts, and the last one being a religious act.'[45] The three separate acts of libation are as follows. First, an act of:

> invitation to the ancestor to enable the ancestor to feel free to actively participate in whatever activity that the living are engaged in or [are] about to commence at the time that the invitation is issued.[46]

Second,

> When the ancestor is presumed to have responded to the invitation, the living [community] issuing the invitation or the person pouring libation gives a welcome address during which the purpose of the invitation is explained. From that point onwards, the ancestor is presumed to have joined the living in taking part in whatever activity that is about to take place.[48]

The point of the welcome address is that since 'ancestors are considered as the heads, both of the living and the dead within the community ... the fatherly address of welcome and greetings as is normally made to the living head of family, is also extended to the ancestral head'.[48]

According to Nana Addo Dankwa, it is these 'customary preliminaries' that 'are at times mistakenly considered as prayers to the ancestors' and he recalls J. H. Driberg's view that 'what we mistake for religious attitude is nothing more than a projection of the African social behaviour ... For no African prays to his late grandfather any more than he prays to his living father'.[49] It is only after these 'purely cultural acts' of invitation, welcome and information have been completed that the third act, the properly 'religious act' of prayer is performed:

> When the roll has been called, that is, when the ancestor has been welcomed and everybody is present and all is set, prayers are made to introduce the particular act for which invitation has been issued.[50]

Nana Addo Dankwa then comments:

It means therefore that the ancestor, who at that moment, has joined the living, also takes part in offering prayers. Under the circumstances, therefore, it is not correct to say that the prayers are made to the ancestor and that the ancestor has been deified.[51]

To illustrate this interpretation of the libation acts, Nana Addo Dankwa gives a sample text to accompany the act of libation appropriate to the occasion of the 'outdooring' of a new-born baby:

Here is water, our revered ancestor; we have invited you this morning to come and help us in outdooring your own grandson. As you know, we cannot undertake such an important customary rite without your participation; you are therefore welcome to assume your role as Abusua Panyin (head of family) to supervise this rite. O Busuburu, on behalf of our ancestor, I am calling you as the clan god to bless this family; we ask for long life and prosperity. We commit this child, about to be named, to your care; give him long life and let him be a good man to the glory of his family. Long life for all the members of the family; blessing to our ancestor(s).

Since, on this interpretation of the acts of libation, the prayer is strictly addressed to 'the deities, Obosom or divinity, Suman or non-personal spiritual force, or the Supreme God, depending upon which one the person offering the prayer subscribes to', Nana Addo Dankwa also felt able to add: 'If therefore the family concerned are Christians, instead of Busumburu, Christ's name could be used.'[52]

Not everybody will agree, and Nana Addo Dankwa himself would not claim to be speaking for all Africa. So insistent is he that ancestors are never worshipped, that he even disagrees with the designation of Ancestor as a Christological title. Reacting to J. B. Danquah's portrayal of God as the great ancestor in his *Akan Doctrine of God*, Nana Addo Dankwa states:

God and Christ are not ancestors in the sense that we Akans consider our forefathers. The Akan will consider any entity as an ancestor only in the situation where the entity concerned during the 1st degree of existence had all the human qualities of the Akan; and interacted with others in the normal way before passing on to the 2nd degree of existence as a mortal being. God has never stayed physically in this world even though he is said to be omnipresent and yet he cannot be considered to be part of the living community. He is our creator. Christ, even though he stayed physically with us, the difference is that his body never saw corruption in the grave. So unlike an ancestor, his spirit is not part of the living community in the sense that we consider our ancestors whose bodies saw corruption in graves. The spirit of Christ which is part of the Trinity cannot be considered as an ancestor.[53]

Nana Addo Dankwa's views on libation and the ancestors will be debated for a long time, not least because his treatment of the subject illustrates the character of an inner dynamic as well as the process of 'sifting' which are features of African religious traditions. For instance, his insistence that in what he calls the 'original cultural libation', the first act was an *invitation* to a departed elder of the community and not an *invocation* of a supernatural being, finds some support in the common practice of not obstructing the main entrance into where libation is being poured, whilst the official himself faces the open doorway. Furthermore, his view that 'the use of alcoholic drinks for libation is of recent origin' is important.[54] The frequent use made of Schnapps, an imported alcoholic beverage (usually from Holland, though it is now also manufactured locally), poses the question as to how truly indigenous the present common practice really is.

While it would be considered the utmost discourtesy to offer drink to living elders by setting it on the ground in their presence, the suggestion that one could in fact give drink to revered ancestors by pouring it on the ground raises very grave questions. The symbolism itself is hard to take. This difficulty with symbolism of drink 'on the ground' goes to support Nana Addo Dankwa's contention that the liquid substance poured on the ground was meant to be water, to wash, symbolically, the dust-covered feet of the invited ancestor. This suggestion must be right if the original liquid substance for libation was, in fact, water, specifically rain water, called in Akan *nyankosu* or *adukrosu* because it collects 'in the hollow of a tree or stone'.[55] For Nana Addo Dankwa then, the mistaken view that libation is 'a completely religious act' within the terms of traditional religious ritual has come about because traditional priests of the old religion and other devotees of the old divinities – the customary depositories of the language of libation – have modified the original cultural libation to suit themselves![56] Here are all the elements for a battle royal over who is preserving and who is distorting the traditions!

Nana Addo Dankwa's views on libation and ancestors do, however, reveal that there is more than one strand running through the particular African tradition he is examining; there is that which is idolatrous and leads to a distortion of truth, and there is that which is enlightened and leads to a sharpening of focus on the truth. In relation to Christianity, there is more than one strand in every pre-Christian tradition; there is that which leads away from Christ and there is that which leads towards Christ, and can be made to serve Christian purposes.

If Nana Addo Dankwa's views raise critical questions for our understanding of the African primal world-view, his opinion also opens fresh avenues for African Christian reflection in particular. In reinforcing Meyer Fortes's main thesis that an ancestor's significance consists in his 'continued relevance for his society, not as a ghost, but as a regulative focus for the social relations and activities that persist ... as a deposit of his life and career',[57] Nana Addo Dankwa also helps us to realise that a Christian theology of ancestors in relation to the Christian community is unavoidable.

Towards a Theology of Ancestors

It has long been realised that an area of Christian affirmation to which African ideas on ancestors could make a significant contribution is the doctrine of the Communion of Saints.[58] E. Fasholé-Luke's article, 'Ancestor veneration and the communion of saints',[59] has the merit of being not just a call for the effort, but an actual attempt at doing so. Beginning with a reference to William Robertson Smith's statement that 'no positive religion that has moved man has been able to start with a *tabula rasa* – as if religion were beginning for the first time'[60] – Fasholé-Luke felt that the incorporation 'into Christian faith and practice' of ideas derived from African ancestral cults was needed in African Christianity. African ancestral cults are 'expressions of the family and tribal solidarity and continuity' and what was needed was 'a theology of the communion of saints that will satisfy the passionate desire of Africans, Christians and non-Christians alike, to be linked with their dead ancestors'.[61] Regarding the vexed question whether Africans 'worship' their ancestors or 'venerate' them, he preferred 'veneration', since African worshippers 'make a distinction between the worship they offer the Supreme Being [God] and the "worship" they offer the ancestors'.[62] While this is an important distinction to make, as we have already seen, by retaining the discussion within the terms of 'qualitative levels of worship', Fasholé-Luke does not get us out of the initial difficulty.

Furthermore, while he rightly identifies the doctrine of the Communion of Saints as a useful 'framework for incorporating African ideas about ancestors into Christian theology',[63] yet his interpretation of the phrase 'communion of saints' to mean 'fellowship with holy people of all ages and the whole company of heaven through participation in the holy sacraments',[64] in the end becomes limiting. He has, necessarily, to draw in notions like receiving the sacraments on behalf of the dead, prayers for the dead, and pleading for the salvation of the dead. These ideas, though interesting, do not lead us to the fundamental questions that need attention.

Perhaps the real problem was to have started with the doctrine of the Communion of Saints as a theological *datum*, a sort of fixed grid of Christian answers into which the African ideas must somehow be made to slot. The fact is, the general meaning given to the phrase in use in the Church does not take account of the questions which the presence of African ideas about ancestors raises for the Christian consciousness.[65] The real task of a theology of ancestors is not about the fate of the departed who were not Christians, or who were not sacramentally linked with the Church; a theology of ancestors is not made necessary because 'many African Christians have ancestors who were not Christians' as Fasholé-Luke wrote.[66] Admittedly these are important considerations, but they cannot be treated as though the saving activity of God were absent in the times prior to the historic proclamation and reception of the Gospel. Rather, a theology of ancestors is about the interpretation of the past in a way which shows that the present experience and knowledge of the grace of God in the Gospel of Jesus Christ have been truly anticipated and prefigured in the quests and the responses to the Transcendent in former times, as these have been reflected in the lives of African people.

A theology of ancestors becomes, therefore, the corollary and unavoidable by-product of the continuity of God in African experience, which was so robustly argued in an earlier phase of African theology. If the God of African pre-Christian tradition has turned out to be the God of the Christians, then it is to be expected that He has not left Himself without testimony in the past.[67] This testimony is not to be confined to those whom the old tradition designated as its ancestors, since the Gospel, itself a 'historical category' in the tradition, introduces new criteria for interpreting the tradition itself. The past can be examined for its anticipations of the present, thus some who would not have been considered ancestors emerge as striking confirmation that the divine initiative had, in fact, been at work in the past. Korankye, a nineteenth-century chief of Fomena in Ashanti, who suffered a cruel death for being a dissenter on the subject of human sacrifice, must be numbered among the ancestors of Ashanti Christianity. He was to have been the bridgehead for Freeman's mission into Ashanti. The countless incidents in African missionary histories of prophecies which were given within the pre-Christian religion, pointing to a Christian future of Africa, assume a new importance and show that in the African context too, God did speak 'to our forefathers through the prophets at many times and in various ways'.[68] It is rather ironic that an African Christian writer like Byang Kato whose theological viewpoint did not predispose him to recognise such positive elements in his pre-Christian background, had to acknowledge that such an event had in fact occurred among the Jaba people of Nigeria. He recounts the story of a prophetess who through spirit-mediumship 'predicted several years earlier that some white people would come to Kagoro and tell them about Gwaza, the Supreme Being'. Kato admitted that 'this prediction was fulfilled' in a vigorous missionary activity which produced a sizeable Christian population in the area; and yet he did not attach any theological value to it.[69] Similar and comparable stories are found in the local Christian histories of many African communities. It is therefore in the light of the experience of the Gospel as an African reality that their true theological significance is made manifest.

I do not wish to give the impression that I consider cross-cultural transmission of the Gospel through missionaries as ceasing to have any value in view of an African theology of ancestors. On the contrary, as is shown by the Jaba story from Nigeria, the missionary dimension of the local Christian history has its specific value, but within a religious history which truly belongs to the African tradition. The cross-cultural transmission came as a catalyst in a process which had preceded it, while the cross-cultural transmission also needed the local context and response to validate it. In missiological terms, this is another way of saying that the cross-cultural transmission did not *bring* Christ into the local African situation. If that were to be the case, then, in African terms, Christ would be a disposable divinity, actually able to be taken, carried and brought ... and presumably also, disposed of if not needed. The deeper insight is, however, that Christ, already present in the situation, called in His messengers so that by proclamation and incarnation, He might be made manifest. The cross-cultural transmission is thus a confirmation of the divine initiative in the local situation, extending its ramifications beyond the range of former horizons, and demonstrating the ecumenical significance of local history. Local history is drawn into the unfolding of the history of the people of God. Local ancestors who prepared the way for the coming of the Gospel emerge as fellow witnesses in 'the multitude that no one could count ...'.[70] A doctrine of the Communion of Saints, in this sense of the cloud of witnesses, therefore becomes the outcome of a theology of ancestors. In the words of Erasmus, cited by Nathan Söderblom in his 1931 Gifford Lectures, *The Living God – Basal Forms of Personal Religion*: 'It may be that the Spirit of Christ goes farther and wider than we think. And there are many in the fellowship of the Saints, who are not in our catalogue.'[71] This leads to my next observation, that an African theology of ancestors cannot be taken to mean that African Christianity has no further need of the Old Testament. On the contrary, it is the Old Testament that validates such a theology of ancestors. For, by presenting us with the history of God's dealings in the lives of His people whose faith was not perfect, the Old Testament itself offers a paradigm by which to understand the similar journeying in our own past. This relevance of the Old Testament has nothing to do with the oft-recalled cultural affinity between the Old Testament range of ideas and world picture and African life and thought.[72]

The relevance of the Old Testament for understanding the place of ancestors stems instead from the fundamental theological affirmation that in Christ, and through faith-union with Christ in the Gospel, we become 'the seed of Abraham and heirs according to the promise', that is, the promise of Abraham[73] and therefore 'heirs together with Israel, members together of one body'.[74] In Christ, then, we receive 'an adoptive past' through our 'Abrahamic link', thus connecting our past with the entire past of the people of God.[75] Thus, the African participation in the Gospel establishes the relevance of the Old Testament to African tradition and opens the way for an African appropriation of the whole Scriptures.

It is, however, important to understand the basis of this African appropriation of the Scriptures. Since the Gospel, in the words of Bishop Kenneth Cragg, 'has to do with men as men, their sins and their fears, and not with Jews as Jews, or Greeks as Greeks' and therefore 'cannot be racially received or culturally confined',[76] Africans appropriate the Scriptures not as Africans, but as human beings. At the same time, it is important to observe that this appropriation of the Scriptures in African Christianity is predominantly through the medium of African languages, enabling each one to hear in his or her own language the Word about the wonderful things which God has done, and therefore sending reverberations and resonances into the African world in ways which only mother-tongues can do.

Thus the Scriptures become *our* story, illuminating our past, reflecting the triumphs of our dependence on God, as well as our failures in disobedience and idolatry. We come to *participate* in the meaning of the scriptural events, as anyone who shares in African Christian worship services knows. The world-view and the religious idiom of the Scriptures themselves, with their ever-renewed stress that the lives and careers of the 'ancestors' – Adam, Eve, Noah, Enoch, Abraham, Isaac, Jacob, Moses, David – have a relevance for every succeeding generation, assuring us that they have something to do with us too. So we too must have had our fathers and mothers, ancestors who like the Biblical ancestors, at critical points in their lives and careers, made choices which went into shaping the destinies of our traditions till in the fullness of time our histories became merged, in Christ, with the history of the people of God.

It is such an appropriation of Scriptures, rooted in a positive theology of ancestors, which enables us to read the Gospel as having something to do with us in the present. The relevance of the Scriptures as the interpreter of the past, therefore, establishes their validity for the present. A theology of ancestors connects with an Ancestor-Christology in which Christ features as Lord among the ancestors too. In this way, the continued significance of ancestors within the life of African Christianity comes to pass through the prism of Christology, revealing in the process, the many-sided manner in which the ancestors have been part of the story of the making of Christian Africa.

Conceivably it could happen, as John V. Taylor wrote nearly thirty years ago, with great insight and deep African sympathy, that: 'when the gaze of the living and the dead is focused on Christ Himself, they have less compulsive need of one another'. However, Taylor felt able also to add: 'But need is not the only basis of fellowship; and Christ as the second Adam enhances rather than diminishes the intercourse of the whole community from which he can never be separated'.[77] In the local Presbyterian Church, called Christ Church, in Akropong in south-east Ghana, a number of seats are reserved for the traditional ruler and his court. On the wall above their seats is a plaque with the following inscription, in Twi, which, in translation, reads:

> To the glory of God, with this plaque we honour our kings, Nana Addo Dankwa I, during whose reign the Gospel was preached and gained a footing in Akuapem, Nana Addo Dankwa II, during whose reign the Presbyterian Church of Ghana attained its centenary; Nana Addo Dankwa III, during whose reign the Presbyterian Church in Akropong attained 150 years.

It is quite possible that an observer might read these words as little more than a piece of dynastic propaganda to bolster the name of the particular ruling house mentioned and yet, the events associated with these rulers, taken together, have massive symbolic significance. The official court history of Akuapem asserts, rightly, that it was the rulers who first welcomed Christianity to the realm. Such a claim, made today, means the ancestors and yet none was a communicant! The plaque in church proclaims that affirmation, even though it is a church which still refuses to grant the king the full privileges of church membership. It is hard to see how the king could come into full church membership without his royal ancestors. Were not they the ones who welcomed and provided for the establishment of Christianity in the first place? And is the king not after all the one 'who sits on the stool of the ancestors'? The dilemma which these questions pose for all concerned is probably the measure of the importance of a Christian theology of ancestors.

Perhaps a resolution of the dilemma may emerge sooner rather than later in African Christianity. In 1989, the Church of the Province of Kenya in the Anglican Communion, published its final version of *A Kenya Service of Holy Communion*.[78] The prayer thanking God for the lives of those departed in Christ reads:

> Gracious Father we heartily thank you for our faithful ancestors and all who have passed through death to the new life of joy in our heavenly home. We pray that surrounded by so great a cloud of witnesses, we may walk in their footsteps and be fully united with them in your ever-lasting kingdom.[79]

Then, later in the service, the introduction to the Sanctus reads: 'Therefore with angels, archangels, faithful ancestors and all in heaven, we proclaim your great and glorious name ...'.[80] In the *Church Times* of 6 April 1980, the Chairman of the Liturgical Committee of the Church of the Province of Kenya, Bishop David Gitari, commented on these parts of the new liturgy in an article under the title: 'An offering from Africa to Anglicanism': 'The introduction to the Sanctus (as well as the prayer thanking God for the lives of those departed in Christ) includes mention of our faithful ancestors – something vital to African Christian Theology ...'. And then he adds: 'not all ancestors are implied, but those who were faithful to the Supreme God, before the arrival of the Gospel, as well as early converts'. The last post-communion prayer, on which for some reason he did not make any comment, perhaps because it speaks for itself, reads as follows:

> O God of our ancestors,
> God of our people,

Before whose face the human generations pass away;
We thank you that in you we are kept safe for ever,
and that the broken fragments of our history are gathered up
in the redeeming act of your dear Son,
remembered in this holy sacrament of bread and wine.
Help us to walk daily in the Communion of the Saints,
declaring our faith in the forgiveness of sins and
the resurrection of the body.
Now send us out in the power of your Holy Spirit
to live and work for your praise and glory.
Amen.[81]

Here, past and present meet, the ancestors are fully within the new community of faith, and the living and the 'living-dead' pray together, indicating what one possible response to the question of ancestors could well be in the meeting of the Christian religion and the African world.

Notes and References

1. Geoffrey Parrinder, *West African Religion* (with foreword by E. W. Smith) London: Epworth Press, 1949.
2. Ibid., p. 16.
3. Ibid., p. xii.
4. See Terence O. Ranger and I. N. Kimambo (eds), *Historical Study of African Religion – With Special Reference to Central and Eastern Africa*, London: Heinemann, 1972, pp. 2f.
5. K. A. Busia, 'The Ashanti', in Daryll Forde (ed.), *African Worlds*, London: Oxford University Press, 1954, p. 205.
6. Geoffrey Parrinder, *West African Religion*, pp. 16ff.
7. J. G. Christaller, *Dictionary of the Asante and Fante Language called Tshi (Twi)*, Basel: Evangelical Missionary Society, 1881, pp. 342f.
8. Patrick Ryan, 'Arise O God! God and gods in West Africa', *Journal of Religion in Africa*, vol. 11, fasc. 3, 1980, pp. 161–71.
9. Ibid., p. 169.
10. *Romans* 3:29f.
11. Kenneth Cragg, *Christianity in World Perspective*, London: Lutterworth Press, 1968; subsequently, also his *The Christ and the Faiths – Theology in Cross-reference*, London: SPCK, 1986.
12. See John S. Mbiti, 'Christianity and East African culture and religion', *Dini na Mila: Revealed Religion and Traditional Custom*, vol. 3, no. 1, May 1968 (Kampala: Makerere University), pp. 1–6; *African Religions and Philosophy*, London: Heinemann, 1969.
13. Anton Wessels, *Images of Jesus – How Jesus is Perceived and Portrayed in Non-European Cultures* (ET), London: SCM, 1986.

14. Lamin Sanneh, *West African Christianity – The Religious Impact*, London: C. Hurst, 1983.
15. Lucy Quimby, in Ranger and Kimambo (eds), *Historical Study of African Religion*, p. 23, no. 5.
16. Andrew F. Walls, 'A bag of needments for the road: Geoffrey Parrinder and the study of religion in Britain', *Religion*, vol. 10, pt 2, Autumn 1980, p. 145.
17. Bolaji Idowu, *African Traditional Religion – A Definition*, London: SCM, 1973, p. 165.
18. Bolaji Idowu, *Olódùmarè – God in Yoruba Belief*, London: Longman, 1962, p. 147.
19. Ibid., p. 62.
20. Ibid., p. 32.
21. Ibid., p. 63.
22. Ibid., p. 209.
23. See John Mbiti, *African Religions and Philosophy*; Harry Sawyerr, *God: Ancestor or Creator? Aspects of Traditional Belief in Ghana, Nigeria and Sierra Leone*, London: Longman, 1970; G. M. Setiloane, *The Image of God Among the Sotho-Tswana*, Amsterdam: A. A. Balkema, 1976; Mulago, *La religion traditionnelle des Bantu et leur vision du monde*, Kinshasa: Faculté de Théologie Catholique, 1980; see also J. B. Danquah, *The Akan Doctrine of God – A Fragment of Gold Coast Ethics and Religion*, London: Frank Cass, 1944 (2nd edition, 1986) for a non-theological writer.
24. See G. Setiloane, 'How the traditional world-view persists in the Christianity of the Sotho-Tswana', in E. W. Fasholé-Luke et al. (eds), *Christianity in Independent Africa*, London: Rex Collings, 1978, p. 406, quoting a Ghanaian woman-theologian.
25. See Byang Kato, *Theological Pitfalls in Africa*, Kisumu: Evangel Publishing House, 1975.
26. See Kwame Bediako, *Theology and Identity – The Impact of Culture on Christian Thought in the Second Century and Modern Africa*, Oxford: Regnum Books, 1992, pp. 386–425.
27. S. N. Ezeanya, 'The Communion of Saints', in Kwesi Dickson and Paul Ellingworth (eds), *Biblical Revelation and African Beliefs*, London: Lutterworth Press, 1969, p. 45.
28. C. G. Baëta, 'The challenge of African culture for the Christian church and the Christian message to African culture', in *Christianity and African Culture* (The Proceedings of a Conference held at Accra, Gold Coast, 2–6 May, 1955, under the auspices of the Christian Council), Accra: Christian Council of the Gold Coast (Ghana), 1955, p. 60.
29. See J. H. Driberg, 'The secular aspect of ancestor-worship in Africa', *Supplement to the Journal of the Royal African Society XXXV*, January 1936; J. V. Taylor, *The Primal Vision – Christian Faith Amid African Religion*, London: SCM, 1963; H. Sawyerr, 'Ancestor worship I: the mechanics', *Sierra Leone Bulletin of Religion*, vol. 6, no. 2, December 1964; John Mbiti, *African Religions and Philosophy*, London: Heinemann, 1969; Bolaji Idowu, *African Traditional Religion – A Definition*, London: SCM Press, 1973; Malcolm McVeigh, *God in Africa – Conceptions of God in African Traditional Religion and Christianity*, Cape Cod: Claude Stark, 1974; Edward Fasholé-Luke, 'Ancestor veneration and the communion of saints', in Mark Glasswell and Edward Fasholé-Luke (eds), *New Testament Christianity for Africa and the World*, London: SPCK, 1974.
30. See Kwame Bediako, 'The Christian tradition and the African God revisited – towards a new African theological idiom', in David Gitari and Patrick Benson (eds), *Witnessing to the Living God in Contemporary Africa*, Nairobi: Uzima Press, 1986; Malcolm McVeigh, *God in Africa*, p. 38.

31. John Mbiti, 'Response to John Kinney', *Occasional Bulletin of Missionary Research*, vol. 3, no. 2, April 1979, p. 68.
32. Ibid.
33. Kwame Bediako, 'Biblical Christiologies in the context of African traditional religions', in Vinay Samuel and Christopher Sugden (eds), *Sharing Jesus in the Two-Thirds World*, Grand Rapids: Eerdmans, 1984, pp. 35–42; see *Colossians*, 1:15; *Ephesians*, 1:13–14.
34. See J. S. Pobee, *Toward an African Theology*, Nashville: Abingdon Press, 1979; C. Nyamiti, *Christ as our Ancestor – Christology from an African Perspective*, Gweru: Mambo Press, 1984; Kwame Bediako, 'Biblical Christologies in the context of African traditional religions', 1984; Kwame Bediako, *Jesus in African Culture – a Ghanaian Perspective*, Accra: Asempa Publishers, 1990.
35. Meyer Fortes, 'Some reflections on ancestor worship in Africa', in M. Fortes and G. Dieterlen (eds), *African Systems of Thought*, London: Oxford University Press, 1965, pp. 122–41.
36. Ibid., p. 122.
37. Ibid., p. 126.
38. Ibid., p. 128.
39. Loc. cit.
40. Ibid., pp. 128–9.
41. Ibid., p. 129, my emphasis.
42. Loc. cit., my emphasis.
43. Nana Addo Dankwa III is himself an interesting person from the standpoint of our present discussion. He considers himself a Christian and often attends public Christian worship in the local Presbyterian Church; but, in view of his official duties which include regular ritual service to his royal ancestors, he is debarred from participation in the sacrament of the Lord's Supper. This is the Church's way of expressing its disapproval of ancestral rites. My sources are, apart from personal interviews, four lectures which the King delivered in November–December 1987 at Trinity College, Legon, on the general theme: 'Christianity and African Traditional Beliefs', and which were subsequently published under the same title. See Nana Oseadeeyo Addo Dankwa III, *Christianity and African Traditional Beliefs*, New York: The Power of the Word Press, 1990.
44. Ibid., p. 31.
45. Ibid., p. 45.
46. Ibid., p. 46.
47. Ibid., p. 46.
48. Ibid., p. 47.
49. J. H. Driberg, 'The secular aspect of ancestor-worship in Africa', p. 15.
50. Addo Dankwa III, *Christianity and African Traditional Beliefs*, p. 47.
51. Loc. cit.
52. Ibid. p. 48. The 'outdooring' is the initial 'rite of passage' at which a child is formally given a name and ritually incorporated into the community.
53. Ibid., pp. 33–4.
54. Ibid., p. 45.
55. See Johannes Christaller, *Dictionary of the Asante and Fante Language called Tshi (Twi)*, 1881, vol. 1, pp. 98 and 344.
56. Addo Dankwa III, *Christianity and African Traditional Beliefs*, pp. 50–6.
57. Meyer Fortes, 'Some reflections on ancestor-worship in Africa', p. 129.
58. See John V. Taylor, *The Primal Vision – Christian Presence Amid African Religion*, p. 106; Malcolm McVeigh, *God in Africa*, pp. 124 and 169.
59. In Mark Glasswell and Edward Fasholé-Luke, *New Testament Christianity for Africa and the World*, pp. 209–21.

60. William Robertson Smith, *Lectures on the Religion of the Semites*, (2nd edn), London: A. and C. Black, 1894, p. 2.
61. Edward Fasholé-Luke, 'Ancestor veneration and the communion of saints', pp. 209–10.
62. Ibid., p. 211.
63. Ibid., p. 214.
64. Ibid., p. 216.
65. J. N. D. Kelly, *Early Christian Creeds*, London: Longman, 1972 (3rd edn), pp. 388–97.
66. Edward Fasholé-Luke, 'Ancestor veneration and the communion of saints', p. 216.
67. See *Acts* 14:17.
68. *Hebrews* 1:1.
69. See Byang Kato, *Theological Pitfalls in Africa*, Kisumu: Evangel Publishing House, 1975, p. 36ff.
70. *Revelation* 7:9–10.
71. Nathan Söderblom, *The Living God – Basal Forms of Personal Religion*, London: Oxford University Press, 1933, p. 263.
72. This fact itself may be of added significance in the establishment of African confidence in the Scriptures as not alienating – an important factor to bear in mind when dealing with the so-called Western character of Christianity in Africa in discussing the whole subject of modern mission.
73. *Galatians* 3:29.
74. *Ephesians* 3:6.
75. Andrew F. Walls, 'Africa and Christian identity', *Mission Focus*, vol. 4, no. 7, November 1978, p. 13.
76. K. Cragg, *Christianity in World Perspective*, London: Lutterworth Press, 1968, p. 48.
77. Taylor, *The Primal Vision*, p. 106.
78. *A Kenya Service of Holy Communion*, Nairobi: Uzima Press, 1989.
79. Ibid., p. 23.
80. Ibid., p. 28.
81. Ibid., p. 33.

I3

Christian Religion and African Social Norms
Authority, Desacralisation and Democracy

Christianity's Significance in African Political History

The following is one African scholar's assessment of the significance of Christianity in African political history:

> [Christian] missionary education in the majority of African countries helped provide the first wave of modern African nationalists. What can all too easily be overlooked is the concurrent influences of missionary education in the direction of global awareness and the beginnings of *pax humana*.[1]

That statement was made over sixteen years ago by one of the most authoritative African analysts of the modern political history of Africa, Ali Mazrui. Sufficient evidence can be gained from different parts of the continent to give a consistent picture: even in the context of the colonial experience and in many places prior to colonialism, Christianity, through giving access to modern Western-style education in its educational institutions, as well as through its unique message about the inalienable right to freedom of the human person, had a creative role in fostering religious and intellectual awakening, which eventually led to the demise of Western political dominance. In other words, the expansion of the intellectual horizons of Africans, eased by Christianity, enhanced a new African self-understanding and self-appreciation beyond the immediate traditional circles of kinship and lineage, and so paved the way for the modern expressions of African nationalism which finally challenged and overturned Western rule.

Mazrui's observation is important. For a writer more renowned for his critical view of the cultural impact of Christianity upon African life, this recognition of the religion's positive role is worth noting. Mazrui is not the only African secular historian to assign a positive role to Christianity in the political history of the continent in this century. The Ghanaian historian Adu Boahen regarded 'the spread of Christianity and Islam and especially of Western education' as an 'important social benefit of colonialism'.[2] According to Adu Boahen,

> the spread of Western education, due mainly to the activities of the Western missionaries ... was mainly responsible for producing the educated elite which not only spearheaded the overthrow of the colonial system but also constitutes the backbone of the civil services of independent African states.[3]

Like Mazrui, Adu Boahen also ascribed political significance to Christianity's role in producing that universalising of African horizons, a process which was crucial in the transition into the expanded world that came with the Western contact. Christianity enabled Africans to participate in the European intellectual discourse and to challenge some of its assumptions; in the process, it helped produce in Africans that early political consciousness – Adu Boahen called it 'this negative nationalism, or anticolonialism ... arising out of anger, frustration, and humiliation produced by the oppressive, discriminating and exploitative measures and activities of the colonial administrators'.[4] Christianity's record, then, has not been one unmitigated tale of collusion with, and manipulation by, colonial administrations. As Mazrui points out, 'A distinction needs to be made between the Christian message and the European *messenger* who brought it'.[5] Christianity has been an active participant in the struggle to regain the independence of Africa. It is the argument of this chapter that African Christianity, now with greater consciousness of its African identity and character, may face an even greater challenge to be of service to Africa in the political realm.

A New Political Task in Africa – from Independence to Democracy

Subsequently, in a statement published in *West Africa*,[6] Mazrui summarised with characteristic clarity the new political task in Africa:

> In the final two decades of the 20th century Africa has been undergoing what does indeed deserve to be called 'the Second Liberation Struggle'. If the first liberation struggle was against alien rule, this new crusade is for African democracy. If the first liberation effort was for political independence, this second struggle is for wider human rights. If the first endeavour was for collective self-determination, this second liberation is for individual fulfilment. Africa fought hard for decolonisation in the first crusade; it remains to be seen if Africa will fight equally hard for democratisation in this second challenge.[7]

Mazrui made this statement in his native Kenya, applying his observations to factors and forces in Kenyan political life which he saw as impediments to democratisation. He described the country as one which, in time past, was 'Africa's flagship against white minority governments' but which now 'is in danger of becoming the dragship which pulls the democratic fleet behind'. Mazrui's comments drew sharp criticism from the Kenyan government which called him 'a misguided foreigner ... who does not know anything to do with his country'.[8] In view of what has happened in Kenyan political life since that exchange of views took place, it becomes clearer that 'the struggle for African democracy' is also at least about the struggle for the legitimacy of dissent in African politics.

Until recently, the post-independence political histories of many African countries could be described as the process of the elimination of political dissent, that is, of organised and recognised dissent. The majority of these began their post-colonial political life in the 1950s and early 1960s as some kind of democracy with a well-defined and recognised opposition both within and outside the legislative structures established to control national political life. By the early 1970s, these arrangements had been replaced by one-party, and in many cases military, governments. It is only at the end of the 1980s that the one-party concept began seriously to be called into question.

This does not mean that post-colonial African politics has lacked a serious presence of alternative viewpoints. Rather, the process which led to the one-party state, in many if not all cases, involved a bitter struggle between contending interest groups in which the winner took all and secured his gains by instituting measures to eliminate and outlaw the loser. This process was usually justified on the grounds that indigenous African political tradition was consensual in character, so the presence of an organised opposition appearing to institutionalise the principle of adversarial politics reflected too closely the political institutions of the former colonial powers. This argument, however, often came in as a justification for actions taken on quite other grounds; it was not an understanding reached through sustained dialogue on the basis of a shared perspective.

My own home country, Ghana, is an illustration of this process. In February 1964, not quite seven years after achieving political sovereignty, the government of Ghana under the first President, Kwame Nkrumah, eliminated organised opposition and declared the country a one-party state, the flag of the ruling Convention People's Party (CPP) replacing the original national flag. The rationale for the change was that the one-party concept was 'in consonance with Ghanaian traditional political institutions which had no tradition of organised opposition and worked through a system of consultation and consensus'.[9] This was despite the well-known fact that such a consensus could not be maintained without political detentions and the removal of the right of opposition parties, *qua* opposition, to participate meaningfully in national political life. Essentially the same argument for consensual politics undergirded the political careers of several other political leaders in the early post-independence era: Leopold Senghor in Senegal, Julius Nyerere in Tanzania, Kenneth Kaunda in Zambia, Jomo Kenyatta in Kenya, Hastings Banda in Malawi, Sekou Toure in Guinea, Modibo Keita in Mali, and Houphouët-Boigny in Côte d'Ivoire. Even in the present quest for new democratic institutions, the same argument for 'African consensual politics' continues to be advanced. A recent sustained attempt at its restatement in order to validate one view in the current debate on the democratic future for Ghana, for instance, is the book published in Ghana by Kofi Awoonor, who also happened to be Ghana's Ambassador in Brazil at the time. The central piece of Awoonor's thesis is stated in relation to the African (extended) family which he takes to be the basic political unit:

> Decisions of the family council are arrived at by consensus. This is the first principle in African democratic practice. In it is enshrined the notion that by consensus, all agreed on a particular line of action; opposition which could be vital for arriving at the decision therefore becomes eliminated in the aftermath of the decision being taken. Opposition as a factor in achieving consensus occurs only during deliberations. If opposition persists beyond these deliberations, then decisions are postponed until further consultations, in order that unbending opponents of the general drift of the council's thinking can be advised and other extra parliamentary tactics employed to end the opposition. The collective and representative authority of the council is the bedrock of the consensus mode of decision-making. It emphasises the unity of the family invoking the ties that bind each member rather than drawing attention to any factors that may divide them.[10]

Awoonor's thesis fails to offer a solution to the problem of how, within this 'consensus mode of decision-making' persons who may have responsible and legitimate grounds for dissenting from 'the general drift of the council's thinking' may express their dissent without infringing the tradition. The contemporary clamouring for multi-party politics in African countries constitutes an implicit challenge to the notion that political opposition, and particularly organised opposition, is somehow *un-African*. On the other hand, the fact that political challenge as such has hitherto been discouraged in African post-colonial politics, may be a pointer to its absence in the tradition of the past. The larger question is therefore whether, in the context of the extended pluralism of political life in modern African nation-states, the traditions and political arrangements that operated in the predominantly homogeneous ethnocultural communities of the past are capable of rendering adequate service, as Awoonor seems to expect.

The Religious Roots of African Post-Independence Political Authoritarianism

K. A. Busia, always a sure guide into the character of African indigenous political systems, has identified the factor of the extension of scale as one of the major problems of political organisation in Africa.[11] (At the time he wrote his book, Busia was in voluntary exile, away from the reach of President Kwame Nkrumah's policies in Ghana. Later he would return to become Prime Minister in the Second Republic, only to be overthrown by a military *coup d'état* after less than three years in office.) Busia pointed out:

> Whereas the bond of union of the tribal community has been that of kinship, a modern state consists of many different tribes. How is one to achieve an extension of the African family spirit to the nation as a whole? How can one shift the emphasis from kinship groups to the state? This is one of the major problems of political organisation in Africa today.[12]

But it was not the difference in scale alone which caused a problem in modern African political organisation. Busia also recognised that the traditional emphasis on solidarity, when projected on to the political institutions of the new nation-state, had an inherent tendency towards authoritarianism or the one-party state. He noted:

> This idea of solidarity has relevance for the growth of one-party states in Africa, ... a strong predilection for a one-party state emanates from the traditional cultural emphasis on solidarity.[13]

But the kinship solidarity of the past was not the only element that was invading the present and bringing its legacy to bear upon political organisation in Africa's new nation-states. In an article published a number of years ago,[14] I sought to show that the issue of authoritarian governments in Africa in the post-independence era needed to be understood in religious terms too. Specifically, the problem had to do with the legacy of certain important religious aspects of the African traditional world-view as they related to authority, power and political governance, particularly the tendency of traditional society to sacralise authority and political office. The failure to recognise this meant that a whole body of evidence was left untouched. One effect of this failure to examine what I would call 'the legacy of the religious factor in African politics' has been that the era of one-party politics has been understood solely in 'cold-war' terms, namely, as Africa's acceptance of the communist prescriptions of democracy.

Basically, this said that democratic pluralism was a luxury that African countries needing to develop their economies fast could hardly afford. This may explain the case of some countries, but hardly all; it certainly cannot explain the existence of authoritarian governments in those countries which did not find communism attractive. Furthermore, it reduced the current surge for multi-party democracy to simply Africa's acceptance of another set of prescriptions – this time, those of the World Bank, the International Monetary Fund and Western governments – following the collapse of communism, and the end of the Cold War.

While such considerations have their place, they fail to take account of forces operating within African societies themselves, chief among these forces being religion. It is interesting that in his treatment of factors to considered in Africa's search for democracy, it was what he called 'the religious heritage' that Busia placed first. He wrote:

> There are many people to whom questions of religion seem irrelevant and out of place in discussing such issues as modernisation and progress. It is our contention that this attitude is prejudicial to a proper appraisal of the problems of Africa as Africans see them.[15]

Curiously, however, though Busia had seen so clearly the pervasive influence of religion in traditional political life, he appeared not to have recognised that the sacralisation of power in traditional society would have any significance for understanding Africa's new problems in politics, nor affect the new search for democracy.

In their introduction to *African Political Systems*,[16] the result of studies of eight traditional African societies widely distributed over the continent, anthropologists Meyer Fortes and Evans-Pritchard drew attention to this factor in traditional politics. They wrote:

> An African ruler is not to his people merely a person who can enforce his will on them. He is the axis of their political

relations, the symbol of their unity and exclusiveness and the embodiment of their essential values. He is more than a secular ruler .... His credentials are mystical and are derived from antiquity.[17]

The explanation for the 'mystical credentials' of the African ruler is the crucial political role of ancestors which is attested to in virtually all African societies, both those with centralised authority and those which lack it. Because the traditional belief is that the well-being of the society depends upon the maintenance of good relations with the ancestors on whom the living depend for help and protection, the ruler fulfils an important function as intermediary between the living and the ancestors. The ruler is the central figure at the instituted religious rituals that ensure the maintenance of the desired harmony between the living and the ancestors. Accordingly, the authority of the ruler in the traditional political system is strictly speaking, the authority of ancestors. In the usage of the Akans (of Ghana), for example, the traditional ruler is 'the one who sits on the stool of the ancestors'.[18]

This crucial role of ancestors in traditional political organisation means that beyond sacralising the office of the ruler, the whole realm of politics is sacralised, since the traditional world-view makes no sharp dichotomy between 'secular' and 'sacred' realms of existence. In the traditional perspective too, the concept of the state is inclusive of both the living and the ancestors. The institutions of political and social organisation consequently acquire a sacral character themselves, through their association with ancestors. As Fortes and Evans-Pritchard observed: 'The social system is, as it were, removed to a mystical plane, where it figures as a system of sacred values beyond criticism or revision'.[19] By thus reckoning the authority of living rulers to be that of ancestors, African tradition appeared to make every challenge to political authority an attack upon the sacral authority of ancestors on whose goodwill and favour the community's continuance and prosperity are held to depend. Any radical political challenge, therefore, would seem to suggest the subversion of tradition and custom; indeed, it amounts to undermining the very foundations of the identity and continuity of the state or community itself. In this way, the ancestor cult, by functioning *inter alia* as the guarantor of the authority of living rulers, becomes perhaps the most potent

symbol of the sacralisation of authority and power in African traditional politics. In Meyer Fortes's words: 'Ancestor worship puts the
final source of jural authority and right or ... jurisdiction, on a
pedestal ... where it is inviolable and unchallengeable, and thus able
to mobilise the consent of all who must comply with it'.[20] It is my
view that the problems of African post-independence politics are not
unrelated to the aspects of African traditional politics that we have
been discussing.[21] In other words, the sacralisation of authority and
political power found its way into the new political ideologies and
the political experiments that were embarked upon in the new
nation-states, though as 'secular' parodies, lacking the kinds of
checks and balances which formed part of the old religious universe
of meaning. The ready justification of the one-party concept mentioned above, the precarious fortunes of political dissent and the
tenacity with which unpopular rulers continued to cling to power, all
suggest that in the politics of independent Africa one was still
encountering the 'old' ancestor who never ceases to reign from the
realm of spirit-power. Certainly the honorific titles and praise-
names of some modern African heads of state seemed to convey
ancestral overtones. To cite the case of my own home country, when
President Kwame Nkrumah adopted the title 'Osagyefo' portraying
himself as 'Saviour' and 'Redeemer', he was not promoting the interests of the old traditional rulers. Instead the title portrayed him as
'Saviour' and 'Redeemer' from the misfortunes of colonialism, and
virtually as the eponymous ancestor-founder of the nation. Ghana's
coins bore his image, with the inscription: 'Civitatis Ghaniensis
Conditor'. President Nkrumah, for all practical purposes, became an
ancestor-ruler in the old sacral sense. As John Pobee has shown, the
President even 'approved of being accorded a supernatural status'.[22]
It would seem that, to varying degrees, this persistence of the
sacralisation of power from the traditional political frame of reference into the era of post-independence politics took place in several
African countries.

For African nations, then, caught between their legacy of the one-
party concept and the perceived need for change in the direction of a
genuine democratic pluralism, the challenge is not simply to 'run a
democracy' by the mere adoption of the external trappings of
democratic reform. It is evident that if African politics in the future is

to be able to integrate a wider political pluralism and to manifest a greater tolerance of dissent, that is, exhibit some of the fundamental assumptions of genuine democratic culture, then African societies are going to need to put in place new conceptions of political authority and power. I am persuaded that in this connection, African Christianity may have some distinctive contributions to offer.

Christianity and the Desacralisation of Authority and Power in History

By the close association of religious (sacred) authority and political power in the person of the traditional ruler, African traditional societies were what Dutch historian Arend van Leeuwen called 'ontocracies', sacralising authority and power with the effectual integration of altar and throne.[23] But, as van Leeuwen has shown, Christianity has been a desacralising force in world history. In Old Testament history, a comparison of the institution of kingship of ancient Egypt and Babylon with the monarchy in ancient Israel provides illuminating examples of the impact that the Hebrew prophetic religion was intended to have on the conceptions of authority and the exercise of power in human society.

Indeed, to the Hebrew prophets, *all* rulers – be they the sacral rulers of Egypt and Babylon, or the unsacral kings of Israel – are mere mortals among fellow mortals, and can be summoned to account before God. To the kingdoms of the world there is an alternative and overarching kingdom, the Kingdom of God, to which the kingdoms of the world must bow and submit. It was the quality of her faith that kept ancient Israel from going the way of her neighbours.[24] The essential thrust of the New Testament is the continuation of this desacralising impact. Undoubtedly, Jesus' message about the Kingdom of God was not perceived as other worldly or as politically neutral by the authorities of his day. They saw him as a threat and a challenge, and had him executed as a political criminal: 'We caught this man misleading our people, telling them not to pay taxes to the Emperor, and claiming that he himself is the Messiah, a king', his accusers said to Pilate.[25] Similarly, when Jesus said to Pilate, 'My kingdom is not of this world',[26] he could not have meant that it had nothing to do with the world. Had he meant that, then at a most crucial point in his career, the fundamental commitment of the mission of Jesus to human history and to its transformation, signified in the doctrine of the Incarnation, breaks down. His meaning could only have been that he held a conception of authority, that is, power in the political sense, which was essentially 'other' than that which Pilate held. Accordingly, Pilate's claim to have 'power either to free or to crucify' Jesus is the indication that his conception of power sacralised the political authority of the Empire. It is a pointer to the nature of all sacralisation: it fails to recognise the essentially derivative character of all earthly power. On the other hand, Jesus' response: 'You would have no power over me if it were not given to you from above' represents Jesus' desacralisation of the Empire itself. Pilate's authority, as that of the earthly Empire, 'like all human authority, is *delegated*; its source is Divine and therefore it is not arbitrary power, which can be exercised capriciously without moral blame'.[27]

Fundamentally, therefore, authority belongs to and derives from the transcendent realm. At this point Christian teaching affirms an important dimension of the African tradition: authority, political power, does not reside with human beings, nor even with the sacral ruler, for is not the sacral king merely 'the one who sits on the stool of the ancestors'? But Christianity would take the argument further. If authority does not reside with the merely human, then why should it be located in the realm of the essentially *human* spirits of the ancestors? So, in the perspective of Christian ideas, ancestors too become desacralised. Authority truly belongs only to God. Pilate's unease[28] in the presence of Jesus can be accounted for as indicating that Pilate, in his attempt to exert his authority by ascribing 'to himself almost the divine prerogative which is actually true of Jesus', only discovers that 'he is confronted with one who is himself at the source of all authority. The tables are turned and Pilate is judged by the one whom he judges.'[29]

The way of Jesus revealed, then, a new political option in the world of his. time. His was not the way of the Sadducees and Herodians who preserved their religion through pragmatism and expediency by collaborating with the Roman occupying forces. His was not the way of the Zealots, the violent revolutionaries out to overturn Roman rule by force. Nor was it the way of the Essenes who chose withdrawal into the desert in order to preserve their religious life intact, nor of the Pharisees who preoccupied themselves solely with their religious observances and segregated themselves politically. Jesus' way was one of engagement and involvement through a new way of overcoming, which arose from a unique concept of power: the power of forgiveness over retaliation, of suffering over violence, of love over hostility, of humble service over domination. Jesus won his way to pre-eminence and glory, not by exalting himself, but by humbling himself, to the point of dying a shameful death. In other words, his conception of power was that of non-dominating power. By making himself of no account, everyone must now take account of him.[30]

Thus, the ultimate clue to what Jesus meant, in his words to Pilate, as well as the logic of his own mind on the question of authority and power, are conveyed by his Cross, the means of his death which Pilate sanctioned and which Jesus willingly embraced. By his Cross, Jesus desacralised all worldly power, relativising its inherent tendency, in a fallen universe, to absolutise itself. But this means also that the Cross desacralises *all* the powers, institutions and structures that rule human existence and history – family, nation, social class, race, law, politics, economy, religion, culture, tradition, custom, ancestors – stripping them all of any pretensions to ultimacy. It is this 'concrete social meaning of the Cross'[31] which illuminates Paul's terminology of 'principalities', 'powers', 'thrones', 'dominions', and their cognate expressions. These categories, far from being the elements of a mythological outlook, have been shown in recent studies by Hendrik Berkhof,[32] J. H. Yoder and others[33] to be in fact relevant to the conditions of modern existence. In the African setting, it is through an African reading of the Scriptures, particularly in African languages, and by paying attention to the resonances of the Biblical categories into the African primal world-view, that the desacralising impact of the Gospel is experienced afresh. In view of the possible affinities that may exist between the primal imagination and the spiritual world of the Christian religion as noted earlier, such an approach to this question could prove fruitful. For example, the Twi reading of an important Christological passage like *Colossians* 1:15–17 is as follows:

Ɔno ara na ɔyɛ Onyankopɔn a wonhu no no suban ne abɔde nyinaa abakan, efisɛ ɔno mu na wɔbɔɔ nneɛma nyinaa, nea ɛwɔ ɔsoro ne nea ɛwɔ asase so, nea wohu ne nea wonhu, nhengua oo, wuradi oo, mpanyinni oo, tumidi oo, nneɛma no nyinaa, wɔnam no so na ɛbɔe, na wɔbɔ maa no. Na ɔno na odi ade nyinaa kan, na nneɛma nyinaa atim wɔ no mu.

The Twi words, *nhengua* (thrones), *wuradi* (powers), *mpanyinni* (rulers) and *tumidi* (authorities), are the categories designating the sacral nature of traditional political authority and rule. If these become appropriate terms for designating the Lordship of Jesus Christ as Christians understand it, then this is bound to have far-reaching implications for the way that Twi-speaking Christians regard political power in the world. Since the roots of sacralisation in African tradition lie in *religion*, it is in terms of *religion*, perhaps another religious principle, that it can be adequately encountered. It is as *religion* that the Christian Gospel is able to meet the African in depth. The primal world-view conceives of religion as power; the Gospel is the power of God.[34] On the basis of the principle of the translatability of the Scriptures, therefore, such an African reading of the Scriptures as I have indicated need not be frustrated by the kinds of alleged hermeneutical distances between text and context which sometimes hamper the hearing of the Word of God. However,

> if Christianity desacralises, it does not de-spiritualise. The African world continues a spiritual world; what changes is the configuration of forces. The human environment remains the same, but the answers to its puzzles are different.[35]

In the present quest for new political arrangements in Africa, the discussion is often distorted, so that it seems as if the choice is between so-called 'Western' forms of political organisation and 'indigenous' African systems and patterns. That distinction may sometimes be valid. It is important to realise, however, that so-called Western democracy is not inherently indigenous to the Western world, nor is it exclusively the preserve of the West, for it has emerged largely under the impact of Christian political ideas. Since many Western nations, under the impact of secularisation, have themselves lost touch with the Christian roots of their political institutions, it is not sufficiently realised that Christianity has, in fact, played a key role in the emergence of freedom in the modern world.

One result of this inadequate appreciation of the role of Christian religion in the world, is that in Africa in particular, political theorists, historians and governments have continued, by and large, to nurse a suspicion of Christianity as somehow alien, alienating and unhelpful in dealing with the modern questions of African political and cultural identity.

A proper understanding of the issues involved shows that the struggle for true democracy in Africa unavoidably involves making room for the 'way of Jesus', the way of non-dominating power, in the political arrangements under which members of society and nation will relate to one another. The mind of Jesus, as related to the questions of politics and power, is *not* a dominating mind, *not* a self-pleasing or self-asserting mind, but rather a saving mind, a redemptive mind, a servant mind. 'For Christ did not please himself.'[36] Jesus' way of dealing with political power represents the perfect desacralisation of all worldly power. The recognition that power truly belongs to God, which is rooted in the Christian theology of power as non-dominating, liberates politicians and rulers to be humans among fellow-humans, and ennobles politics and the business of government into the business of God and the service of God in the service of fellow humans. It is this perspective which provides the only genuine and abiding foundation for any serious quest in Africa for a sustained culture of freedom and justice in a genuine democracy. 'Without such a conception of power as Jesus held, taught, and demonstrated by the Cross, the hope of achieving a real sharing of political power in any society will remain elusive.'[37]

What are the indications that Christian Africa will be in a position to rise to this challenge in the coming decades? In 1969 Harold Turner published an article in *The Journal of Religion in Africa*[38] under the title, 'The Place of Independent Religious Movements in the Modernisation of Africa', in which he sought to counter the view that these movements, mainly the new independent churches of Africa, were ignorant and reactionary, compensating people for their miserable lot in life in a turbulent Africa by diverting energies from national development and modernisation. He was able to show, on the contrary, that these movements had made some significant contributions not only to the rise of modern African nationalism, to the transcendence of ethnic allegiances, but also to areas of positive social and economic transformation. They had also contributed to the desacralisation of political life in Africa, by not, on the whole, becoming the spiritual arm of the new nationalisms.

I am aware that we must guard against making exaggerated claims for Christianity in Africa. Nevertheless, it seems appropriate that one can apply Turner's observations across the whole range of the Christian presence in Africa, especially as the distinctions between independent and missionary-connected churches have, with time, become less meaningful.

The Christian churches of Africa live to a large extent in contexts of relative material poverty, amid some of the most vulnerable economies in the world at the present time. Consequently, as the churches have registered growth in membership in course of time, so have the burdens grown which they have had to carry to sustain their witness and ministries. But the increasing social and economic hardships have also been accompanied by a deepening of Christian consciousness, especially in relation to various pressing national issues and the need to be relevant to questions at the grassroots of society. When the need has arisen, the churches have, on the whole, not been ill-prepared.

The subject of this chapter has been the desacralisation of political power in African society and the contribution Christianity can make to this process. The evidence that this is already happening can be found in the careers of Archbishop Tutu and other church leaders in South Africa in the struggle against the white ontocracy of apartheid, of church leaders in Kenya in the struggle for democratic pluralism and open government, in the united stance of the Christian Council of Ghana and the Catholic Bishops' Conference against the curtailing of human rights in Ghana, just to cite a few instances.

Over the last five years or so, as country after country has embarked upon the path of democratic pluralism, it has been the Christian churches, their bishops, moderators and other official leaders, who have been called upon to stand in the breach to act as interim chairmen and presidents of the numerous negotiations and national conferences held to smooth the way into the new political dispensation. It is as if the embarrassment of the colonial connection, real or imaginary, which was Christianity's burden in the immediate post-independence era, has been effectively lived down. The Christian churches are now being recognised as institutions with genuine commitment to African concerns, coupled with a deep understanding of African problems from an African perspective, which arises out of their Christian convictions.

But Africa has not produced and is not likely to produce, a new Christendom. The Christian ontocracy in Ethiopia has gone, as has the white Christian ontocracy in South Africa. All Christian churches in Africa exist in contexts of religious pluralism and, in such contexts, they will have to learn to continue to worship God and His Christ, witness to the Gospel, learn to survive in joy, and strive for peace and justice and democratic freedom for all. Therefore Christian evangelisation, Christian nurture – and hence the church – are essential elements in the process whereby a society's outlook, value-systems, thought patterns and social and political arrangements become permeated with the mind of Jesus. The church, as the first fruit of the new humanity, created through the reconciling – by the Cross – of hostile groups,[39] needs to manifest the victory of the Cross in the concrete realities of her own existence in society, and to demonstrate that she has begun to be liberated from bondage to the 'powers' which rule human existence and the cosmic order in that context. Therefore, Christian conversion and Christian discipleship need to find concrete expression in response to the 'elemental forces' – ethnicity, race, social class, culture and customs – which shaped individual and social identity and destiny in the old order.

The major challenge now facing the Christian churches in African in the political sphere is to raise to consciousness in the wider society the connection between the Church's message of righteousness, love and justice, and the search for sustainable democratic governance though the churches must continually remember that the search for democracy is not an end in itself. As the end of human existence is the Biblical vision of *shalom* in the Kingdom of God, the arrival of democracy is not the coming of the Kingdom.

Notes and References

1. Ali Mazrui, *Political Values and the Educated Class in Africa*, London: Heinemann, 1978, p. 168.
2. Adu Boahen, *African Perspectives on Colonialism*, Baltimore: Johns Hopkins University Press, 1987.
3. Ibid., p. 104.
4. Ibid., p. 98.
5. Ali Mazrui, *Political Values and the Educated Class in Africa*, p. 153.
6. *West Africa*, 2–8 September 1991.
7. Ibid, p. 1450.
8. Loc. cit.
9. Kofi Awoonor, *Ghana – A Political History from Pre-European to Modern Times*, Accra: Sedco, 1990, p. 202.
10. Ibid., p. 9.
11. K. A. Busia, *Africa in Search of Democracy*, London: Routledge & Kegan Paul, 1967.
12. Ibid., p. 20.
13. Ibid., p. 3.
14. Kwame Bediako, 'Biblical Christologies in the context of African traditional religions', in Vinay Samuel and Chris Sugden (eds), *Sharing Jesus in the Two-Thirds World*, Grand Rapids: Eerdmans, 1984, pp. 81–121.
15. K. A. Busia, *Africa in Search of Democracy*, pp. 1f.
16. Meyer Fortes and E. E. Evans-Pritchard (eds), *African Political Systems*, London: KP (in association with the International African Institute), 1987. (First published in 1940.)
17. Ibid., p. 16.
18. See K. A. Busia, *The Position of the Chief in the Modern Political System of Ashanti – A Study of the Influence of Contemporary Social Changes on Ashanti Political Institutions*, London: Frank Cass, 1968, pp. 36f. (First published in 1951.)
19. Meyer Fortes and E. E. Evans-Pritchard (eds), *African Political Systems*, p. 18.
20. Ibid., p. 137.
21. See Kwame Bediako, 'Biblical Christologies in the context of African traditional religions'.
22. J. S. Pobee, *Kwame Nkrumah and the Church in Ghana: 1949–1966 – A Study in the Relationship Between the Socialist Government of Kwame Nkrumah, the First Prime Minister and First President of Ghana, and the Protestant Christian Churches in Ghana*, Accra: Asempa Press, 1988, p. 146.
23. Arend Th. van Leeuwen, *Christianity in World History: The Meeting of the Faiths of East and West*, (English translation by H. H. Hoskins), London: Edinburgh House Press, 1964, pp. 165ff.
24. H. Frankfort, *Kingship and the Gods – A Study of Ancient Near Eastern Religion as the Integration of Society and Nature*, Chicago: The University of Chicago Press, 1948.
25. *Luke* 23:2.
26. *John* 18:36.
27. J. H. Bernard, *The Gospel According to St John* (The International Critical Commentary) (2 vols), Edinburgh: T. and T. Clark, 1928, p. 619.
28. Or 'fear', see *John* 19:8.
29. Barnabas Lindars, *The Gospel of John* (New Century Bible), London: Oliphants, 1972, p. 568.
30. *Philippians* 2:10–11; see J. H. Yoder, *The Original Revolution – Essays on*

Christian Pacifism, Scottdale: Herald Press, 1971, pp. 13–33.

31. J. H. Yoder, *The Politics of Jesus*, Grand Rapids: Eerdmans, 1972, p. 134.
32. Hendrik Berkhof, *Christ and the Powers*, Scottdale: Herald Press, 1962.
33. See J. H. Yoder, *The Politics of Jesus*; also Walter Wink, *Naming the Powers – The Language of Power in the New Testament*, Minneapolis: Fortress Press, 1984; *Unmasking the Powers – The Invisible Forces that Determine Human Existence*, Minneapolis: Fortress Press, 1986; and *Engaging the Powers – Discernment and Resistance in a World of Domination*, Minneapolis: Fortress Press, 1992.
34. *Romans* 1:16.
35. Kwame Bediako, 'Christ in Africa – Some Reflections on the Contribution of Christianity to the African Becoming', in Christopher Fyfe (ed.), *African Futures* (Proceedings of a conference held in the Centre of African Studies, University of Edinburgh, 9–11 December 1987), Edinburgh: Centre of African Studies, 1987, p. 456.
36. *Romans* 15:3.
37. Kwame Bediako, *Jesus in African Culture – A Ghanaian Perspective*, Accra: Asempa Publishers, 1990, p. 29.
38. Harold Turner, 'The place of independent religious movements in the modernisation of Africa', *Journal of Religion in Africa*, vol. 2, fasc. 1, 1969, pp. 43–63.
39. *Ephesians* 2:14.

14

The Place of Africa in a Changing World
The Christian Factor

Africa as 'Laboratory' for the World

An observation made nearly thirty years ago by John Ferguson, at the time Professor of Classics in the University of Ibadan, Nigeria, may helpfully set the framework for this discussion. Ferguson was commenting on the place and value of a Classics department in a Nigerian university:

> Our Classics department is set in one of the few parts of the world where you can still consult oracles, where there are tonal languages (as Classical Greek was tonal), where there is a living tradition of religious dance-drama (what is Greek tragedy in origin but that?), where sacrifice is understood, where contemporary society offers many fascinating parallels to ancient Greek and Roman society. Nigerian scholars, if they will look at the classics with Nigerian and not European eyes, can interpret the classics to us in ways that no European scholar can do.[1]

For 'Nigerian scholars' I should like to put 'African Christian scholars', as well as any non-African Christian scholars with African sympathy, and for 'the classics', I should like to put 'the Christian religion'. Expressed in these terms, the statement becomes an immense claim: Africa as laboratory for the world. I do not wish to exaggerate the significance of the African dimension in the present global transformation of Christianity. Yet, it seems that the sheer surprise-element in the emergence of that continent as a major base of the Christian faith at the close of the twentieth century makes it important that we seek to understand what this might mean both for Africa and for the Christian faith too.

Africa as Privileged Arena for Christian and Religious Scholarship

In the last few years, there has been much allusion to the marginalisation of Africa, especially following the end of the Cold War era when there has been an expectation that Africa will hold a less strategic place in a world no longer dominated by the ideological rivalries between West and East, between capitalism and communism. It is possible that Africa's current economic problems may make really serious external involvement too costly to contemplate; on the other hand, it is to be doubted that the continent's potential will make it easy actually to ignore her altogether. What is certain is that in one particular respect, and perhaps in others too, Africa will not be marginalised, and that is in the field of scholarship, and specifically Christian and religious scholarship.

It is true that the present shift in the centre of gravity of Christianity to the non-Western world involves more than Africa. The whole of the non-Western world is important in the present phase of the cultural history of the Christian faith, and in each of the contexts of its manifestation, non-Western Christianity gives access to the exploration of valuable lessons and features of the Christian presence in the world.

It can be argued, however, that the African Christian field, not least because of its massiveness and its diversities, offers quite distinctive opportunities for Christian scholarship. In 1974, Harold Turner published an article on 'The contribution of studies on religion in Africa to Western Religious Studies' in the volume of essays in honour of Prof. Harry Sawyerr of Fourah Bay College, Freetown, Sierra Leone, entitled *New Testament Christianity for Africa and the World.*[2] In that article Turner sought to show that in all the regular Christian religious disciplines – Biblical studies, Christian history, missiology and ecumenics, systematic theology and Christian ethics, as well as in the general phenomenology and history of religion – the African field, and in this case, particularly the 'independent' churches and other new African religious movements, threw new light on old issues, because they yielded data which were both vital and contemporary. With regard to Biblical Studies, Turner pointed to the independent churches' ability to penetrate into and participate in the realities of the Biblical world in their modern circumstances, citing the experience of dreams 'as a means of revelation at many critical junctures and for many prominent figures' in the Scriptures. Did not the evidence from these new churches lead to a new appreciation of the Bible as 'indeed a book for all cultures', Turner asked, so that when the Bible ceases to speak 'to our culture at this point, we learn more about ourselves than about the Scriptures?'[3] In relation to Christian history, these new churches and movements give new insights into earlier and parallel movements in the history of the Church; areas of earlier Christian history which are poorly documented might well profit from the study of living manifestations of identical phenomena in modern times. With regard to missiology, the remarkable expansion of some of these churches 'without the usual resources of men and equipment organised by some sending body', could shed fresh light on questions relating to 'how churches grow'. As to the African churches, Turner wrote:

> The essence of their answer seems to be that they find a mandate in the revelation to their founder or prophet, and a gospel in their offer of spiritual power from the God who has given the revelation and who continues to manifest himself in healing or guidance or deliverance from the forces of evil. For their method they have preaching and testimony set in the context of joyous worship and for their chief instrument, the Scriptures.[4]

For systematic theology, the African churches' stress on an ecclesiology – though this is often a lived rather than a written reality – of a community of the Holy Spirit, or a 'spiritual church', organised around Christ who is perceived as the source of abundant life and divine power, according to Turner, raised important questions in relation to 'what is meant by the criteria of the Church'. For Turner, in the light of the African evidence of a more dynamic nature arising from dynamic and vital Christian life, 'the classic notes of the Church as one, holy, catholic and apostolic, ... the different credal forms, or the Reformation marks of preaching, administration of the sacraments and the exercise of godly discipline, help us little'.[5] Turner, therefore, commended the study of the African evidence 'to all the Western religious disciplines not merely as a highly specialised field of enquiry, but as a field pregnant with new ideas, new methods

and procedures, new categories and points of view, for use throughout their work'.[6]

Once again, it should be stressed that what Turner wrote of the
independent churches can now be applied equally to the broad
spectrum of the Christian presence in Africa. His specific appli-
cations to the independents were valid, however, in so far as it was
the independents who were indicating the direction in which African
Christianity was generally moving.

Before leaving Turner's article, it is important to understand the
basis upon which he was commending the study of the African evidence. Inasmuch as that basis has nothing to do with the projection
of the ascendancy of African Christianity over other manifestations
of the Christian faith in the world, I share it fully, as the grounds on
which I too wish to argue for the significance of the Christian factor
in Africa, and its consequent importance for Christian scholarship.
Turner stated his position clearly, and to quote him fully:

> Theology as a science depends upon access to its appropriate
> data in their most authentic and vital forms. If we regard the
> data of theology as being the revelations and acts of the Divine,
> the post-biblical and contemporary manifestations of these
> data will occur less vividly in a dispirited Western Church with
> declining numbers and morale. On the other hand, the data will
> be more evident and accessible in unsophisticated churches
> where the living God is taken seriously as present in the healing
> and conquering power of the Spirit, with a gospel-generated
> growth and a spiritual creativity and confidence. Here at the
> growing edges of Christianity in its most dynamic forms, the
> theologian is encouraged to do scientific theology again,
> because he has a whole living range of contemporary data on
> which to work. It is not that these dynamic areas of the Chris-
> tian world are free from imperfection; but being full of old and
> new heresies they need theology and offer it an important
> task.[7]

The Quest for Christian Identity – a New Creative Stage in Theology

Once this recognition of the theological significance of African Christianity (as of other non-Western manifestations of Christianity) is granted, it becomes clear how it is that 'the Christian interaction with the cultures of the South therefore marks a new creative stage in Christian theology', as Andrew Walls has written. Christian theology is being taken 'into new areas of life, where Western theology has no answers, because it has no questions',[8] that is, at least in its more recent endeavours.

My own studies in the formative stages of modern African theology brought me to the conclusion that the issue of identity lies at the heart of the process by which the Christian theological enterprise is actually carried forward.[9] As it emerged in the post-missionary context of African Christianity in the 1950s and 1960s, the question of identity entailed not only confronting constantly the problem of how 'old' and 'new' in African religious consciousness could become integrated in a unified vision of what it meant to be Christian and African. The issue also forced the theologian to become in himself or herself the point of intersection of this struggle for integration through an inner dialogue which became infinitely personal and intense, if it was to be authentic. African theology, therefore, by becoming 'something of a dialogue between the African Christian scholar and the perennial religions and spiritualities of Africa'[10] was thereby a struggle for an appropriate Christian discourse which would account for and hold together the total religious experience of Africans in a coherent and meaningful pattern.[11] Identity itself thus became a theological category, so that the development of theological concern and the formulation of theological questions were linked as the inevitable by-product of a process of Christian self-definition.

My discovery of a similar process in the origins of the development of Christian thought in the Graeco-Roman world strengthened for me the significance of the African evidence. For in both contexts, marked by a transposition of the Christian faith from one cultural framework into another, theology clearly answered to 'the need to make Christian decisions';[12] to be engaged in the Christian theological enterprise was also to give account of one's Christian self-consciousness; one's theology was also one's *apologia pro vita sua*.

Equally important for me was the discovery of another feature in the contexts in which Christian theology was being articulated in both modern Africa and in the second and third centuries of the Christian era. It was because both contexts can be described as religiously pluralistic that the question of identity occupied such a central place in the articulation of Christian thought. It is essential for us to understand that for the early Hellenistic Christian theologians as for the modern African theologians, religious pluralism is their *experience*; Christian identity is the *issue*. Religious pluralism therefore does not lie outside of theological existence itself. It is when the context of religious pluralism is succeeded by a *corpus Christianum*, a Christendom from which all possible alternatives are presumed eliminated, not only from the context, but from theological existence too, that the theological enterprise ceases to need to make Christian decisions. Because no other kinds of decisions are conceivable, the character of theology itself becomes changed. Within such a changed frame of reference there is little that a Christian theologian can say about his or her faith to a person of another faith, while a person of another faith cannot encounter Christ except on the terms of a Christian theology whose categories have been established with little reference to the faiths of others. In recent Christian history this process has occurred most prominently in the context of the Christian theology of the West. What has happened to Christianity in Africa (as in the rest of the non-Western world) has subverted it.

In Harold Turner's article mentioned above, Turner included the general phenomenology and history of religion as one of the areas where he expected studies on Religion in Africa to make a contribution. Turner stated the matter thus:

> It becomes apparent, especially in new movements that cannot be called independent churches, that the traditional tribal religions must also be investigated since these provide a major component of the new developments. Thus the history and phenomenology of religion are being led into an area that has largely been left to the anthropologists.[13]

From what we now know about the significance of primal religions generally in the history of Christianity, to which Turner has himself made an important contribution,[14] we may be a little surprised to find a suggestion here that the study of the 'traditional tribal religions' of Africa may have less to do with Christianity's future. But more important still, what Turner failed to note was that in African religious scholarship too, it was African *Christian* theologians who were being led into the 'area that has largely been left to the anthropologists', as any cursory glance at the bibliographical lists of African theology reveals. To those who have criticised African theologians for doing with the material of African primal religions what anthropologists do not do,[15] the simple response is that African theologians did not set out to do what anthropologists do. It has not been generally recognised that the kind of study that the African theologian makes of African religious tradition cannot be compared with 'a clinical observation of the sort that one might make about Babylonian religion; he is handling dynamite, his own past, his people's present'.[16]

For the anthropologist, the subject-matter is quite often exotic. For the African theologian, however, the traditional religions, even if they constitute his past, are of the nature of an 'ontological' past, which means that together with the profession of the Christian faith, it gives account of the same entity – namely the history of the religious consciousness of the African Christian. Theological investigation of the traditional religions therefore also becomes a quest for what Bishop Kenneth Cragg calls 'integrity in conversion: a unity of self in which one's past is genuinely integrated into present commitment, so that the crisis of repentance and faith that makes us Christian truly integrates what we have been in what we become'.[17] Paradoxically then, virtually all of Africa's leading theologians, trained in theology on a Western model, have, with one notable exception, been forced by the very demands of Africa's religious pluralism, to move into areas of theological activity for which no Western syllabus prepared them.[18] The one notable dissenter was Byang Kato, who unlike his colleagues retained his Western model for his theological career in the African context, and failed thereby to establish a tradition of creative thought.[19]

African Theology – Communicative, Evangelistic, Missionary: a Benediction to the West

It could be argued, however, that in the process, African theologians have gained rather than lost. For, being forced to theologise in the interface of their Christian faith and the perennial spiritualities of their own African primal traditions, as well as having to internalise that dialogue within themselves, African theologians have recaptured the character of theology as Christian intellectual activity on the frontier with the non-Christian world, and hence as essentially communicative, evangelistic and missionary. It is this character of African theology which Dutch theologian and missiologist, Johannes Verkuyl, recognised.[20]

In the process, African theology may well be discovering new conceptions of the role and the task of the Christian theologian, conceptions which are different from those which have hitherto been dominant. As Kwesi Dickson puts it:

> Is the Christian theologian to be concerned solely with Christian faith in his theologising, or is he to put Christianity into the wider context of religion as an acknowledgement of God's rule over mankind?

Or again,

> Is the theologian adequately defined as a spokesman for a particular religion, that is Christianity? Or is he one whose understanding of the revelation of God has been tempered and enriched by an insight into God's self-disclosure in other religious traditions? Is the term theology fully meaningful when used in relation to the life and thought of strictly one group of people, that is, Christians?[21]

If it is true that 'it is not Christianity that saves, but Christ',[22] then such questions as these cannot be unimportant for any tradition of Christian theology anywhere.

Yet it may also be part of the 'surprise story' of Christian Africa in the twentieth century that having emerged largely as a result of the impact of the West, African contributions to Christian scholarship may now become a benediction to the West.

The main thrust of African Christian scholarship has been the argument that 'conversion' to Christianity must be coupled with cultural continuity'.[23] In its specific application to Africa, the argument has meant that against all odds, space had to be made for a positive pre-Christian religious heritage in the African Christian consciousness on the grounds that 'religion informs the African's life in its totality'.[24] To the extent that the African endeavour has been successful, it may hold promise for a Western Church which is now also asking seriously how the Christian faith may be related to Western culture, indeed, how the West may be converted.

Paul Bohannan may well be right when he says that 'African culture shares more of its traits, its history, its social organisation with Europe than Asia shares with Europe, and certainly more than the North American Indians share with Europe'.[25] In relation to our present discussion, it is worth recalling that Europe shares with Africa an identical pre-Christian heritage in the primal religious traditions of the world. But it is in Africa (as in the rest of the non-Western world) that the significance of the primal religions in the history of Christianity has been seen for what it is. In the case of Europe, Christian mission appears to have proceeded on a basis of substitution to such an extent that the primal traditions were virtually completely wiped out. What this has done to the Western religious memory may probably never be fully recovered. But at least it raises to prominence the matter of learning the lessons of history for today's mission.

The modern question posed regarding the West is: 'Can the West be converted?' From a missiological point of view, however, an equally valid question could be: 'Was the ancient West given the opportunity to be converted?' We know that in the conversion stories of many of the ancient peoples of northern Europe particularly, 'although the issue might be discussed in the assemblies, it was not necessarily decided by a vote, for the king could dictate that the alternative to baptism was combat or death', as Gordon Donaldson has pointed out.[26] Iceland gives us an instance of a fully discussed and democratically decided outcome, though not without some prior pressure from King Olaf Trygvasson of Norway.[27] The general picture, as Donaldson indicated, was rather that 'marriage, miracles, conquest and compulsion seem, wherever we look, to have been the recurring factors'.[28]

In the light of this history, one might be forgiven for thinking that the old primal religions of Europe quickly became a spent force. But the fact that Christians continued to name the days of the week after pre-Christian deities, that pre-Christian elements and notions made their way into the celebration of church festivals, notably Christmas and Easter, and in several other ways too, must be indicators that the old beliefs had not entirely lost their hold upon people's minds.

It is in Africa that the opportunity for a serious theological encounter and cross-fertilisation between the Christian and primal traditions, which was lost in Europe, can be regained; and Africa may well be the place for redeeming wrongs done not to her alone in the name of mission.

By overturning virtually every negative verdict passed on African primal religion by an ethnocentric Western missionary enterprise, Africa's Christian theologians have contributed in no small measure to reaffirm the place of *religion* itself in the Christian theological enterprise. By all indications, in Africa it is religion – and the findings in the history and phenomenology of religion – which have become the handmaid of theology. As Kwesi Dickson put it, the theologian who fails to:

> recognise the structures of religion as revealed by the historian of religions ... may not notice the absence of religion from his theology. In the context of Africa, Christian theology must of necessity take account of that understanding of religion which bears the stamp of an authentic African contribution [that means, the primal religions].[29]

This relocation of African primal religions 'at the very centre of the academic stage', as Adrian Hastings noted about twenty years ago,[30] is what may prove a benediction to Western Christian theology as it also seeks to be communicative, evangelistic and missionary in its own context. If it has any validity, the African vindication of the theological significance of African primal religions also goes to affirm that the European primal heritage was not illusory, to be consigned to oblivion as primitive darkness. The nature of the meeting of Christianity with European primal religions may hold more significance for understanding the modern West than may have been assumed. A serious Christian theological interest in European primal traditions and early Christianity amid those traditions, could provide a fresh approach to understanding Christian identity in Europe too, as well as opening new possibilities for the theological enterprise today. The primal imagination may turn out to be not so alien to Europe after all, even in a post-Enlightenment era.

For the signs of what appears to be a post-modernist rejection of the Enlightenment, seen partly in the resurgence of the phenomenon of the occult as well as some of the other features of the 'New Age', bearing the marks of a primal world-view, are sufficient indicators that a primal imagination suppressed rather than purged and integrated, rises to haunt the future. In other words, even in the context of a post-Enlightenment critical outlook with which all Christian theologies must now contend, the theological enterprise is also about finding new ways in which we may affirm the reality of transcendence, and demonstrate wholeness as its fruit. In this connection, the viability of a Christian consciousness fully anchored in the primal imagination, as we noted earlier in Prophet Harris (in West Africa) and in Archbishop Emmanuel Milingo (from Zambia), as well as the theological cross-fertilisation between the primal world-view and Christian faith that is evident in African theology are all an implicit challenge to the notion that humanity can be fully defined in exclusively post-Enlightenment terms. In Europe, as in Africa and elsewhere in the non-Western world, the religious traditions that have been most closely associated with the continuing Christian presence in the world so far, may yet again point the way into the Christian future. If so, the African contribution will have been an important one.

To return to Africa, however, it is in African Christianity that the primal heritage in Africa is most likely to acquire a more enduring place in African religious consciousness. Religion, it seems, especially the Christian religion – in belief as in its manifestation in social and cultural behaviour – will remain an important indicator for understanding African life.

Consequently a general secular intellectual outlook which is suspicious of religion may be unable to determine the place of religion or its significance or otherwise in African history, or its shaping of African destiny. In a world which has seen a great deal of religious fanaticism, it is also possible to find the winsome face of religion. As the centre of gravity of Christianity has shifted into the non-Western world this century, so also the majority of Christian martyrdoms, apart from the instances of religious persecution under the former communist regimes of Eastern Europe, have been in the non-Western world; Africa too has had her share of them.

We noted earlier the role that Christianity played in the first liberation struggle of African peoples against colonialism. In more recent years too, Christian leaders and councils of churches have achieved prominence in Africa's 'second liberation struggle' for wider human rights in the post-independence nation-states. The indications are that in several African countries, Christian leadership will continue to be sought for guidance, as these countries feel their several ways towards the new and more open political arrangements that are expected to materialise in the near future. In the absence of the trappings of Western imperial patronage, or of Western missionary tutelage, African Christian maturity will continue to be tested for what it is. There is no reason to conclude that African Christianity will lack the spiritual resources that will be required, or that African religion will not continue to display the resilience it has often shown.

It is all the more surprising, therefore, that in recent general studies of Africa, African Christianity has not attracted as much attention as its massive presence in Africa would appear to require. It is as if in becoming less associated with Western dominance – imperial or missionary – Christianity also ceases to appear important as a social force. Lest it be thought that only Western scholars might be held guilty of this, Busia too, for all his insistence on the importance of Africa's religious heritage, failed to recognise that Christianity could have any positive significance in *Africa's Search for Democracy*, in his book of that title. He was much more impressed by the notion that 'the establishment of Islam and Christianity has made religion a potential or actual factor of tensions, and religious freedom has acquired a new significance as a democratic right'.[31] Busia so consistently interpreted Christianity in Africa as a 'veneer', that, leading Christian layman that he was, he could not entrust to Christianity the 'expression of Africa's way of life'.[32] Christianity has not fared much better at the hands of other African social scientists and historians. African Christianity then, at least with regard to the attention it receives, must be said to share the predicament of the continent in 'the dark tunnel' that Adrian Hastings pictured her traversing.[33] In that 'dark tunnel', African Christianity must work out her own salvation and her future.

For Hastings, 'one cannot be too sure' what African Christianity will become at the other end. Be that as it may, we will do well not to confuse African Christianity with the scholarly literature on it. We need to recall that one of Africa's leading theologians who berated the African Church in the 1960s for lacking a theology[34] would, twenty years later, write: 'The Christian way of life is in Africa to stay, certainly within the foreseeable future', and that: 'African Christianity cannot wait for written theology to keep pace with it. Academic theology can only come afterwards and examine the features retrospectively in order to understand them.'[35]

We began with John Ferguson's statement about an African setting, an African university in Nigeria, as the laboratory for teaching the classics of ancient Greece and Rome. I adapted that statement to serve my purposes. Now I should like to quote an African scholar whose comments relate more closely to my subject. Ali Mazrui concluding his wide-ranging study of cultural conflicts in his *Cultural Forces in World Politics*[36] comes to focus on Africa, again as a 'laboratory', this time, not for learning how we may understand the past, but rather how we may prepare for the future. In this case too, Christianity is part of the picture.

> But in recording these conflicting trends we may have to look more widely around the world for areas of cultural reconciliation and for creative opportunities. Cultural experiments may have to be conducted partly in Africa precisely because that is the one continent where the rival cultural forces of the human species have to learn the secrets of accommodation and synthesis.

Then, after commenting on each of the continents with regard to the relative strengths in them of Marxism and capitalism, Islam and Christianity, Mazrui continued:

> In geographical distribution, Islam is primarily an Afro-Asian religion. Christianity is primarily an Afro-Western religion in dispersal. The area they share is the 'Afro' part. The two religions continue to compete for the soul of Africa. Africa is

destined to be a laboratory of both religious ecumenicalism and ideological co-operation – Marxism, capitalism, Christianity and Islam are well represented in African conditions.[37]

Mazrui's book was written before the collapse of communism and the eclipse of Marxism as a viable ideological rival to capitalism. The world is not likely to be dominated again by the ideological rivalry between East and West, between communism and capitalism. But that leaves the religious element, the 'religious ecumenicalism' of Christianity and Islam' in Mazrui's terms. Curiously, Mazrui leaves out of consideration the continent's primal religions, although it must be because he regards both Christianity and Islam as originally external to Africa.

I have no wish to minimise the strength of Islam in Africa. One may hesitate, however, about describing Christianity at the close of the twentieth century as 'Afro-Western'. By becoming a non-Western religion, Christianity has also become a true world faith, and in the African context, the depth of the inter-penetration between Christianity and Africa's primal religions points to the significance of the Christian factor.

An important dimension of Africa's role as 'laboratory' for the world may, therefore, include the vindication in the modern world of the viability of Christian religious discourse, as not outworn and to be discarded, or about which to be embarrassed, but rather as fully coherent with human experience, and fully meaningful within the history of the world's redemption. How effectively African Christianity will bear its part of this responsibility, thankfully, does not depend upon human energies alone.

Notes and References

1. John Ferguson, quoted in Robin Horton, 'Philosophy and African Studies', in David Brokensha and Michael Crowder (eds), *Africa in the Wider World – The Inter-relationship of Area and Comparative Studies*, Oxford: Pergamon Press, 1967, p. 269.
2. H. W. Turner, 'The contribution of studies on religion in Africa to Western Religious Studies', in Mark Glasswell and Edward Fasholé-Luke (eds), *New Testament Christianity for Africa and the World*, London: SPCK, pp. 169–78.
3. Ibid., p. 170.
4. Ibid., p. 175.
5. Ibid., p. 176.

6. Ibid., p. 178.
7. Ibid., pp. 177f.
8. Andrew F. Walls, 'Structural problems in Mission Studies', *Intenational Bulletin of Missionary Research*, vol. 15, no. 4, October 1991, pp. 147f.
9. See Kwame Bediako, *Theology and Identity – The Impact of Culture upon Christian Thought in the Second Century and Modern Africa*, Oxford: Regnum Books, 1992.
10. Adrian Hastings, *African Christianity – An Essay in Interpretation*, London: Geoffrey Chapman, 1976, p. 50.
11. See Edward Fasholé-Luke, 'The Quest for an African Christian Theology', *The Ecumenical Review*, vol. 27, no. 3, 1975, pp. 259–69.
12. Andrew F. Walls, 'Structural problems in Mission Studies', p. 147.
13. H. W. Turner, 'The contribution of studies on religion in Africa to Western Religious Studies', p. 178.
14. H. W. Turner, 'The Primal Religions of the world and their study', in Victor Hayes (ed.), *Australian Essays in World Religions*, Bedford Park: Australian Association for World Religions, 1977, pp. 27–37.
15. Benjamin Ray, *African Religions – Symbols, Ritual and Community*, Englewood Cliffs, New Jersey: Prentice Hall Inc., 1976.
16. Andrew F. Walls, 'The Gospel as the prisoner and liberator of culture', in *Faith and Thought*, vol. 108 (1–2), 1981, p. 49.
17. K. Cragg, 'Conversion and convertibility, with special reference to Muslims', in John R. W. Stott and Robert Coote (eds), *Down to Earth – Studies in Christianity and Culture*, Grand Rapids: Eerdmans, 1980, p. 194.
18. See Andrew F. Walls, 'The Gospel as the prisoner and liberator of culture', p. 49.
19. On Byang Kato, see Kwame Bediako, *Theology and Identity – The Impact of Culture upon Christian Thought in the Second Century and Modern Africa*, pp. 386–425; cf. Paul Bowers, 'Evangelical Theology in Africa: Byang Kato's legacy', *Evangelical Review of Theology*, vol. 5, no.1, April 1981, pp. 35–9.
20. 'African theology does all the things which theology in general does, but in African theology (as in Asian) all these other functions are embraced in the missionary or communicative function. It is not primarily an intra-ecclesiastical exercise, but a discipline whose practitioners keep one question central: How can we best do our theology so that the Gospel will touch Africans most deeply?' (Johannes Verkuyl, *Contemporary Missiology – An Introduction*, Grand Rapids: Eerdmans, 1978, p. 277.)
21. Kwesi Dickson, *Theology in Africa*, London: Darton, Longman and Todd, 1984, pp. 30 and 42f.
22. Andrew F. Walls, 'The first chapter of the Epistle to the Romans and the modern missionary movement', in Ward Gasque and R. P. Martin (eds), *Apostolic History and the Gospel* (Biblical and historical essays presented to F. F. Bruce), Exeter: Paternoster Press, 1970, p. 357.
23. Edward Fasholé-Luke, 'The quest for an African Christian Theology', p. 267.
24. Kwesi Dickson, *Theology in Africa*, p. 29.
25. Paul Bohannan, 1966, quoted in Robin Horton, 'Philosophy and African Studies', p. 263.
26. Gordon Donaldson, *The Faith of the Scots*, London: Batsford, 1990, p. 16.
27. K. S. Latourette, *The Thousand Years of Uncertainty, AD 500–1500* (A History of the Expansion of Christianity, vol. 2), Grand Rapids: Zondervan, 1970, pp. 134–6. (First published in 1938, New York: Harper and Row.)
28. Gordon Donaldson, *The Faith of the Scots*, p. 16.
29. Kwesi Dickson, *Theology in Africa*, p. 46.
30. Adrian Hastings, *African Christianity – An Essay in Interpretation*, p. 50.

31. K. A. Busia, *Africa in Search of Democracy*, London: Routledge and Kegan Paul, 1967, p. 12.
32. Ibid., p. 169.
33. Adrian Hastings, *African Catholicism: Essays in Discovery*, London: SCM Press, and Philadelphia: Trinity Press International, 1989, p. 10.
34. John Mbiti, *African Religions and Philosophy*, London: Heinemann, 1969, p. 232.
35. John Mbiti, *Bible and Theology in African Christianity*, Nairobi: Oxford University Press, 1986, p. 229.
36. Ali Mazrui, *Cultural Forces in World Politics*, London: James Currey and Nairobi: Heinemann Kenya, 1990.
37. Ibid., pp. 256–7.

Index

Abraham, William, 183
African theology, 81–5
  achievements, 4, 82, 177–8, 192, 260–2
  and ancestors, 216–30
  Christology, 83–5, 176, 217, 228
  Damuah's view, 77
  early developments, 76–7, 114–19,
    225
  identity as theological category,
    256–8
  impact of vernacular, 33, 59–60, 72–3,
    79, 246
  as missionary theology, 129, 259
  new challenges, 82–6, 263–5
  and primal religions, 83, 97–106, 177,
    258, 262
  as theology of inculturation, 177
  as theology of the people, 159
Africanisation of Christianity, 4–5
Africanness, 14, 20, 29
Afrikania
  Blyden's legacy, 14, 17
  challenge to African Christianity,
    33–6
  as critical reaction to Christianity, 77
  cultural heritage, 29
  ethnicity, 81
  foundations, 28
  leading ideas, 30–2
  political scene, 20
  rise and establishment, 4, 17
Afrocentrism, 30
afterlife, 94–5
Aggrey, J. E. K., 211
Akan
  ancestors, 219–23
  Christaller's observations, 54–5, 79–
    80, 213
  Danquah's observations, 24, 28,

    78–80
  death, understanding of, 56
  and missionary movement, 68–9
  monotheism, 54–5, 213
  spiritualism, 81
  political organisation, 241
  spirituality, 81
Akrofi, Clement Anderson, 52–3, 56–7
Akropong school of Christian
  historiography, 46, 47
Akropong Seminary, 46, 48, 49, 52
Akuapem, 219, 228
Akyem-Abuakwa Traditional State
  Council, 56
Allen, Roland, 164
Ambedkar, 139
Amu, Ephraim, 52
ancestors, 210, 212, 216–30
  desacralisation, 244
  in church liturgy, 229–30
  political aspects, 181, 241–2
  theology of, 223–30
Animism, 193, 200–1
anthropocentrism, 100, 101
anthropological poverty, 144–5
Antubam, Kofi, 25
Armed Forces Revolutionary Council
  (AFRC), Ghana, 19
Asante, David, 40, 46
Ashanti
  ancestors, 219, 225
  dynamic in history, 212
  Freeman's mission, 225
  MacCarthy's death, 45
  Rattray's observations, 34
  Reindorf's observations, 40
Asia, 173–4
authoritarianism, 236–7, 239–43
Awoonor, Kofi, 237–8

268

Index

Index

Index

Index

Index

Index

Index

Index